INTERNATIONAL POLITICAL ECONOMY SERIES

General Editor: Timothy M. Shaw, Professor of Political Science and International Development Studies, and Director of the Centre for Foreign Policy Studies, Dalhousie University, Halifax, Nova Scotia

Recent titles include:

Laura Macdonald
SUPPORTING CIVIL SOCIETY: The Political Role of Non-Governmental
Organizations in Central America

Stephen D. McDowell
GLOBALIZATION, LIBERALIZATION AND POLICY CHANGE: A Political
Economy of India's Communications Sector

Juan Antonio Morales and Gary McMahon (editors)
ECONOMIC POLICY AND THE TRANSITION TO DEMOCRACY: The Latin
American Experience

Ted Schrecker (editor)
SURVIVING GLOBALISM: The Social and Environmental Challenges

Ann Seidman, Robert B. Seidman and Janice Payne (editors)
LEGISLATIVE DRAFTING FOR MARKET REFORM: Some Lessons from
China

Kenneth P. Thomas
CAPITAL BEYOND BORDERS: States and Firms in the Auto Industry,
1960–94

Caroline Thomas and Peter Wilkin (editors)
GLOBALIZATION AND THE SOUTH

Geoffrey R. D. Underhill (editor)
THE NEW WORLD ORDER IN INTERNATIONAL FINANCE

Henry Veltmeyer, James Petras and Steve Vieux
NEOLIBERALISM AND CLASS CONFLICT IN LATIN AMERICA: A
Comparative Perspective on the Political Economy of Structural Adjustment

Robert Wolfe
FARM WARS: The Political Economy of Agriculture and the International Trade
Regime

International Political Economy Series
Series Standing Order ISBN 0–333–71110–6
(outside North America only)

You can receive future titles in this series as they are published by placing a standing order.
Please contact your bookseller or, in case of difficulty, write to us at the address below with
your name and address, the title of the series and the ISBN quoted above.

Customer Services Department, Macmillan Distribution Ltd
Houndmills, Basingstoke, Hampshire RG21 6XS, England

Institutions and Institutional Change in China

Premodernity and Modernization

Fei-Ling Wang

The Sam Nunn School of International Affairs
Georgia Institute of Technology, USA

First published in Great Britain 1998 by
MACMILLAN PRESS LTD
Houndmills, Basingstoke, Hampshire RG21 6XS and London
Companies and representatives throughout the world

A catalogue record for this book is available from the British Library.

ISBN 0–333–73080–1

First published in the United States of America 1998 by
ST. MARTIN'S PRESS, INC.,
Scholarly and Reference Division,
175 Fifth Avenue, New York, N.Y. 10010

ISBN 0–312–21360–3

Library of Congress Cataloging-in-Publication Data
Wang, Fei-Ling.
Institutions and institutional change in China : premodernity and
modernization / Fei-Ling Wang.
p.   cm. — (International political economy series)
Includes bibliographical references (p.   ) and index.
ISBN 0–312–21360–3 (cloth)
1. Social change—China.   2. Social change—Study and teaching.
3. China—Social conditions.   4. China—Politics and government.
5. China—Civilization.   6. China—Economic conditions.   7. Economic
development—Social aspects.   I. Title.   II. Series.
HN733.W35   1998
303.4'0951—DC21   97–48642
                                                                              CIP

This book is printed on paper suitable for recycling and made from fully managed and
sustained forest sources.

10   9   8   7   6   5   4   3   2   1
07   06   05   04   03   02   01   00   99   98

Printed and bound in Great Britain by
Antony Rowe Ltd, Chippenham, Wiltshire

To Yvonne and Justin

May the old wisdom of five millennia
continue to enrich your lives
in a young nation of three centuries

Contents

List of Tables and Figures

Preface

A quarter of humankind is struggling to reach modernity in the grand process of Chinese modernization. The millennium-old Chinese domestic organizational structure is experiencing some of the deepest and most consequential institutional changes in human history. This book is about that event. Exploring the institutional continuities and changes in China, I use an innovative analytical framework to describe the peculiar institutional premodernity in that nation and examine the currents and the prospects of Chinese modernization. An inquiry of Chinese labor allocation patterns and their changes serves as the indicators for the institutional analysis. On the track of a state-led modernization, the dragon of China is found to be institutionally entering the nets of the market economy and international relations.

In a conceptual discussion of the notion of modernity, this study aspires to construct and demonstrate, through the case study of China, a general analytical framework that may be used to study issues of modernization in other national and historical settings. The varied routes to, and forms of, modernity, the issues of the latecomer's modernization and "post-modernity," and other methodological issues are examined.

More specifically, this book analyzes the institutional relationship among the Chinese economy, polity, and social life. It addresses issues such as why China was a backward nation for so long, what institutional continuities it has today, and what kind of domestic organizational structure the Chinese are likely to acquire in the near future. It concludes, among other findings, that China has had a super-stable and undifferentiated domestic organizational structure centered on a family-like state for centuries, including most of the PRC era, as reflected by the dominant existence of a family-based traditional labor allocation pattern and its variations. Premodern China was forced by external influences to start an alien but urgent state-led modernization in the nineteenth century. This modernization, however, was plagued by its own institutional legacy, imperialist foreign forces, policy and human errors, and bad luck. Only in the last two decades of the twentieth century has this course become truly promising, as a distorted but effective market advances rapidly to be the leading, if not yet dominant, economic institution. A profound institutional differentiation of the Chinese economy from the Chinese sociopolitical complex is under way. Though its arrival is not guaranteed, a *Chinese* modernity is now visibly on the horizon. As a dragon entering the institutional nets of a "Chinese style" market and the international political economy, a modernizing China appears to be an increasingly prosperous and rapidly transforming (yet still modest) player that is likely to be conforming to existing international institutions.

ORGANIZATION OF THE BOOK

This book is a combination of a theoretical discourse on human institutions, institutional changes and labor allocation patterns (Chapters 1 to 2) and a study of the Chinese case (Chapters 3 to 5). Historical analyzes constitute the bulk of the case study, substantiated by information collected from interviews and field studies conducted from 1989 to 1997. Publications consulted are listed in the attached bibliography, while many additional sources of information are indicated in the corresponding notes.

Chapter 1 discusses an institutional approach to the study of modernization. After a short survey of the relevant literature and a conceptual discussion on human behavior and human institutions, this chapter defines the notion of modernity as a certain domestic organizational structure with a differentiated yet interactive relationship among the economy (the market), polity (a participatory and effective nation-state), and social life (an autonomous civil society). The varieties of, and the routes to, modernity are clarified. The issues of a latecomer's modernization, so-called "postmodernity," and the possibility of destruction of modernity are discussed. Other important concepts like the market, the state and the "developmental state," culture, and civil society are examined or redefined.

Chapter 2 proposes a theory on labor allocation patterns (LAPs). LAP and its three historical types are conceptually defined, discussed, and proposed as indicators for our observation of the institutional features and changes in a nation's domestic organizational structure.

Chapter 3 is an examination of Chinese domestic organizational structure through a historical review of the Chinese LAPs. It attempts a review of Chinese institutional history with the hope of explaining certain peculiarities of Chinese civilization, such as its continuity, dynasty cycles and long-term stagnation. The main finding is that there has been one major LAP for most of Chinese history since the Qin dynasty (third century BC): the family-based traditional LAP in various forms. That reflects well the institutional nature of Chinese organizational structure as a super-stable, family-like, premodern one that has an undifferentiated relationship among the economy, polity, and social life. Confucian culture, the internalized Chinese institutions, served as a major protector of Chinese premodernity. Long international isolation and domestic political unity made a market-driven modernization impossible in China. By the nineteenth century, affected by external influences, new LAPs began to emerge in China and a state-led modernization became a historically more appropriate alternative. Mao Zedong's CCP (Chinese Communist Party) merely inherited this course, but attempted to accelerate it in a new but wrong direction by eliminating rather than emancipating the market. An authoritarian state LAP pushed the family-based traditional LAP to the extreme. In a way, the CCP forcefully interrupted the Chinese modernization course and further rigidified the Chinese premodernity.

Chapter 4 links the study of Chinese modernization to an examination of the Chinese LAPs mainly their institutional significance, based on the sister volume of this book studying labor allocation in contemporary China (Wang 1998). What Deng Xiaoping and his fellow reformers have achieved in the past two decades is a change of direction on the track of a state-led modernization: to introduce and "utilize" the market institution. Since the mid-1980s, four LAPs have coexisted in the PRC: a restored family-based traditional LAP, an authoritarian state LAP, community-based labor markets, and a national labor market. That reflects the mixed and transitional nature of the Chinese domestic organizational structure. The continuity of institutional premodernity in China is reflected by the existence of the restored family-based traditional LAP and the authoritarian LAP. The family-based traditional LAP, numerically the largest LAP, has restored much of the Chinese premodernity to the majority of the Chinese in the rural areas. The new development of this LAP in the 1990s, however, indicates its instability and stagnation – just like its ancestors in the past. The authoritarian LAP is still a cornerstone for the current CCP-PRC domestic organizational structure, especially the authoritarian political system. Practiced by urban collective enterprises, many state-owned enterprises, and especially the massive and thriving township and village enterprises, the community-based labor markets (CLMs) are now numerically the second largest LAP in China and are growing very rapidly. Economically very viable and fairly efficient, while politically and socially less "threatening," the CLMs are expected to be the dominant LAP in the near future; thus a distorted but functioning market institution will become the dominant economic institution in China. The development of the CLMs appears to hold special significance to the national unity of China. The rapidly emerging national labor market has been primarily practiced by foreign-invested enterprises and native private employers. The process in which Beijing gradually gave in to the demands of foreign investors concerning the "importing" and development of this new LAP demonstrates the crucial role of external influences in Chinese modernization. As the fastest-growing LAP, though still relatively small, the national labor market has had a disproportionately great institutional impact on Chinese domestic organizational structure, helping to facilitate a differentiation of the economy from the sociopolitical complex.

Chapter 5 summarizes the main findings and assesses the analytical framework used in this study. A few speculative assertions are made concerning the future of Chinese modernization and the likely characteristics of a *Chinese* modernity. Possible impacts of a modernized China on the world, among other related issues, are considered.

The Appendix is a methodological discussion on Chinese statistical data.

Acknowledgments

For the sprouts of ideas, critical comments, kind encouragement, and invaluable support, I want to thank my mentors, colleagues, and friends at the University of Pennsylvania, the United States Military Academy (West Point), Georgia Institute of Technology and other places: Robert Barnett, Linda Brady, Peter Brecke, Tom Callaghy, Tom Christensen, William Clark, John Garver, Avery Goldstein, Joanne Gowa, Chong-Sik Lee, William Long, Arvid Lukauskas, Dan Kaufman, Fritz Kratochwil, Richard Matthews, Jack Nagel, Dick Norton, Dan Papp, Steve Wilkins, and Brian Woodall.

The Sam Nunn School of International Affairs at Georgia Tech has provided a wonderful working environment for me. The librarians and staff at the East Asian Section of the Library of Congress, the Harvard-Yenching Library of Harvard University, and the East Asian Library of Columbia University have always offered great help to me when using their collections. The five field trips I took from 1992 to 1997 financially benefitted from, among others, the following generous sponsors: the Penfield Fellowship of the University of Pennsylvania; the Faculty Research and Development Fund of the United States Military Academy; the Center for International Business Education and Research at Georgia Tech; the Georgia Tech Foundation; the Center of International Strategy, Technology and Policy; and Cable News Network (CNN) International.

Many people have helped my field research in China and other East Asian countries yet I can only list some of their names here: Chen Fei, Chen Ping, Chen Siheng, Chen Ying, Chu Shulong, Guang Li, Guo Henchui, Guo Wanqing, He Ming, Miyuki Ishii, Jung-Bock Lee, Jong-Chan Rhee, Ma Min, Yang-Ho Kim, Li Canli, Li Lei, Li Qian, Li Wei, Liu Ji, Liu Xianling, Liu Wanqing, Ming Chu-Cheng, Hakson Paik, Sheng Fumin, Sun Hui, Sun Qi, Tang Jinping, Wang Guanying, Wang Liya, Wang Subei, Wu Sou-Chang, Xu Minqi, Zhang Lanting, Zhang Nan, Zhang Xinming, Xu Yibo, Zhang Yan, Zhong Yongsan, and Zhou Renwei.

Finally, I would like to gratefully mention my family especially my wife Yan, daughter Yvonne, and son Justin, for their love, patience, understanding, and support – without which I would never be able to finish this book.

F.L.W.
Roswell, Georgia
USA

List of Abbreviations

This list contains some Chinese terms and abbreviations that are frequently used in this book. Italicized terms are phonetic translations of Chinese terms or abbreviations.

CBEs (社队企业): commune and brigade enterprises
CCP: the Chinese Communist Party
CLMs: community-based labor markets
CNPC or NPC: the Chinese National People's Congress
COCs: coastal open cities
dangan (档案): personal dossier
danwei or *danweis* (单位): unit or units
diannong (佃农): tenant farmers
FDI: foreign direct investment
FESCO: foreign enterprise service corporation
gaogan (高干): senior cadre
getihu (个体户): individual household (private family economy)
guanxi (关系): connections
gudinggong (固定工): permanent employees
guanshang (官商): state-owned/run business
gunong (雇农): hired peasants
hukou (户口): household or residential registration system
juntian (均田): (re)distribution of land
KMT: Kuomintang or Gumindang, the Chinese Nationalist Party
LAP: labor allocation pattern
liumin (流民): migrating and unemployed peasant
LSEs: labor service enterprises
mangliu (盲流): blindly (uncontrolled) floating/migrating people
mu (亩): 0.1647 acre
PLA: the People's Liberation Army
PRC: the People's Republic of China
qiye (企业): enterprise (for example, a factory, shop, or a company)
rencai jiaoliu zhongxin: talent/professional exchange center
Renmin Ribao: People's Daily
Renmin Ribao-Overseas: People's Daily-Overseas Edition
rmb (人民币): renminbi – currency of the PRC
sanzi (三资): foreign investment of three kinds (equity joint

ventures, cooperative joint ventures, and wholly owned enterprises)

SEZs: special economic zones

shiye (事业): institution (for example, a school, hospital or governmental agency)

SSB: the State Statistical Bureau

TVEs (乡镇企业): township and village enterprises

xiagang (下岗): off-duty (dismissed with minimum pay for limited time)

xiahai (下海): plunge into the sea (engage in business activities)

Xinhua: the (official) Xinhua News Agency

yigong yinong (亦工亦农): semi-worker semi-peasant

zhuanyehu (专业户): specialized household (a family specializing in one industry)

zigengnong (自耕农): landowning farmers

1 Institutions, Institutional Changes and Modernization: A Conceptual Framework

The history of human civilization has been a history of organized human behavior. How are people organized? What are their goals or objectives? What are their mental and physical capabilities? What is the natural environment? These are questions of essential relevance to a good understanding of any specific human behavior, including economic activities, social and political changes, modernization, and the development of human civilization in general. If we accept the presumption that all humans have similar behavioral goals since they have universally similar needs and largely similar desires, and if we believe that different peoples potentially have essentially equal mental and physical capabilities, then variations in human behavior and their consequences can be sufficiently explained by variations in their organizational structures or their institutional arrangements.[1] Basic questions in the study of modernization – What is the goal of modernization? How does a nation get there? – can, therefore, be adequately addressed if we can ascertain the domestic organizational structure of a group of people or a nation.

From such an institutional perspective, this chapter presents an analytical framework for the study of modernization in general and for an inquiry into Chinese modernization in particular. Essentially, it can be read as a note on methodology in the study of political economy. It proposes that an analysis of alterations in a nation's domestic organizational structure enables us to observe and study issues of economic development, sociopolitical changes, and modernization. The notion of *domestic organizational structure*, the human organizational structure of a nation, refers to the institutional arrangement of people or the human institution within a nation as the primary human grouping. It has conceptual similarities to a number of existing concepts, such as Karl Marx's "social relations," "societies" or "modes of production"; Emile Durkheim's "conscience collective" and institutionalized contract of differentiated units based

1

on an "organic solidarity"; Talcott Parsons's "social systems" plus "culture systems" in his general theory of action; Jürgen Habermas's "realms" of human life; and Kenneth Arrow's "social worlds."

The notion of modernization needs to be treated differently from the concepts of development and economic development. Development is understood as a process of expansion, improvement, invention, or enlargement of human behavior. Economic development thus refers to the growth, quantitative and qualitative, of human economic activities and outcomes. Modernization is suggested by this book to be the institutional changes towards the optimization of the human institution with a particular form of the human institution – modernity – as its identifiable goal. If political democracy, an important albeit secondary feature of modernity, "can be initiated at any level of [economic] development" (Przeworski & Limongi 1997, 177), modernity can be reached at any level of development as well. Development and economic development can take place in a premodern or a modernized institutional setting with, naturally, different performance or pace. Development and economic development are endless processes that can take different directions with progression and regression both possible as long as the human civilization continues, while modernization has an institutionally identifiable point of completion. A regressive "modernization" or the destruction of modernity is hence also possible conceptually and practically.

Section I reviews briefly the existing theories on modernization and introduces an analytical framework that focuses on alterations of domestic organizational structure. Sections II and III discuss in depth the institutional approach to the study of modernization, the notion of modernity, the routes to modernity, and the variety of modernity. Important concepts such as the market, the state, and civil society are clarified or redefined. Section IV addresses the issue of timing and other remaining methodological issues. Section V provides a summary.

I. MODERNIZATION: THE ARGUMENTS

Though it is nearly a household word, modernization denotes very different things to different people, or to the same people in different settings. It is often used to describe almost any progressive, goal-oriented human behavior, including mere "renewing" or technologically "updating" efforts. To some, modernization refers to a process of economic development that yields more material benefits. To others, it means social and political changes, usually in emulation of the particular institutional arrangement or division of labor in some other nation. As one of the most frequently addressed topics in social sciences, modernization has drawn attention from anthropologists, economists, historians, political scientists, sociologists, and of course politicians in and out of power. Consequently, there have been countless theorizing efforts that have produced profound conceptual frameworks for the study of modernization. Among others, Barrington Moore ([1967] 1993), in the tradition of Karl Marx, Max Weber and Karl Polanyi (1957), made serious and fruitful efforts in constructing general models to observe modernization and social changes. The Frankfurt School (Habermas 1979 & 1987) attempted to revitalize the Marxian theory of historical materialism to explain the process of modernization. Douglass North (1981) built an institutional model for the study of economic history. Talcott Parsons (1951a & b, 1964 & 1967) attempted construction of a general theory of action that explored the institutional aspects of human "social systems." Other classic works of "modernization theory" include those by Alexander Gerschenkron (1964), Samuel Huntington [1968, 1970], and W.W. Rostow ([1960] 1990). Related to the traditional modernization theory, a "neo-evolutionism" school believes that modernization should be understood as a multilinear process based on the differentiation of the "societies" like the biological organisms.[2] The rational choice approach (Samuel Popkin 1979 and James Scott 1976) yields significant findings by examining political and economic changes through the patterns of human behavior.

The traditional "modernization theory"[3] based on the logic of classic or neoclassic economics, understands modernization essentially as a process of economic (the accumulation of capital and the efficient utilization of the accumulated capital) and sociopolitical changes that is nationally based, but is linear in all cases and has its own inherent, universal, observable (thus comparable), and predictable characteristics. Nations essentially follow the same road to reach "modernity." The problem for the developing countries, or "less developed countries," however, is that they started the process late and proceeded slowly on this trajectory because of their adherence to traditional values and institutions.[4] W.W. Rostow implies rather explicitly that modernity is something that can be achieved along quite the same road by all peoples – the model of "taking off."[5] Modernization is thus often interpreted as the transition from agricultural to industrial civilization.[6]

A clear dichotomy of modernity versus traditionality is a key component of the traditional modernization theory. Although "traditional" or "premodern" situations can be described with relative accuracy, the crucial concept of "modernity" has been at best nebulous, often biased, and severely ethnocentric; thus it is unscientific, and mainly finds its usefulness in the discourse of classic philosophy.[7] It is often associated with the *current* status of nations generally viewed as rich, technologically advanced and powerful, politically democratic, and socially liberal. Major – or even trivial – characteristics of those nations and their people have often been mingled into the concept of modernity. Subject to everyone's interpretation, the term has thus lost its analytical usefulness. The unilinear view of the traditional modernization theory may have been disputed by, primarily the neo-evolutionists and other sociologists and anthropologists, but its "crude" understanding of modernity (Sklair 1995, 34), still remains. The "universal" principles and prescriptions offered by the powerful logic of modernization theory, therefore, suffer tremendously from this conceptual defect.

Critics, especially the schools of dependency and world systems, have long argued that traditional modernization theory is biased, inaccurate, and severely ethnocentric. They argue that economic development and social progress of nations, especially in the twentieth century, have much to do with the existing international political structure and the distribution of capabilities across nations. Recent political history and the existing worldwide division of labor are crucial variables that are largely overlooked by modernization theorists.[8] Marxists, or neo-Marxists, suggest that modernization has its own inherent, almost predestined, logic that is defined by modes of production and driven by ceaseless class struggle leading to changes in relationships among the elements of production, mainly between capital and labor (Cox 1987). The Weberian school believes in a comprehensive approach to understanding modernization, with emphasis on social actions and organizations of individuals, who are assumed to be sovereign, rational or "controlled," but definitely self-conscious. "Rationalization" is viewed as the core of a modernization process.[9] Certain types of domestic political structure and cultural environment, such as a "bureaucratic-authoritarianism" or "developmental state," are found by some to be important to our understanding of the modernization process.[10] The technical advantages of the latecomers have prompted some to describe a so-called "catching-up" modernization model featured with an accelerated economic growth based on massive introduction of state-of-the-art technology from those advanced nations.[11] To a lesser extent, we also see various culture-analysis approaches based on the findings of anthropology, sociology and even human psychology.[12]

By the end of the twentieth century, however, a striking fact is that most existing conceptual models still appear to be unsatisfactory in explaining modernization or economic development. They are especially weak in explaining concurrent successes *and* failures of modernization efforts. Useful analytical concepts such as the dichotomy of modernity versus premodernity and the issue of rationalization often became conceptually problematic and practically useless, primarily because of the lack of concrete definitions for those terms.[13] As with many other discourses in social sciences, our overall understanding of modernization is still filled with conceptual confusion, ideological biases, methodological problems, and practical irrelevance. Most analytical models derived from theories concerning modernization, economic development and political democratization have been reductionist in nature. There is no good conceptual framework to incorporate those reductionist theories, some of which are excellent models that could be very useful and powerful. Coexisting successes and failures are often explained by a variety of "cultural reasons" that are equally mystical. This is especially true in the study of Chinese modernization, where so many frustrations have made the field an elusively fertile one, yet barren in terms of theoretical construction.[14] Clearly, we need a new analytical approach to make our study of modernization more coherent and scientific, and thus more fruitful than it has been. This is an especially urgent task for China scholars, who seek to answer extremely important questions such as: Will Chinese modernization succeed? What kind of modernized China can be expected in the twenty-first century? Are there any lessons for other premodern nations, developing or socialist ones, since China bears characteristics of both?

An Alternative Analytical Framework

This book revises traditional modernization theory by offering an institutional definition of the crucial concept of modernity.

Modernization is a collective human behavior, which, as the central subject of all social sciences, can be scientifically studied through exploring the behavior-constraining human institution. Accepting the dichotomy of modernity versus traditionality or premodernity, this book views modernization as the process of institutional changes approaching modernity – a specific kind of domestic organizational structure that is composed of the three basic spheres or elements of the human institution: polity, economy, and social life, which are functionally and organizationally distinguishable. As an intended contribution to modernization theory, this book defines modernity as, primarily, a differentiated and interactive relationship among polity, economy, and social life. To a lesser extent, modernity also refers to certain optimally developed internal structures of the three institutions: an effective and participatory nation-state or political democracy, a market economy, and a civil society.[15] Modernity institutionally enables maximum fulfillment of human needs and highest satisfaction of human desires – the goals of human behavior. Fulfillment and satisfaction are then mainly limited by the natural conditions and the accumulation of knowledge (levels of technology at the given time). With the same natural and technological conditions, economic development and the development of human civilization in general have qualitatively different performances and paces in a premodern and a modernized nation. Modernity ensures the collective survival and evolution of the three elements of the human institution that may be functionally and/or organizationally in conflict with one another.

Due to the varied institutional "distances," patterns and velocity of interactions among a nation's economy, polity and social life – caused by different timing and routes of modernization – a variety of modernities is possible in different historical and national settings. How the three institutions are arranged against each other determines the features of a particular modernity. Institutional barriers that exclude some groups of people within a nation from modernity determine another set of varied characteristics of that nation's modernity. Modernity, as a specific and optimal human organizational structure, is by no means guaranteed for every nation or every human grouping; there are historical examples of the destruction of modernity. Modernization, then, is defined as the process of establishing and/or expanding a differentiated yet interactive relationship among the economy, polity, and social life. As Samuel Huntington (1968, 32–34) pointed out, modernization

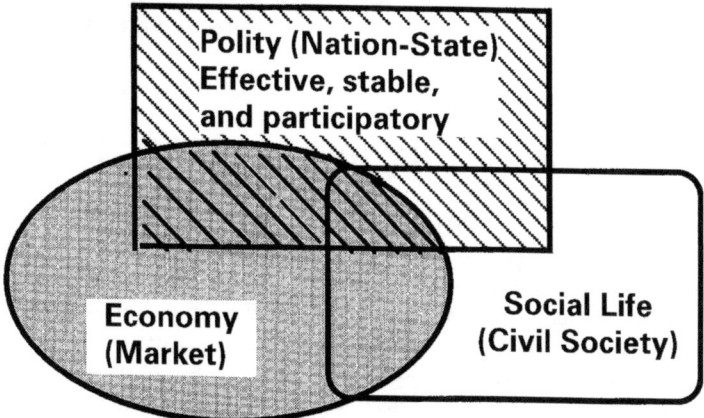

Figure 1.1   An institutional understanding of modernity

is "a multifaceted process involving changes in all areas of human thought and activity" from traditionality to modernity.

The road to modernity varies. Which one of the three institutions emerges first as a relatively autonomous engine that drives modernization depends primarily on the starting point of the process – namely, the existing domestic organizational structure and the external environment. Different routes to modernity and various strategies for modernization are, therefore, identifiable. Modernity is achieved whenever a differentiated and interactive relationship among a nation's economy, polity, and social life is established. Historically, market driven modernization occurred in much of Western Europe and North America, while state-led modernization took place in Germany and much of Eastern Asia. This study hypothesizes that a state-led route and a strategy of guided marketization are more appropriate for modernizing efforts of "latecomer" nations. Since the market institution needs to survive within a particular international political system of anarchy, modernity tends to be a national or group-based phenomenon; a world modernity appears to be a desirable but infeasible goal until viable human space colonies can be established.[16] Furthermore, constant interaction of the three institutions can be caused by changes of conditions such as population (the simple growth, migration or the elimination of institutional exclusions) and knowledge (technology); thus, modernity may be demolished by its own momentum, external forces, or human design or error.

The rest of this chapter discusses and elaborates on this general conceptual framework for observing modernization and institutional changes.

II. HUMAN NEEDS, BEHAVIORS AND INSTITUTIONS

Our institutional approach to the study of modernization starts with a three-part assumption: first, that human behavior is the central subject of all social sciences, including the study of modernization and sociopolitical changes; second, that all human behavior is constrained by man-made formal and informal institutions; third, that the human institution has primarily three spheres or elements – economy, polity, and social life, with their distinguishable structures, functions, scopes, values, and objectives. An institutional analysis that examines these elements and the relationships among them is suggested as an avenue to advance the study of human behavior. This approach offers potential for integrating social or natural scientific explanations, reductionist or systemic, for some of the most fundamental human behaviors. Modernization, democratization, economic development, war and other social changes are clearly cases and/or consequences of institutionally defined and constrained human behavior. To elaborate on this approach, we will first examine the concept of the human institution based on an understanding of human needs and behavior. The important notions of institutional legitimacy and the appropriate unit for institutional analysis are discussed, followed by a clarification of the important terms of market, the state, and social life.

Human Behavior and Human Institutions

Humans are born to interact with each other and nature to meet their needs and satisfy their desires. People are, therefore, organized for goal-oriented actions. Goal-oriented (as well as non-goal-oriented or random but consequential) human behavior has been the central subject of the social sciences.[17] Human behavior is motivated by needs, such as nutrition and safety, and desires, such as comfort and freedom. Needs are largely biologically defined and are basically universal and stable. A fairly exhaustive list of human needs can be obtained scientifically and accurately measured with relative ease. Biology and biochemistry, among other scientific endeavors, have contributed fundamentally to this accomplishment.[18] Based on relevance to human life and the cost of achieving them, needs may be ranked into "higher," such as spiritual pursuits (which may be actually desires rather than needs), and "lower" or basic needs, such as food and air (Maslow 1948).

Important thinkers on history and political economy have long used need as a central concept in constructing their theories on human institutions and behavior.[19] An "optimization" of need gratification is the motivation for people's organized behavior (Parsons 1951a, 5–6, 24–67 & 1951b, 8–10). Using needs as the premise for theoretical discourse may run into technical difficulties. The functionalists have been criticized for this, but their alleged problems may have more to do with the theorists' objectives than the approach itself. Our understanding of human needs naturally cannot explain completely the story of human behavior, since it is difficult to ascertain what needs are responsible for what human behavior at a given time in a given environment. But the theory of human needs nonetheless lays a solid foundation for a general understanding, as it reveals the basic particles of the universe of human behavior. It is, therefore, "essential to any logical theory of behavior."[20]

Human desires are more diverse, ambiguous, dynamic, and subjective than needs. The efforts of social and natural scientists have yet to produce an adequate understanding of the content, formation and changes of human desires.[21] Desires, however, are functionally secondary to human needs, and many can actually be reduced to needs. For example, greed is basically a reflection of the need for security/survival, while the desire for celebrity or "power" can be viewed as basically a reflection of the need for reproduction. It is, therefore, safe to assume that human needs, clearly identifiable and relatively stable, are the most important motivation of human behavior.

At the risk of simplification, it is further assumed that the most fundamental human goals are survival and reproduction. For the satisfaction of those goals, three basic sets of needs are universally identifiable: materials and services for physical survival; cooperation with and security from others to survive, produce, and reproduce; and reproduction or transmission of individual genes or characteristics. Human needs and desires can be categorized into these three sets. For a particular individual, naturally, the self-determined order of importance of his numerous needs and desires may not start with these three.[22] As Emile Durkheim found in his famous sociological study of suicides, man has a powerful internalization, interpretation and interpenetration of information and even his own needs to form expectations and motivations for action.[23] Distortions and anomie are, therefore, common companions of needs-driven human behavior. Thus we see individually rational but objectively irrational (and even suicidal) behaviors, still needs-driven, for which the heaviest penalty would be that an individual simply loses his life, hence forgoing all his needs and desires.

Since the dawn of human civilization, human behavior has been constrained, or bounded, by the human institution because humans are organized beings.[24] The basic human needs, starting from reproduction, can only be effectively met by organized behavior of at least two people – male and female. Institutionalized organization and division of labor have been the most important sources of strength and achievement of human civilization.[25]

Here, the human institution is defined as a set of "humanly devised constraints that shape human interaction," and "a set of rules, compliance procedures, and moral and ethical behavioral norms designed to contain the behavior of individuals in the interest of maximizing the wealth or utility of principals."[26] The human institution can also be viewed as human organization itself.[27] It refers to the organizational arrangements of humans, formally and/or informally, in their interactions with nature and with each other. "In general, institutions are settled or routinized practices established and regulated by norms."[28] A hierarchical grouping, a family structure, an accepted social or political stratification, a norm of conduct, a contract or treaty, an "anarchic" international political order, and a moral code are all examples of the human institution. Things commonly referred to as "cultural" or "psychological" constraints or perimeters of human behavior can be interpreted as internalized, usually informal but often very powerful, human institutions that are passed across generations through education, socialization, and indoctrination.[29] The term "group/national culture," including habits, religions and customs, refers to the internalized and individualized domestic organizational structure. Unlike Talcott Parsons (1951b, 22), this work considers culture systems to be secondary or extended but integrated parts of the human institution rather than independent from the latter.

All human behavior, including that which is non-goal-oriented – such as random, "insane" or "abnormal" activities – is constrained by the human institution. The constraining power of different aspects of the human institution naturally varies. More deeply, desires are clearly conditioned, shaped, defined and even created by the human institution. Even some human needs are historically and practically affected by the human institution (Parsons 1951b, 9). The powerful role played by "culture" on the formation of many needs and desires, such as dating rituals or a green lawn, is rather obvious. Therefore, analysis of the human institution is as important and basic as the study of human needs to social sciences.

The human institution can be analyzed scientifically because, like basic human needs, it is relatively universal, stable, and measurable – in contrast to the diversity and ambiguity of human desires and individuals' "rationality." More important, due to its plasticity and dynamism, the human institution contains rich information about the variety of human behavior, much more so than human needs. Thus, institutional variables are key pieces of the puzzle of human behavior, which is the central subject of social science. Institutional analysis, combined with behavioral studies based on human needs, has been consciously or unconsciously a very fruitful approach in social science. Major works in social science from Adam Smith, Karl Marx, Max Weber, to Talcott Parsons have all been essentially studies on human institutions with varied understanding of human needs. Formal theories like game theory study the patterns of human behavior, the choice-making of humans, which is a part of the human institution. Normatively, institutional analysis is fully justified because the human institution is man-made, hence can be devised or altered for maximization of goal achievements or for minimization of costs.

Goal-oriented behavior, aimed at meeting human needs and satisfying human desires, can be conceptually categorized into three groups: economic activities, political actions, and social interactions. These respectively address the three most basic sets of human needs and desires mentioned above: materials and services needed for survival, cooperation with and security from others for sustenance, reproduction and the related aspirations of "self-realization." An elaboration of the differences among the three domains of human behaviors will be attempted shortly. Accordingly, the human institution has primarily three spheres or elements: economy, polity, and social life or "society" – three basic institutions.

The lack of a standard vocabulary among social scientists naturally tends to blur this conceptual typology. For example, the word "society" refers to organizations such as the family in some eyes while meaning "nations" or human groupings to others, yet it has been generally used as the overall notion of the human institution. This book uses the word, perhaps more appropriately, as only one part of human institutional or organizational life. In order to avoid unnecessary confusion, however, the term "social life" will be used instead of "society." Many secondary human needs and desires that develop over time often tend to obscure the boundaries among the three spheres of the human institution. The historically heavy influence of religious beliefs in social sciences, especially in philosophy, may make this categorization of the human institution unacceptable to many. They may contend it "ignores" those predestined "spiritual pursuits" thought by many to be an independent and major, if not primary, purpose of human behavior. Empirically, confusions about this typology are almost inevitable since many human actions may actually contain one, two or all three aspects at one point. For example, education in the United States may be an economic behavior, but strong social interactions and even political activities are also visible in American schools.

Essentially, the three spheres of the human institution are ways to organize people engaging in the three domains of human behavior. These three institutions of economy, polity, and social life constitute the organizational structure of human behavior, life, or civilization. Structural and important differences are identifiable between those different institutions. Naturally, as will be discussed later, the boundaries between the three are not always clear-cut. Furthermore, the boundaries between the three institutions are not exactly the same as the empirical boundaries between government, firms, and family: certain governmental actions are economic in nature and certain family activities are economic and/or political. Analytically, nevertheless, a conceptual typology is clearly evident. Most of us may not see the fact that the same basic elements and mechanism make up the great variety of living things, from a tree to a human, but modern chemistry and biology could not have advanced without a clear and sound typology of the elements of matter.

To view the human institution as being composed of polity, economy, and social life is not new. Max Weber may be credited as among the first to analyze the institutional distance between polity, economy, and society (1978, 52, 333–7, 941–47). Talcott Parsons (1951a, 136–50, 153–7; 1951b, 28–9) analyzed government, economy and kinship as "sub-social systems" and their "differentiation." Jürgen Habermas, among others, explored conceptually the links among the various domains of the human institution in his discourse on modernization.[30] Some recent works in history, political science, economics, and sociology have employed this typology in various ways and under different names.[31] Although this typology may have been taken for granted by many, our understanding of the three domains of human behavior and the three basic institutions is clearly underdeveloped. A re-emphasis and clarification are, therefore, in order to gain new knowledge about the human institution.

Three Institutional Domains of Human Behavior

The systemic differences and similarities of human behavior under the three institutions – economy, polity, and social life – can be summarized as follows: different objectives or purposes, different institutional values, different organizational scopes, different organizational principles, and similar behavioral patterns dictated by the three institutions.

Different objectives
All human behavior under the three institutions has a similar goal: to meet human needs and to satisfy human desires. The needs and desires that are fulfilled by the three domains of human behavior, however, are somewhat different. For the economy, the primary purpose is the production of material goods and services that have utility in meeting a whole set of human needs and satisfying a variety of human desires. The primary purpose of polity is twofold· the provision of order and security for the members of the community, and the establishment of an authority structure governing and regulating necessary interpersonal interactions. The primary purpose of social life is also rather specific: to meet human reproduction needs, including family life; to secure emotional feelings such as caring and love, which are necessary for the continuation of human life; and to develop an individual identity and at the same time, paradoxically, an acceptance of socialization, thus to "reproduce" the individuality.

Those objectives can be harmonious with or supplementary to each other. But more often, though all serve the same general goal, they are in conflict with each other due to the scarcity of resources and time, the multifaceted nature of human desires and needs, the difficulty of acquiring information, and the naturally disproportionate intensity of certain human needs and desires at a given time. Therefore, for example, it is natural to see many political actions in conflict with economic pursuits.

Different values
Accordingly, the three institutions emphasize different values. Namely, individuals are rewarded or penalized according to different criteria under each different institution. In economy, mainly in a market economy, people value productivity (efficiency) and innovation. In politics, people value effectiveness and stability of the governing bodies, and appropriate or "equal" treatment of the members of the group/nation. In social life, however, people value social harmony, individual rights and privacy, emotional security, personal sacrifice based on satisfaction-inducing altruism, family integrity and kinship. All those different values are clearly tied to the different objectives of the three institutions.

Those values, once again, can be in harmony with each other and are often mutually reinforcing, but are commonly in conflict with each other. In addition, there are substantial transaction costs involved for individuals to acquire the needed information in order to have a commonly accepted system for weighing the different institutional values.

Varied scope and content
The three institutions have different scope and content. In economy, humans interact with nature and with each other concerning the allocation and utilization of resources: natural resources, man-made products, information and labor – the working ability of the people. Politics is about interpersonal interactions among non-blood-based groupings, concerning the articulation of public interests and the construction and execution of political authority. Social life is about interpersonal interactions based on blood and/or identity or geographical groupings, concerning family, social associations and socialization, and individual self-realization.

Those scopes can and often do overlap with each other. But, just as important as the realization of the inherent links among the three, meaningful boundaries can be conceptually identified and analyzed. Several social sciences actually draw their disciplinary lines here.

Different organizational principles
The internal organizational structures of the three institutions are very different and change over time. For economy, the organizational

principle is a free exchange of property rights (or not so free if the economy is nonmarket) based on a division of labor and dependent on knowledge accumulated (technology levels). The organizational principle of polity is a hierarchical transferring and exercising of authority and the monopoly of the legitimate use of force by the state as the highest form of political grouping. Social life is organized by natural bonds (blood or kinship) and/or voluntary participation based on socialization.

Those organizational principles arrange individuals vis-à-vis their fellow human beings differently in different domains of life at any given time. Essentially, a certain "alienation" type of sophistication, or differentiation, of an individual's place is established. In a nation where the three institutions are all present, one can be a loving and sacrificing parent and a generous volunteer to some; a tough, stingy, and hated competitor on the market; and still be a law-abiding, patriotic, and taxpaying army reserve officer to the state.

Same behavioral patterns
Humans essentially have three identifiable behavioral patterns: strategic or interdependent, dependent, and independent. The strategic behavioral pattern refers to the situation under which the actors are mutually influenced. Their behavior is based on the perceived actions of others as rivals or simply colleagues, the calculation of the impact of the others' actions, and the expected consequences of those actions. In the dependent pattern, one person's actions are conditioned by the actions of others. The independent pattern implies that one actor's behavior is basically free, neither conditioned nor directly impacted by any other specific actors.[32]

Interestingly, the three institutions, depending on their varied internal structures, almost all sanction the same three behavioral patterns for individuals. In economy, human behavior tends to be strategic in an oligopoly situation of an "imperfect market," or in a small-scale moral/traditional economy. There may also be dependent behavior by individuals/firms facing a monopoly of the market, or independent (nonstrategic or price-taking) behavior in a perfect or near-perfect market economy. In politics, human behavior is typically strategic. We may also see clear political dependence of individuals/groups in an authoritarian or totalitarian system. Independent (nonstrategic or price-taking) political behavior is possible in a massive democratic setting such as national direct elections. In social life, human behavior can be either strategic (interdependent) in the family and/or small social groups, or dependent for a beneficiary in the family and/or the social groups. Independent (nonstrategic or price-taking) behavior is relatively rare in social life.

All those basic patterns of human behavior are present in all three institutions. Thus good models describing behavior under one institution, developed by one social science discipline, can conceivably be applied to understanding behavior under other institutions by other disciplines. The use of the same methodologically sound models in the study of human economic, political, and even social behavior is, therefore, possible. The attempt by some to use certain neoclassic economic models in political science is an example. Naturally, certain substantive and sometimes very difficult modifications are needed due to institutional differences that may have profound impacts on what seem to be the same type of human behavior. Institutional variables such as the right of legitimate use of force and limitations of behavioral options often incapacitate the poorly modified "borrowed models" in a different institution.[33] Without a good understanding of the institutional differences, theoretical insights based on studying human behavior patterns, such as the now famous game theory, can have only limited utility.[34]

Human Groupings and the Unit of Institutional Analysis

Human behavior can only be adequately understood in an institutional context. As a first step, one must conceptually establish an appropriate unit of analysis. Since at least two people are required to form a human institution, groupings rather than individuals are, therefore, the essential unit of institutional analysis.[35] Human groupings vary in scale and size across the three institutional settings. The human institution, therefore, is built upon a great variety of groups that can be as small as two and as large as over one billion people. Institutional mechanisms, historical fortuitousness, locational rationality and external influences play important roles in determining the size of a particular human grouping. The smallest grouping, naturally, may be found in social life, that is, in a two-person family. The largest human grouping exists perhaps in the realm of economy, that is the much talked about "integrated international market." Politically, despite the substantial growth of international organizations and the increasing democratization of political processes, the most important human grouping has remained since the seventeenth century the sovereign nation-states. The institutional arrangement of nations, the international political anarchy, is a human institution built upon the largest but loosest human "grouping" of sovereign nations. This grouping has little group cohesiveness and group identity, in the absence of, say, extraterrestrials.

As in other sciences, how to select samples for an institutional analysis depends primarily on the nature of the task. In order to understand human reproductive behavior, for example, the family and its variations would be the best human grouping to study. To understand economic behavior, firms are the most appropriate groupings to start with. Political issues, and many related economic and social issues, need to be analyzed on the national level. The basic unit of institutional analysis in the social sciences, especially in political science, is the nation or nation-state. The main reason for this is the unique grouping nature of nation-states.

A *nation* is commonly defined as "a relatively large group of people who feel they belong together by virtue of sharing," most importantly "a common language" and "such traits as a common race, culture, history, or set of customs and traditions."[36] *Nation-state* is commonly defined as "a polity in which all citizens share a sense of common identity (nationhood) and in which sub-units . . . are under the domain of a central government" that monopolizes the legitimate use of force (Migdal 1988, 18–19). The size and ethnic composition of a particular nation-state, however, may be subject to external factors *and* changes in its own domestic organizational structure. Some nations, usually large ones, may actually consist of several "nations" that either do not have the ability or do not want to be independent at the time for a number of reasons. The integration of the world economy and the democratization of national politics, for example, may cause the breakup of existing large "multinational" nation-states or even "single-nation" states. (Alesino and Spolaore 1995)

The political grouping of a nation has the unique functions of using force, including force to terminate an individual's or a human grouping's life; taxing every individual and group in the nation; and maintaining the most rigid mutual exclusivity among any human groupings – national borders. The nation thus shall be treated as the most independent human grouping of all. Because the size of nations is sufficiently large, most institutionally constrained human behaviors can develop to their fullest within a nation's boundary, and hence can be observed most fully. No one can really claim to be a "world citizen" and no individual or other human grouping can escape from the "sovereign" power of one nation-state or another. Therefore, nations, rather than any other human groupings, have become the most important basic unit of institutional analysis for social scientists. A nation's domestic organizational structure, or the human institution within the nation, is suggested as the basic unit for an institutional analysis exploring important human behaviors such as economic development, modernization, even war and peace. External institutions, such as international politics and the international market, are by no means ruled out. On the contrary, as this book will demonstrate later, those external factors must be taken into consideration for a good institutional analysis of the domestic organizational nature of a particular nation.

Institutions and the Issue of Institutional Legitimacy

A key issue in the study of the human institution has been the issue of institutional legitimacy.[37] As mentioned above, the human institution and its internalized versions – culture systems – are man-made, and their behavior-constraining or facilitating functions are subject to the acceptance of the members of a human grouping or a nation. An institution's legitimacy is indicated by the number of people who believe in its merits or propriety, not necessarily by its effectiveness.[38] The issue of legitimacy is even more important when there is an alteration of an institution, especially a drastic and comprehensive alteration like those often associated with rapid economic development and revolutionary sociopolitical changes. An institutional change could not last without gaining sufficient legitimacy. Institutions could not effectively function to constrain or facilitate human behavior without their legitimacy. They could not even survive long without sufficient legitimacy. The internalization of a particular set of institutions, the formation of culture systems, would not happen in the absence of legitimacy for those institutions.

Why and how people accept some institutions while rejecting others naturally deserves our attention. How to translate an institution's legitimacy into its effectiveness is perhaps equally important to social scientists and practitioners. Many believe that institutions, especially formal ones, gain their legitimacy and effectiveness through their representation of their governed subjects. The fullest possible participation by the subjects in the decision-making of a particular organization, such as the state, tends to yield the highest institutional legitimacy.[39] Thus, a participatory state or political democracy would have the greatest legitimacy a state can get, and a free market would have the most legitimacy as an economic institution. Others argue that institutional legitimacy depends heavily on the ways in which an institution is "created" by the group members or "imposed" upon them. The former is presumed to be more legitimate, though not necessarily more effective, than the latter (Young 1979). A type of "charismatic legitimacy" is important in the evolution of many legal norms and rules (Kratochwil 1989, 183). A hegemonic rule or "leadership" may be crucial to the emergence and legitimacy of a particular regime or institution (Kindleberger 1973; Keohane 1984). Knowledge, experts, and existing institutions can greatly affect the legitimacy of a new or existing institution (Haas 1964). Douglass North stated straightforwardly that, historically, institutional changes were usually and most effectively "started by the rulers" and then legitimately imposed upon the subjects (1981, 26–8). Existing "legitimate" political and social institutions (they are legitimate at least because they are existing and functioning) can be used to grant an instant legitimacy to a new institution, which may or may not acquire a legitimacy on its own.

In short, institutions, especially those newly emerged, need to gain legitimacy to endure and to function. Institutional legitimacy has its roots deep in pre-existing institutions and the relationship between new and old institutions. By virtue of existence and operation, existing institutions tend to have an important legitimizing or illegitimizing impact on the new. This may especially be the case for political institutions, which may use coercion to force institutional legitimacy effectively, efficiently, and rapidly into people's minds and to break down resistance from the institutions and individuals replaced or reduced.[40] The intrinsic merit or value, internal organization and functional utilities of an institution create the foundation for its acceptance; but skillful and effective leadership by those who create or impose it matters perhaps even more, especially at the crucial beginning. Time, however, appears to be the key to institutional legitimization (Putnam 1993, 8). Over time, an existing and functioning institution accumulates confidence just by being there and functioning, even though it may not be very effective. People need time and experience to feel the value and utility of an institution, and thus to accept and protect it. They also need time and experience to learn how to behave in the institution and to develop the habits and "culture" of such behavior.[41] The transaction cost of demolishing and replacing an institution appears to grow in proportion to its age and scale. The appropriate timing and speed of institutional changes may also be of crucial relevance to the legitimacy of an institution. Therefore, the fate of modernization, understood as a process of institutional changes, may lie more in the legitimization of the new institutions than in their initial quality. Just as there is a distance between the effectiveness and legitimacy of an institution, there is also a practical distance between its "quality" and legitimacy. Other factors affecting the institutional legitimacy of a nation's domestic organizational structure, such as external influences, are too obviously important and relevant to require further discussion here.

Market, Premodern Social Life, Civil Society, and the State

Four key concepts – market, traditional or premodern social life, modern social life or civil society, and the state – need to be clarified.

Market
The term "market" is understood as more than a "gathering of people for buying and selling things."[42] In an ideal sense, it refers to certain organizational principles governing human economic behavior and possibly other kinds of activities. These principles have the following important features: (1) a legitimate purpose of maximizing profit for each producer; (2) the opening of the economy to everyone's entry with an ideal of free flow or exchange of all economic resources; (3) trading of economic resources and products based on mutually exclusive individual, or *legalis homo*, property rights; (4) a changeable price system determined primarily by supply and demand; (5) effective protection and enforcement of market transactions such as contracts; and (6) sufficient independence of economic activities from most of the noneconomic concerns people may have.[43]

Among these features, mutually exclusive property rights and autonomy of the economic activities are perhaps the most important. The ideal "free flow" of economic resources, especially labor, commonly viewed as the essence of the market, is not the defining character of the institution. "Hierarchical" economic institutions, such as firms, as described by Oliver Williamson (1975 & 1985), should be viewed as differently organized and perhaps better equipped actors in the market rather than a substitute for it because, unless a meaningful monopoly is reached, firms do not alter the basic institutional characteristics of the market outlined above. Intrafirm economic exchanges are basically distorted market-based exchanges with the ultimate purpose of competing better on the market, national or international. If a monopoly or an authoritarian type of central planning is established, then the market is distorted, replaced, or even destroyed. A market institution, by definition, cannot exist and function without a political and social framework providing primarily a contract-enforcing mechanism and (especially after the era of the gold standard) a medium of exchange. Thus a perfect or "free market," often interpreted as a free flow or exchange of all economic resources based purely on supply and demand, is only an ideal and practically an impossibility.

The archetypal market described above, if it exists, naturally adapts itself to different social, political, and even natural environments; thus we see some differences in markets of different historical and national settings, but they share the basic characteristics stated above. The influence of societal forces, especially state power, is the key to understanding the inevitable unique aspects of national or regional markets. The classically stated "hidden hand" of the market should, therefore, be understood as a sanction of human behavior generated by the combined forces of the market *and* the political and social institutions.[44]

The market, even if not necessarily a complete or perfect one, makes the allocation and utilization of resources much more efficient than any other known economic system. Although an authoritarian central planning system or a monopolizing giant firm may get a better static utilization of resources by exploring the advantages of a hierarchically structured organization,[45] the market system is definitely superior in maintaining a dynamic optimal resource allocation and utilization over time. This is largely due to the distinctive advantages a market has in generating both technological and organizational innovations. These advantages are deeply rooted in the very dynamic competitive and experimental nature of the market (Cui 1991, 61–2, 66–7). The whole history of modernization has been indispensable to the emergence of the market as the main economic institution. That is, the overall economic system emphasizes the production for the market-based exchange rather than for specific needs (North 1981 and Cox 1987). A market economy *needs* diversity and autonomy in the decision-making of its participants as the basis for competition.

Unfortunately and inevitably, a market institution tends to destroy itself eventually. Market-based competition tends to eliminate competitors by transferring assets to the hands of a decreasing number of winners. This process tends to erode differences, eliminate independence of the participants, and thus suffocate real competition, which is the basis for a viable market economy. Market competition, coupled with ceaseless expansion of production and a search for cost reduction in blind pursuit of maximum profit, results in the transfer of physical and human assets, which leads to overconcentration of property ownership.[46] The related "internalization" or "vertical integration" of firms in substitution for the market may be attractive to individual firms because it saves certain costs involved in market transactions and reduces the risk of asset specificity caused by investment in specialization. But this also tends to contribute to the incapacity of the market mechanisms such as price determination and free entry of competitors (Williamson 1977, 112–22 and North 1981, 34). The market then deteriorates into oligopoly or even monopoly with an inefficient economy. Structurally, this behavior of firms tends to affect state policy making, thus yielding a much more damaging impact on the whole national market. A "self-destruct tendency of the market system," argued Douglass North (1981,183–4), is therefore inherent.

This natural process of self-destruction of the system is a leading path to market failures.[47] First, there is an institutional corrosion of the mutual exclusivity of decision-making by the participants in the market.[48] Second, there is an erosion of the competitive environment for market actors, such as reduced significance of the price mechanism and increased obstacles to the flow of resources. The market itself, unfortunately, cannot correct these two problems, which are either natural products of the operation of a market economy or results of market-related external responses. External intervention to prevent the self-destruction of the market is, therefore, clearly desirable. Nonmarket institutions, particularly hierarchical organizations such as the state, could prevent or correct a market failure by rearranging property rights, modifying or even nullifying certain economic contracts, devising or demolishing obstacles to resource flow, and providing effective guidance or planning supported by the state's legitimate use of force.

Furthermore, a domestic market economy needs to be guided or even "governed" by the state and/or social institutions for other important reasons. While it is the most efficient and innovative economic institution, the market does not necessarily serve other essential needs of human beings. A genuine market tends to damage many other vital human organizations. A major complaint from authors such as Karl Marx and Joseph Schumpeter has been the issue of "alienation" due to the highly specialized division of labor (North 1981, 182–3). Profit-driven short-term behavior, exploitation of the weak and the disadvantaged, environmental devastation, and the commercialization of the family and many other social and political institutions are some examples. The market also tends to produce substantial inequality because of the inevitable differences in individuals' willingness, ability, equipment, accessibility, and pure luck in market-oriented competition. In short, the much cherished "invisible hand" of the market cannot secure the achievement of many noneconomic objectives for humans, although a fast-growing economy powered by the market may provide more economic resources for that achievement. A genuine market-based economy tends to hamper such an achievement by adding new social and political problems. Therefore, profound social and political interventions are justified to moderate externalities of the market that work against people's noneconomic concerns. To economists, this "is probably the most important argument for government intervention" in the market (Cowen 1988, 1).

Domestic markets, except in very rare cases, have, therefore, been largely controlled markets to various degrees (Gerschenkron 1964; Hall 1986). For newly emerged market economies, such as the NICs (newly industrialized countries), domestic markets are especially governed or distorted by political forces (a "strong" or "hard" state) (Wade 1990; Haggard 1990). In other nations, social forces (a "strong" society) may have markedly different controls over the markets (Migdal 1988). In the case of the NICs and similar countries, the states are essentially "working" with their distorted markets to achieve maximum economic growth through efficient international competition. Clearly, they have purposefully paid considerable social and political prices for their fast growth. A bona fide international market now exists governing economic interactions among nationally based firms and individuals and among all nations (Wang 1995). Thus, we observe a two-strata market as the human economic institution: the inevitably distorted domestic markets (or even nonmarket domestic economic systems) and a more authentic international market. To unify the two and create a single "world market" to govern the world economy is an ideal that may never be institutionally feasible.[49]

Traditional or premodern social life and civil society

The term "society" has been commonly used to describe the whole domestic organizational structure of a human group (a nation or a group of nations) and may be defined as "an established pattern of human interaction that persists over time; a division of labor [roles] and rewards [values] that assigns each individual or group of individuals a position vis-à-vis the whole."[50] In this book, unless specified, the word "society" is used in a narrower sense as a general designation to describe social life – the noneconomic activities mainly outside the political realm. It includes personal life, nonpolitical organizations and events, cultural activities and the family. Jürgen Habermas called it "the life-world of self-organized public spheres based on solidarity and communication."[51]

Authors as early as John Locke, Rousseau, Hume, and Hegel have dichotomized human society into antithetical ideal types: the traditional and the modern. This dichotomy has been essential to the study of modernization in our times. Briefly, traditional or premodern social life or society, located in a variety of domestic organizational structures ranging from primitive tribes to highly developed agrarian empires to the "developing" nations of today, is said to be "predominantly rural" and "illiterate." Its social structure "is based upon the extended family" and is "characterized by poorly differentiated, agrarian, family-based, barter economies which neither utilize nor generate innovative technology." Political authority is justified "ascriptively on the basis of lineage, religion, or tradition," and the cultures of premodern nations "reinforce the perpetuation of the traditional social order by stressing the values of passivity, fatalism, and conformity."

"Modern" or "civil" society, often found in "developed" nations, has the features that compose the notion of "modernity": a highly urbanized, well-supplied and universally educated population that is organized in "a highly differentiated network of specialized socioeconomic and political units." The culture of the civil society "stresses the values of political participation, achievement, creativity, nationalism, and other values essential to the operation and perpetuation of modern economic and political systems."[52] Jean Cohen summarized the features of a "modern civil society" as equivalent to "*legality* (private law; civil, political and social equality and rights), *plurality* (autonomous, self-constituted voluntary associations), and *publicity* (spaces of communication, public participation, the genesis, conflict, reflection on, and articulation of political will and social norms)."[53]

The list of contrasting features of the traditional social life and civil society can go on much longer. More confusion is created when some authors actually use the term "civil society" to describe the whole domestic organizational structure of a particular type: a modernity. Nevertheless, the fundamental differences that set a civil society apart from premodern social life are two: how the societal institutions are organized and what their main functions are. A civil society (*civilis societas*) features a clear presence of personal freedom, mobility, and equality based on a basically exclusive property rights definition (Polanyi 1957).[54] Unlike hierarchical political institutions and economic organizations, societal institutions are made up of largely voluntary and equal participants that reserve the right and ability to leave and/or regroup. A significant exception to this organizational principle is the family, where personal choice of regrouping is limited. The functions of the institutions in a civil society are much more exclusively social in that they usually do not have stated economic or political objectives. People generally have individual mobility, both horizontal and vertical. In short, a civil society is "an eclectic variety of noneconomic organizations" (John Keane 1988a, 19; Black 1984) that exist mainly for the purpose of reproduction of individual genes and characteristics. The state and the market economy have taken political and economic functions away from those social organizations.[55] The Italian "civic communities" and "less civic regions," reported by Robert Putnam (1993, 86–92, 182–3), are some recent examples of the notions of civil society and premodern social life, respectively. Civil society, as a convenient name for social life in a modernity, perhaps first emerged in the West but is not exclusively a European phenomenon.[56]

The state
The state is defined by Theda Skocpol (1979) as "a set of administrative, policing, and military organizations headed, and more or less well coordinated by, an executive authority" that "controls a specific territory." A Weberian definition of the state holds that:

> it is an organization, composed of numerous agencies led and coordinated by the state's leadership (executive authority), that has the ability or authority to make and implement the binding rules for all the people as well as the parameters of rule making for other social organizations in a given territory, using force if necessary to have its way.[57]

The state, therefore, is "an institution – an organization – enforcing regulations, at least in part through a monopoly of violence" (Migdal 1988, xiii). It may "autonomously impose collective goals distinct from the private goals generated within the social system itself."[58] The state, Migdal says, can create new social orders and maintain them to foster great social and economic changes since it has "the capabilities to penetrate society, regulate social relationships, extract resources, and appropriate or use resources in determined ways." Whether states have the capability to "achieve the kinds of changes in society that their leaders have sought through state planning, policies, and actions" becomes the criterion to distinguish "strong states" from "weak states" (Migdal 1988, 4–5). Migdal (1988, 18–19) further proposed four major attributes of an ideal "stateness": the monopoly of the principal means of coercion;[59] "the autonomy from domestic and outside forces"; the "significant differentiation of its components"; and explicit coordination of its components, that is, "a coherence of the parts of the state and shared purposes."

The state exists in all sovereign human groupings, ranging from tribes to today's nation-states. In many cases, it may be just an extension of a particular social institution like the family, or effectively captured by a particular social force like religion or an economic force like the market. As the most prominent political institution, the state has a primary function of fulfilling people's political needs, namely the provision of order, security and public authority. Often, however, for a number of reasons and in a variety of ways, the state engages in nonpolitical activities such as economic development and regulation of social life. As the autonomous and sovereign political and administrative organization of a particular human grouping called nation, the state, with its monopoly on coercive means, has always exercised great influence upon the rest of the domestic organizational structure, namely, the economy and the societal institutions.

III. AN INSTITUTIONAL UNDERSTANDING OF MODERNITY AND MODERNIZATION

Having clarified the concept of the human institution, I turn now to discuss an institutional notion of modernity, followed by a conceptual examination of the contents and routes of modernization.

Modernity: An Institutional Notion

Modernization, wrote Samuel Huntington (1968, 32–4), is "a multi-faceted process" towards modernity that ought to be understood on psychological, intellectual, demographic, economic, and political levels. He defines one aspect of modernity – the concept of political modernity or modernized internal structure of polity – as "rationalization of authority, differentiation of structure, and expansion of political participation." Practically, argues Dean Tipps (1973, 223–4), modernization is usually initiated for obvious functional purposes and clearly has multidimensional and even multidirectional features. Monte Palmer (1980, 24, 40–1) also attempted to define "modernity":

> the term *modernity* . . . refers to an ideal pattern of social, economic, and political arrangements that is yet to be achieved but is approximated by the world's more economically developed states. [Thus] *modernization* refers to the process of moving toward the idealized set of relationships posited as *modernity*.

He then listed eight categories and forty-three contrasting characteristics of "ideal traditional and modern societies" to further elaborate the comprehensive concept of "modernity."

Given the multifaceted nature of human needs and desires and given the potentially conflicting human institutions and behaviors, a key to the advancement of social sciences apparently lies in our ability to understand the relationships and interactions of the three elements of the human institution and the three domains of human behavior, which are both conceptualized as economy, polity, and social life. How have they been linked together historically? How can we conceptually capture the various internal structures of the three that have existed in history? What is responsible for the different relationships among the three and their different internal structures over time and geographic span? Can we make any normative judgment about the various types of relationships and interactions among the three, as well as their divergent internal structures for the purpose of maximizing collective and individual human interests? A good answer to those questions will undoubtedly facilitate our endeavors in social sciences. As a contrast to premodernity, modernity, or the goal of modernization, is understood in this book as a specific kind of human organizational structure,

usually nation-based. Namely, modernity refers to the internal structure of the three elements of the human institution – economy,
polity, and social life – and, more importantly, the way in which
they are arranged externally vis-à-vis each other.

The internal structures of human institutions
Historically, human economy, polity, and social life have been internally organized very differently. Many different forms of these
three institutions are observable. For example, there have been
market and nonmarket economies, democratic and nondemocratic
politics, and civil and traditional societies. Naturally, different types
of the three institutions have different impacts on human behavior.
For most social scientists, those varied internal structures of human institutions have been the focus of their work. By definition,
therefore, most of the outstanding social science findings tend to
become reductionist theories. A bridge may be found between those
reductionist theories and the overall mission of explaining human
behavior by exploring how the three institutions, with varied internal structures, relate to and interact with each other. One place to
start is to ascertain the origins of those varied structures. A hypothesis of this study is that the varied internal structures of the
three institutions are primarily the product of the varied relationships and interactions among the three. Two groups of people are
organized differently in their economic activities, for example, primarily because their economies are linked differently to their poli-
ties and their social lives.

Concerning the effectiveness of constraining and facilitating respective behaviors to fulfill the three basic collections of human
needs outlined before, we may be able to identify one optimum
internal structure for each of the three institutions. Such a conceptualization is necessary for an institutional understanding of the
notion of modernity, although it may invite methodological criticism on the grounds of functionalism or normativism.

The market has been viewed by many as the optimum organizational structure for the human economic institution. Historically, a
market economy is a result of separating the economic institution
and behavior from social and political concerns; that is, the market represents an autonomy of economy. It reflects an extensive
differentiation of human institutions and behaviors based on a more
specialized yet flexible division of labor. As mentioned earlier, the
market tends to yield the highest possible dynamic efficiency and

the most innovations over time in allocating and utilizing resources for human needs and desires. But an inherent tendency toward self-destruction through monopolization and the production of significant negative externalities is structurally associated with the market (Williamson 1977, 112–22; North 1981, 34, 183–4). The much criticized ills of capitalism, as forcefully stated by the Marxists, are largely those negative externalities caused by a market economy.

For polity, the prime type of institution has been a nation-state that is internationally sovereign. An internally participatory or "democratic" nation-state tends to have a higher degree of legitimacy if not necessarily effectiveness. A modern nation-state emerges primarily after human political concerns and behaviors are shielded from social and economic concerns; that is, the state acquires a certain autonomy vis-à-vis social and economic institutions such as families and firms. Such a political structure offers effective governing power and lasting political stability if it has acquired sufficient institutional legitimacy through, usually, extensive political participation, thus meeting the human needs for security and order. An extensive and sophisticated political system, however, does not necessarily mean a modern nation-state. For example, the very sophisticated bureaucratic system and authority structure of ancient China was primarily a family-type political system, a "bureaucratic empire,"[60] rather than a modern nation-state. The effective, internally participatory and internationally sovereign nation-state enables optimal achievement of the human political values (stability, order, and equality). Although justified in their interventions in a market economy (Cowen 1988), modern participatory nation-states can be economically costly and inefficient. They also may excessively distort the market and control social life because it is often difficult to avoid abuse of political power based on the legitimate use of force.

The superior institutional form for social life has been a civil society based on functional families and voluntary social associations (for example, contemporary churches). As discussed earlier, the main components of a "modern civil society" are individuality, the relative autonomy of voluntary associations based on socialization, and the family. The boundary between premodern or traditional social life and a civil society is primarily determined by the relationship between social life and the other two basic institutions (polity and economy) since civil society is separated from traditional social life by the relative autonomy of social organizations such as family, social associations, and individuality. Although it has the optimal ability

to fulfill human social needs and social desires centered on reproduction, a civil society is nonetheless not always conducive to a market
economy and may often compromise the effectiveness of the state.

*The differentiation and interaction of the three institutions: to
understand "premodernity" and modernity*
Human economy, polity, and social life have historically been arranged very differently against each other. They may have relative
autonomy and thus the ability to develop fully their own internal
structures. They may also be largely undifferentiated or very poorly
differentiated with almost no visible institutional boundaries among
them and similar, if not identical, internal structures. Historically,
primitive tribes, totalitarian political regimes, or a dominant "free"
market tend to organize the three institutions in such an undifferentiated fashion. Given the known advantages of division of labor,
we may easily understand that such an undifferentiated human institution tends to be a poor maximizer of the various institutional
utilities we need and desire. An individual's behavior, therefore,
becomes political, economic, and social at the same time and is
judged and rewarded or penalized in a uniform and singular way.
Institutionally, those undifferentiated domestic organizational structures are typically viewed as "premodern" (Figure 1.2). Here, perhaps only the "free market" type of premodernity needs a little
explanation, since the premodern domestic organizational structures
of a tribe and an authoritarian or totalitarian nation are relatively
well-known. Due to the self-destructive nature of the market institution, a "free market" premodernity may rarely last long enough
for observers to describe it. Nevertheless, a journalist's comment
on the American judicial system may help to illustrate the impact
such a "free market" premodernity is likely to have on the polity:

> For [it has been] demonstrated perhaps more starkly than ever
> before that in the American justice system, as in so much else in
> this country, money changes everything and huge amounts of money
> change things almost beyond recognition.[61]

Visible damage from a "free market" premodernity or "post-
modernity" may have already happened to the social life of the
United States, as reflected by the decay of communities and functional families, the rapid increase of brutal criminals, and the development of disastrous psychological "diseases."[62]

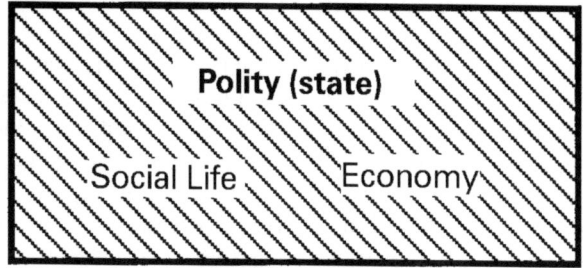

**Type I – State dominance:
A totalitarian nation**

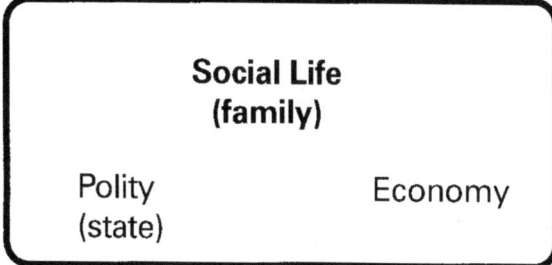

**Type II – Social institution
dominance: a tribe-nation**

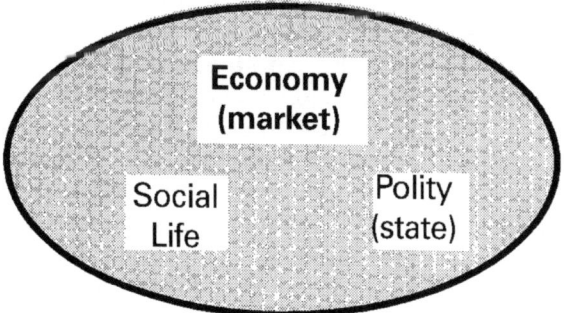

**Type III – Economy
dominance: a "free" market**

Figure 1.2 Premodern organizational structures

For the aggregate optimality of human behavior, therefore, it is a goal for people to have all three ideal forms of institutions present and interacting in a coordinated way to ensure the maximum fulfillment of human needs and satisfaction of human desires – to have a modernity of a particular human grouping.[63] Modernity, therefore, refers to a particular institutional arrangement of the domestic organizational structure of a human grouping (a nation). Under such an arrangement, all three institutions are established in a way that offsets the others' negative externalities and ensures the healthy survival and evolution of one another. The aggregate human behavior is thus differentiated, yet coordinated to meet needs and satisfy desires to a maximum extent. Modernity thus has an observably objective definition: a differentiated yet interactive relationship among the economy, polity, and social life (Figure 1.2). A modernity of domestic organizational structure institutionally fixes the market as the autonomous main economic institution while guaranteeing the existence of nonmarket economic institutions based on social and even political rationales. Market-like exchanges find their places in politics and even families as long as the market is not the dominant institution of polity or social life. Social institutions such as families and voluntary associations are the main institutions of social life, and they can exist and even be influential in economic and political activities. Meanwhile, the autonomous and participatory state is the dominant political institution, which may also have significant influence on the nation's economic and social activities.

Historically, such an institutional goal may be reached through often unconscious behavior, sanctioned by the process of competitive selection among the human groupings (that is, international competition and migration) and based on the human ability of learning and changing. The process of change and development of the human institutional structure approaching modernity is hence called modernization. And the establishment of a differentiated yet interactive relationship among a market economy, a nation-state, and a civil society is the accomplishment of modernization, the arrival of modernity. An institutional understanding of the notion of modernity is therefore proposed to save this useful concept of the traditional modernization theory from vagueness and ethnocentric biases. Such a conceptualization of modernity may make our study of modernization and social changes a more scientific, and thus more fruitful, endeavor.

The Routes to Modernity

Our conceptualization of modernity does not assume a "universal" image of modernity, or insist on the practical feasibility of having all three institutions differentiated and interacting at once, or assert that history ends when the three institutions are established in a differentiated and interactive relationship. On the contrary, the logic of the institutional analysis approach depicts the various internal structures and relationships of the three elements of the human institution in different human groupings or nations, caused by the constant, dynamic and profound interactions among the three. It is entirely possible to have a variety of modernities across national boundaries and at different times. There is no guarantee that every nation, as a human grouping that enjoys sovereignty, can reach modernity before it disappears from history.

In the same logic as Jon Elster's "impossibility theorem" (1993), it is "impossible" to gain a market economy, a participatory polity and a civil society all at once. One of the three institutions can serve as the driving engine for modernization by being relatively autonomous first, and then affecting the other two. Historically, we have had a market-driven modernization route and a state-led modernization course. Although theoretically a society-led modernization is possible, there is no known successful case in history.[64] It needs to be clarified here that the idea of "route" is not the same as "the trajectories" of economic development. Stephan Haggard's (1990, 24–7) three trajectories – import-substitution industrialization, export-led growth, and entrepôt growth – were actually three development strategies that could be used by nations undergoing a modernization process, market-driven or state-led. These two routes, concerning the different degrees and nature of political intervention in the economy, are roughly comparable to what Robert Wade termed "free market," "simulated market," and "governed market" (1990, 297).

A market-driven modernization
As Figure 1.3 shows, in a market-driven modernization a market, essentially spontaneously, emerges as the main economic institution and then causes changes in the whole domestic organizational structure, leading to a differentiation of polity and social life. Historically, the Western European–North American modernization has followed this route.[65] In Western Europe and North America, a

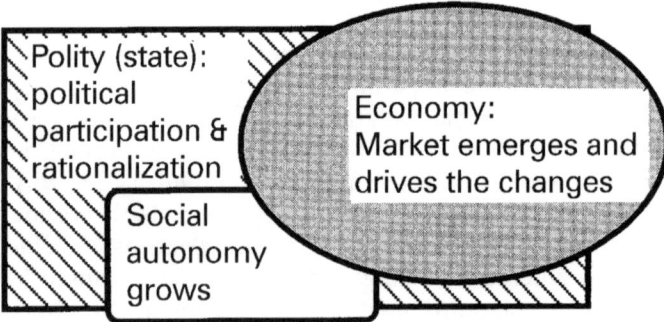

From a state dominant premodernity

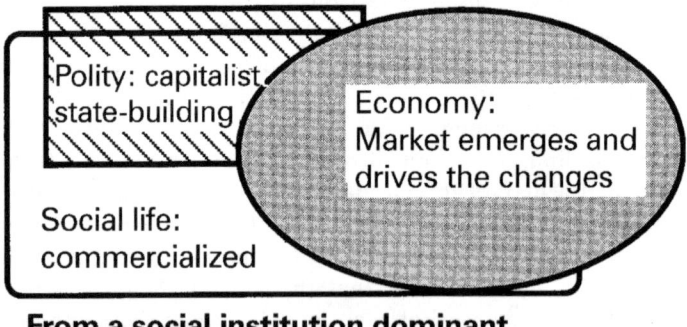

From a social institution dominant premodernity

Figure 1.3   A market-driven modernization

market gradually separated itself from the premodern domestic organizational structure and the whole process of modernization started.[66] During a relatively short period of human history, these nations experienced great increases in economic output, productivity, and innovation. Based on economic and technological developments, social and cultural lives improved enormously. The market demanded and facilitated development of a new set of foundational sociopolitical institutions centered on mutually exclusive property rights. In Marxian terms, the market economy had its social and political impacts which caused a commodification of social relations in general. This commodification, historically and practically, is done through the capture of the state by a certain class or political group; these groups in turn use the state to consolidate the market as the main economic institution. From this process, a "market-driven" modernization succeeded. Thus the establishment of a capitalist market signals the entrance into the realm of modernity. Historically, not only a capitalist market with its "commodification" is important, but that an effective state, independent from the economic and social institutions, is crucial to the development of European modernization. The economically empowered people, soon unsatisfied with the negative externalities and the self-destruction tendency of the market, started to forcefully employ the autonomous state to shield polity and social life from the market *per se*, and started to regulate the economy. As a result, there was the emergence of a differentiated and interactive relationship among the economy, polity, and social life. Almost as a rule of history, however, modernity arrived, at least initially, at the expense of excluding many of the people in the nation who were economically weak, socially and culturally marginal, and politically powerless.

The separation of the state from social life, caused by market-driven institutional changes symbolized by commodification, is viewed by many as not only the process of modernization, but also the very essence, a *sine qua non*, of democracy in complex societies (Keane 1988a, 25). Thus the market institution led to the transformation of the premodern domestic organizational structure. The differentiation of the state and social life is a crucial component of the birth and existence of modern democracy.[67] Liberal interpretation of a market-driven modernization, however, has downplayed the role of the state and stressed the pure function of market under the "invisible hand."

In short, the "market-driven modernization" pattern is characterized by the emergence of a market economy from the premodern social institutions and its autonomy from the state. This market then causes the old sociopolitical complex to transform by "capturing" the state and "commercializing" societal institutions. Political actions and social resistance contributed to the eventual completion of the modernization process.

A state-led modernization
Figure 1.4 shows a state-led modernization referring to an effort by the state as an autonomous political institution to create a market

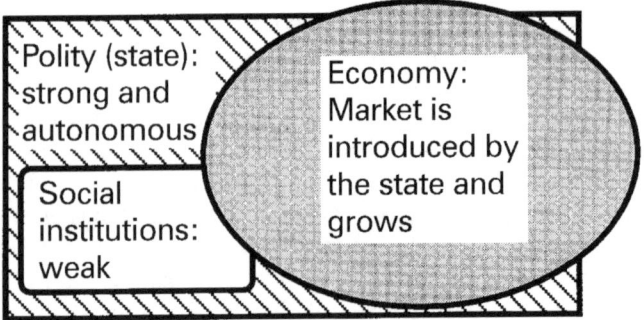

For a state dominant premodernity

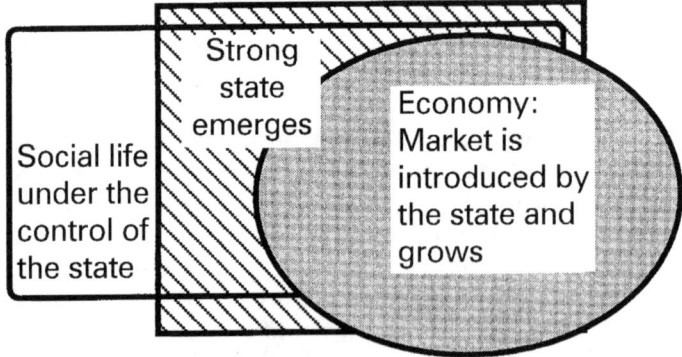

For a social institution dominant premodernity

Figure 1.4 A state-led modernization

economy forcefully, and thus to start the differentiation of the premodern domestic organizational structure. German modernization in the nineteenth century, Japanese modernization after the Meiji Restoration in 1868, and the growth of the East Asian NICs are successful cases of state-led modernization.[68]

A state-led modernization route can be seen as a two-stage process. First, the state uses its political and administrative power to alter the existing domestic organizational structure in order to "modernize" or "develop" the nation. Here, the state can go two ways:

introducing and utilizing the market, or suppressing or even eliminating it. In the second stage, the state continues its leading role in guiding and promoting market-oriented economic development while transforming itself and its relationship with the market and social life. In a successful state-led modernization, an autonomous and strong or "hard" state[69] first introduces, "plants," and even directly "creates" the market economy, breaking the premodern domestic organizational structure. In the process, it creates new institutional arrangements or "contextual conditions" for the market economy to grow *without* fundamentally changing the old sociopolitical complex itself.[70] Then the state uses its "public power,"[71] in the form of an effective, knowledgeable, willing, but usually authoritarian administration, to guide or manage the market according to certain strategies and policy goals. The state and the existing but changing domestic organizational structure hence rapidly inject much-needed institutional legitimacy into the emerging market institution. For this purpose, the state may also project "public power" in the form of an effective and appropriate legal system. Different development strategies, with different economic performance, are often adopted due to differences in "state strength." State strength, in turn, is determined by three important variables: "state-society linkages," "organizational characteristics," and "the range of policy instruments the state commands" (Haggard 1990, 45–6).

Although the initial market-creation or introduction is crucial, it is often the second stage that determines the fate of a state-led modernization effort. This is especially true for those so-called "latecomer" nations. A constant "guidance of the market" is empirically a major defining feature which separates a market-driven modernization from a state-led one. The state must undergo substantial transformation of its internal organization and enhance its ability and effectiveness in facilitating and guiding the emerging market. Yet, many latecoming states did not or could not maintain an effective guidance of the new market in an era of international markets: those nations generally would not have a successful market-driven modernization. A newly emerged market institution on its own would lead the national economy directly to "dependent development" or "underdevelopment" that develops by importing certain new technologies and capital while trailing behind under a "new" but still premodern domestic organizational structure.

As an inevitable byproduct of the institution-altering pressure of the advancing market, a separation between the state and social life gradually takes place, completing the achievement of a distinctive and interactive economy-polity-social life relationship, that is, a modernized domestic organizational structure. The state, however, often continues its traditional hold on the nation's social life in the form of a "sociopolitical complex." There is much less development of a civil society and the associated civil liberties and personal freedom. Political democracy is often sacrificed, at least temporarily, for political stability and effectiveness. Nevertheless, the crucial emancipation of the market has occurred and it is protected by the almighty state, which permits a remarkable pace of economic growth and development of technology, education and social welfare. The market is the engine, but it is the state, not the invisible hand of the market, that directs the engine. The price is the often seen political distortion of the market.

Such an understanding of state-led modernization has cast doubts on the "classic" understanding of modernization as a mere function of economic development and technological progress.[72] It explores the political factors behind economic and social developments. This understanding implies a strong possibility of "conscious" modernizing efforts made by a political regime based on the knowledge of its "needs" and its environment. It also questions the conventional notion that economic development, social liberalization, and political democratization are inseparable in a modernization process.[73] In practice, many national leaders, especially those of the NICs, realize the significance of a separation between economy and politics, but much less the necessity of a division between the state and social life. They achieved a state-led economic and social development program without first fundamentally changing their sociopolitical complex.[74] They favor a modern market economy with basically the traditional state-social life relationship, in which the state plays a dominant role vis-à-vis the social institutions and even the economy.[75]

Having discussed the two different routes to modernization, we certainly should not dismiss "the possibility of an eventual convergence" (Moore 1967, 159). Indeed, the institutional understanding of the notion of modernity clarifies the meaning of this possible convergence. Still, modernized nations will have varied modernities, that is, their "modernized" domestic organizational structures will differ meaningfully from each other. Furthermore, although market-driven or state-led modernizations may all work, not all of them are feasible or desirable for a particular nation. It is obviously important to distinguish the different routes available, though the ultimate destiny may be roughly the same.

The Variety of Modernity

Modernity exists in a variety of forms. The routes to modernity obviously play a crucial role in shaping the specific character of a modernity in a particular nation. Different routes to modernity will necessarily sanction different human behaviors, produce different intended and unintended consequences, achieve different end results, and require very different strategies and conditions to succeed. Different routes and other varied conditions may lead to a variety of modernities as the distances and interactions among the three institutions vary and the internal structures of the three differ. As long as institutional distances *and* linkages are identifiable between the economy and the state, between the economy and social life, and between the state and social life, a nation achieves its institutional modernity. The exact distances among the three institutions may vary and are subject to adjustment by the forces of one, two, or all three of them. Therefore, the main differences that set apart the various modernized domestic organizational structures are the distances, patterns and velocities of the interaction among the three institutional components of that domestic organizational structure: economy, polity, and social life. How the three institutions are arranged against each other determines the features of a particular modernity. For example, Japan and the United States can be considered modernized nations, but they have distinctively different arrangements for the three institutions. While the Japanese state is seen as being intrusive in a "friendly" way, even intertwined with the Japanese market economy (Johnson 1982), Washington has been a historically distrusted, "necessary evil" in the eyes of corporate America. A similar comparison can be drawn for European cases.[76] As long as an institutional differentiation and interaction are established among the economy (generally market-oriented), polity (generally an effective nation-state with massive and meaningful participation of the citizens) and social life (a civil society), a modernity is present even though the various distances and the various patterns of interactions among the three may empirically portray considerably different types of modernity.

The variety of modernity is also reflected in the fact that, once established, a differentiated and interactive relationship among the economy, polity and social life in a particular nation may not include every member of that human grouping. A historical and institutional exclusion or even discrimination against sizable sections of a particular nation illustrate the variety of modernity at different times of that nation's history. The American modernity enjoyed by the wealthy and educated white males of the United States as early as two hundred years ago is very different from the American modernity by the time of the Great Depression and the American modernity in existence today.[77] Even if the arrangement among the economy, polity, and social life has been basically the same in the United States for the past two centuries (a simplistic assumption for the sake of argument), the American modernity has changed over that time by gradually dismantling the exclusions and discriminations against various segments of the population, such as women and ethnic minorities. The whole idea of promoting American "values" and institutions around the globe can, therefore, be interpreted essentially as an effort to establish American modernity worldwide. That would eliminate the differences between the national modernities and enable a world modernity. This noble ideal, however, may never be achievable since the foundation of a world modernity, a genuine "world market," is highly undesirable and basically impossible (Wang 1995).

In short, modernity varies with time, geography and especially grouping. In order to understand those variations of modernity, especially *"ad hoc"* ones, we may need to have a time-conscious, group-based and issue-specific approach in our institutional analysis of modernization.

The Issue of "Post-Modernity"

After the arrival of modernity, modernization is not finished, because people continue to desire and adopt adjustments. The "coverage" of modernity also changes over time as exclusion and discrimination practices change due to migration, education, and political struggles. Knowledge, ideas, and technology play profound roles in this endless process of modernization, or "post-modernization." Modernity can be acquired through modernization; it needs to be maintained and adjusted through "post-modernization." It can also be "lost" through a "post-demodernization," in which the distances among the economy, polity, and social life shrink below meaningful levels or the linkages among the three are somehow severed.

A well-established differentiated and interactive economy-polity-social life relationship can be further adjusted or "destroyed" – "moving forward to the past." Historically, modernity may be "extinguished" by forces from within or without a particular human grouping. The Greeks two millennia ago achieved a remarkable domestic organizational structure resembling a modernity in places like Athens, but that was accomplished on the basis of excluding the majority of the population – the slaves. The mechanisms of the slavery system led to the necessity and even glorification of wars which eventually destroyed the Greek modernity, together with the sovereign "nations" including Athens. Similarly, the modernities reached in the developed nations are in no way guaranteed. Nazi Germany, with its aggression during World War II, is a well-known example of the destruction of modernity domestically and internationally on a horrendous scale.

Modernity can be further affected by the accumulation of knowledge and by technological change and innovation, which cause alterations in human behavior and thus in the delicate interaction among economy, polity, and social life. The variations of units also have a significant impact on the shape and longevity of modernity.[78] The discourse on modernization concerning such things as inductive or hindering conditions, working mechanisms, intended or external consequences of human behaviors, and ways and means to create and maintain a modernity is far from being exhausted. Therefore, an institutional understanding of the notion of modernity sheds new light on the field while opening new horizons.

IV. TIMING AND OTHER REMAINING METHODOLOGICAL ISSUES

There are at least two major routes to modernity – market-driven or state-led – and that is the origin of the variety of modernity. Why do some nations take one route while some take the other? Which route is more appropriate for a specific nation? To answer these questions, a discussion on the timing of institutional changes, that is, modernization, is imperative. The methodological issue of the unit of analysis is revisited here. It is then hypothesized that a state-led route is more appropriate for the so-called "latecomer" nations, as demonstrated by the successful developments of Germany, Japan and other NICs. Some remaining methodological issues need to be considered in order to clarify further the premises of the application of this institutional analysis perspective. The purpose of doing so is to report some methodological uncertainties this perspective may have (King et al. 1994, 31–2).

The Issue of Timing in Institutional Analysis

Like the issue of the unit of analysis, the issue of timing is methodologically crucial to an institutional analysis. As chaos theorists believe, the results of a complex system all have a "sensitive dependence on initial conditions" (Gleick 1987, 311). This book will consider the role of both absolute and relative timing in our institutional understanding of modernity and modernization. Absolute timing refers to a particular point of a human grouping's history: How long has the grouping been in existence before the institutional changes take place? Relative timing means the historical position of a grouping in comparison to others: Has any other nation started modernization or even reached modernity?

The question of when, absolutely or relatively, one of the three institutions emerges autonomously holds enormous significance to a modernization process. This understanding provides a solid conceptual foundation for the criticisms against the ethnocentric problem of many traditional works on modernization.[79] The absolute timing is important because the pre-existing domestic organizational structure, institutions and internalized institutions – the culture, has varied degrees of legitimacy at different "ages"; this significantly increases or decreases the difficulty of an institutional transformation, depending on whether the existing institutions are resisting or facilitating the changes. The relative timing is even more important, primarily because nations, currently the highest level of human hierarchical grouping, do not exist and develop in a vacuum. International relations make the relative timing of institutional changes in a particular nation extremely consequential.

The disparity between an "anarchic" international political order and a market-based international economy only enhance the importance of timing for a particular nation, since economically powerful nations can build up monopoly positions on the international market to the detriment of the latecomer nations. The existence of a near "free" international capital market, accompanied by an absence of international labor market, for example, has made the late-comer nations to face extraordinary difficulties in developing their market economies. Unfavorable influences by the advanced nations, such as enticing people in developing states to premature consumerism, is unfortunately magnified by the shrinking distances among nations. As long as national sovereignty still has legitimacy, group-based human behavior, including the evolution of the human institution, is nationally bounded and subject to foreign influences that are often justifiably viewed as a "threat" to the security and welfare of the nation. Thus, approaching modernity as a trailblazer or a latecomer makes a tremendous difference concerning the selection of routes and strategies and the chance of success. As with the theory of relativity in physics, time is everything to social scientists observing modernization.

To latecomers, commonly doomed to "duplicate" the perceived advanced nations, a proper sequence is especially important. Which comes first – political democracy or a market economy or a liberal social life?[80] Do they have to come in pairs or triplets? The value of T_0 ("time zero"), "the starting point," holds crucial information to answering those questions. If a premodern nation has a T_0 of three years for absolute timing (that is, the nation has only been in existence for three years) and 100 years for relative timing (that is, some interacting nations have reached modernity 100 years ago), chances are the nation would have a weak state and a poorly developed domestic organizational structure due to the lack of seasoned institutional legitimacy and a heavy, usually unfavorable, economic dependence on the international market. This institutionally weak latecomer would then find it very difficult to "catch up" with the developed nations economically, politically and even socially. "Conventional" modernization efforts may actually cause more hardships for the people.

A major task, then, is to ascertain the values of T_0, T_1, T_2, ... and T_n for a nation. Just like any construction work, institutional building and its legitimacy require different actions at different stages of the process. New knowledge and better technology may present possibilities for acceleration and perhaps a better result, but can hardly nullify this rule. Many variables matter very differently to the fate of an institutional change simply because of the different values of T_0. This is why the critique of the traditional modernization theories by the dependency school and world system theorists[81] offers valuable contributions to our understanding of the modernization courses in those latecomer nations. The detrimental impact of international power disparities between the developed and the developing nations, insisted upon and even exaggerated by the dependency scholars, is one of the uniquely unfavorable conditions for a latecomer. To consider the important role of timing in analyzing institutional changes may substantially help us to understand modernization by incorporating the insights of the dependency theory and the world system theory.

Empirically, we see several unique conditions that require more creativity and strength for a latecomer's modernization effort to succeed. The early modernizers could proceed by trial and error and enjoy the luxury of having time on their side. The latecomers are often under crashing pressure of time to "copy" the tangible benefits a modernized nation provides. Altered political geography now determines the general lack of places for population emigration. The dominant culture and media of the early modernizers have imposed an often suicidal cost of institutional exclusion especially political discrimination inside the latecomers. Institutional changes need strong existing institutional forces for innovation and construction, and time is essential for building up legitimacy to support new institutions. Unfortunately, most latecomer nations have neither. Many modernization strategies and tactics prescribed by Western scholars for developing nations are analogous to suddenly giving a supersonic jet to a lifelong driver of a horse-drawn wagon – hardly a desirable or comfortable, let alone manageable, situation. The predictable consequences are two: stagnated real progress due to the inability in "taking off," or a disastrous crash. This simple logic explains the failures and even disasters of many developing nations that have tried to copy the advanced nations instantly or "efficiently."

The task for the latecomers, then, is to devise new institutions such as a market and put them into an interactive relationship with existing institutions as soon as possible, while preventing the whole domestic organizational structure from collapsing. Human behavior without institutional constraints is hardly constructive to the establishment of new institutions. As Douglass North elegantly put it, "institutional changes can hardly be achieved by the unguided and unconstrained masses" (1981, 27). To have an institutional differentiation of the premodern domestic organizational structure is a very delicate and time-consuming task, because legitimacy and effectiveness of any human institution can only be acquired through the accumulation of experience over time. Institutional changes are difficult and potentially explosive.[82] Therefore, perhaps ironically, the strength of certain aspects of the old institutions such as the state and the family structure is crucial for the establishment and growth of new ones. Excessive external "help" and/or demands, even with good intentions, tend to weaken or destroy existing institutions in a reckless way and thus become counterproductive to the modernization efforts of latecomers. Explosive change and shock therapy, being costly and dangerous, in no way guarantee the birth or growth of new institutions. While rightfully urging progress on the latecomers, advanced nations need to be aware of the possibility that they could be traveling on a time machine, moving "forward to the past" by destroying the interactive and differentiated relationships among their markets, nation-states under international political anarchy, and civil societies.

Why a State-led Route?

The value of gradualism and decreasing institutional exclusion during the process of modernization is indeed a major historical lesson that is largely forgotten by many. For latecomers, it is especially important to have effective and legitimate institutional exclusions (mainly a political one) for a considerable time so that newly emerging institutions such as the market can grow and gain legitimacy over the natural resistance from the political actions by the people who are used to the old institutions.[83] The emergence of the market, like the emergence of a democratic polity, causes tremendous alterations of old institutions and cultures; combined with the large scale of human dislocation, there is a greatly increased risk of instability, especially political. That is likely to lead to a loss of institutional constraints that are absolutely crucial to any directional, goal-oriented human behavior.

Naturally, resistance to institutional changes (such as the emergence of a new pattern of labor allocation) seeks to stop or distort the process through political means. Therefore, an autonomous, thus necessarily "discriminatory," determined and capable state is a must for latecomers to overcome the resistance of institutions and the inertia of individuals sanctioned and legitimized by the old domestic structure. The state is perhaps the only institution which can, based on its use of force, effectively introduce and protect the new market institution without causing a massive institutional meltdown.

Unfortunately, an effective and stable state is not a common phenomenon in latecomer premodern nations. Extraordinary pressures for nonexclusive political and economic policies, exemplified by the advanced nations and magnified by modern communications and transportation, have powerfully set the "modernized" West as a tempting but elusive reference for the latecomers. The much greater and more urgent demand for an appropriate and active state role, arising from the need for introducing and guiding a national market, tends to overburden, even destroy, the poorly institutionalized, barely rationalized, and often weak (because of insufficient legitimacy caused by the unpopularity of maintaining institutional exclusions) political systems in those nations. Thus we see so much chaos, mischief, and disappointment.

An erroneous sequence of establishing the three institutions can, therefore, be fatal to a modernization effort. Competent, innovative, and pragmatic national politics, under proper strategic guidance, then become a key to success. Therefore, as a major working hypothesis, this book suggests that, for a latecomer nation like China, a state-led modernization with a well-designed sequence and strategy is an appropriate route. In a seeming paradox, latecomer nations need a state to lead the modernization that requires the predominant role of a market.

In the twentieth century, especially since World War II, almost all "backward" nations have been trying to develop their economy through state leadership. It may look as if all were pursuing a "state-led" modernization. In fact, many of these states, such as the former Soviet Bloc and China before 1978, were only on a "state-led" track that was in the wrong direction – to eliminate rather than to emancipate the market. Many others have perhaps been both on the appropriate track (state-led) and heading in the right direction (to introduce the market). But, because of a lack of capability or the willingness to take political risks, they have been ineffective in "guiding" and utilizing the market. They have largely failed to move beyond the first stage of a state-led modernization. For them, an intended state-led modernization course gradually disintegrated into an undesirable, often chaotic, generally infeasible and ineffective market-driven endeavor.

State-led modernization often started as a state's political effort to develop the economy for its political security. What happened initially in Germany, Japan and the East Asian NICs has been such. By the late twentieth century, however, such a perhaps unintended pattern for the evolution of the human institution has become rather archetypal. To compensate for the disadvantages caused by the timing factor, latecomer nations thus all have the tendency to rely on the state which is often the institution that has some power. The initial purpose was often to secure the political regime or safeguard the national independence. Threatened by the real or perceived colonialism and various "neo-colonialism," latecomer nations naturally started to use their political power to "protect" and develop their economy, aiming at both economic development and national political independence. Mercantilist or neomercantilist policies are popular in developing nations.[84] The lack of capital, technology, and managerial skills prompted latecomers to look for state-of-the-art technology, knowledge and capital in the West. It also prompted them to use their political and administrative capabilities to improve their position in competing with the developed economies for those resources.[85] Planning, coordination, mobilization, fundraising, and protectionism have been the major weapons used by states in the developing nations. Most newly born states in premodern nations are "compelled" to modernize their countries, as the ruling élites usually appreciate the differences between their nations and the West, though not all of them fully understand the causes of the differences. Interactions across national boundaries, greatly enhanced by modern communication and transportation, make such an urge almost politically irresistible to many national leaders.

Usually, the states in premodern nations are capable of leading their modernization course to a certain extent, especially at the first stage – introducing the market. Their performance, however, varies a great deal at the second stage, that is, in guiding and utilizing the market while transforming state and social institutions. Therefore, many states have tried state-led modernization but, so far, very few have succeeded. The key here is the state: Does it have what it takes to complete a state-led modernization?

The notion of "developmental state"

Robert Wade's "governed market (GM) theory of East Asian success" emphasizes an active role for the state in intervening and even "distorting" the market for the purpose of economic growth (1990, 24–9). This GM model, while capturing only part of the conceptualization of state-led modernization, contains a useful notion of "developmental state," a term coined by Chalmers Johnson. The reason why some developing states did not or, more frequently, could not pursue a state-led modernization is that they were not a developmental state, which is a key to the success of a state-led modernization. A developmental state has the following characteristics:

- The top priority of state action is economic development, defined in terms of growth, productivity, and competitiveness rather than in terms of welfare.
- The state actively leads and guides the market in accumulating and directing investment.
- The state is committed to private property and the market, and limits its intervention to conform with this commitment
- The state guides the market with instruments formulated by an élite economist bureaucracy.
- The state is engaged in numerous institutions for consultation and coordination with the private sector.
- The state relies mainly on bureaucrats to "rule," under the "supervision" of the politicians – a "soft authoritarianism."
- The state is heavily colored with "hard" or "soft" authoritarianism and corporatism. (Robert Wade 1990, 25–9)

Three major components or conditions are therefore hypothesized as being responsible for a successful state-led modernization: an effective and usually strong state (even authoritarian state as it is capable of maintaining institutional exclusions and legitimizing new institutions primarily the market) authority committed to economic development; emergence of the market as the main economic institution; and, more important, continuous, willing and capable guidance of the market from the state, which is transforming itself and its relationship to the rest of the domestic organizational structure.

Some Remaining Methodological Issues

As in any social science endeavor, the findings of a study based on institutional perspective are inferences that tend to have limits of certainty. Good empirical tests and further conceptual work are needed to validate hypotheses and reduce uncertainties. For example, at least two methodological tasks still need further work. First, it is necessary to develop units of measurement across historical and national settings in order to observe, record, analyze, and compare institutional changes and to evaluate the results – the variety of distances and interactions among the three elements of the human institution. For instance, how should one measure the distance between the state and market in Japan versus that in the United States? This is very important for any attempt at demonstrating the distance, independence, differentiation *and/or* interactions among a nation's economy, polity, and social life. A good quantification of those units of measurement will conceivably increase the certainty of the findings of an institutional analysis significantly. Existing tools such as fuzzy mathematics may have great potential to enhance the quantitative techniques of institutional analysis in social sciences.

Second, we need a proper treatment for the theoretically possible and practically very meaningful issue of analyzing the "sub-institutions" within the three institutions of economy, polity, and social life. Within polity, numerous sub-institutions such as political participation, law-enforcement, and special protection of minorities demand our attention. Questions such as how they are and should be arranged against each other contain extensive information about the human institution in a nation and its changes. The application of the institutional perspective becomes more elaborated, more practical, and more sophisticated, however, if we take into consideration the "cross-institutional" interactions among the sub-institutions. For instance, many important policies can be improved with a good knowledge of how family life affects law enforcement in the area of labor force production (child-bearing and education). A unified scientific methodology is needed for an adequate analysis of these sub-institutions, utilizing the substantial achievement of social sciences on those subjects.

V. SUMMARY

This chapter has presented an institutional approach for the study of modernization. It suggests that modernity should be understood as an arrangement of three basic elements of the human institution – economy, polity, and social life – in a differentiated yet interactive way. The market, an effective and participatory nation-state, and a civil society are viewed as the ideal types of internal organizations of the three institutions respectively, although internal characteristics of the three institutions are secondary to the notion of modernity. Depending on which institution emerges first as an autonomous engine to drive the separation of the three, there are historically different routes to modernity with a variety of consequences. Timing and sequence of modernization make a great difference in selecting the right route and the proper strategies. For latecomers such as China, a state-led route appears to be more appropriate.

A state-led modernization, however, places heavy demands on the capacity of the state in introducing, establishing, and guiding the market to become the main economic institution. This task, in turn, demands substantial changes of the state in terms of legitimacy, mobilization skills, administrative effectiveness, decision-making autonomy, technical know-how, and legal construction.

NOTES

1. Natural and technological conditions, of course, matter. But they should be viewed as only limited factors in explaining the great variation of human behavior since (1) most nations have basically a functionally similar natural endowment and climate; (2) the varied levels of technology/knowledge are first the results of human behavior before becoming a factor affecting human behavior. For a discussion on the limited impact of high technology on human behavior, see "Does it Matter Where You Are?" in *The Economist*, London, July 30–August 5, 1994,13–14.
2. The leading views of neo-evolutionism can be found in Eisenstadt 1971 & 1973.
3. For a good summary of the traditional modernization theory by sociologists, see Harrison 1988.
4. Rostow [1960] 1990, Hirshman 1977 & 1981, Black 1966, and Almond & Coleman 1960.
5. Rostow 1960 and, similarly, Black 1960. The philosophical origins of such a linear and universal idea of modernization can be easily traced back to Karl Marx and Friedrich Hegel. Some well-known studies of Chinese modernization are based on a similar line with an emphasis on the issue of China's "opening" or "closure" to Western economic and cultural exchanges (Fairbank et al. 1960). As an alternative understanding of modernization, the "dependencia" school presents one important critique to the neoclassic "conventional" theories, and raises the concept of underdevelopment. (Amin 1974, Frank 1967, Evans 1979, and Cardoso & Faletto 1979).
6. Some defined modernization as a qualitatively fast "process of economic and social change" that leads to a "modern society" that is "characterized by a belief in the rational and scientific control of man's physical and social environment and the application of technology to that end." (Kautsky 1980, 20) Similar nebulous and unsatisfactory conceptualizations of the notion of modernization can be found in some other "traditional" works on the subject such as Lener 1958 and Neil Smelser in Etzioni 1964, 258. For a Chinese attempt to add some "national character" to this type of understanding of modernization, see Chen Zhengchang: "Shilun xiandaihua de shijiexing yu minzuxing"

[On the universality and nationality of modernization], in *Xibei daxue xuebao* [Journal of the Northwestern University], Xian, No. 4, 1994, 101–6.

7. For a recent philosophical examination of the notion of modernity, see Winfield 1991, ix & 130–2. For a Chinese understanding of the notion of "modernity," see Liu Xiaofeng: *Xiandaixing wenti yu xiandai Zhongguo* [The issue of modernity and modern China], Hong Kong, Oxford University (China) Press, 1996.

8. Cardoso & Faletto 1979, Evans 1979, Wallerstein 1980, and Chase-Dunn 1989 & 1990.

9. See Weber 1977 and Bendix 1967 & 1977. For a Chinese view of modernization as the realization of "rationality" or "scientific rationality," see He Zhonghua: "Xiangdaihua guanglian de luojiyiyun jiqi lishi biaozhen" [The logic content and historical expression of the notion of "modernization"] in *Tianjin shehui kexue* [Tianjin social sciences], Tianjin, No. 1, 1995, 19–25.

10. For examples, see O'Donnell 1979, Johnson 1982, Haggard 1990, and Wade 1990.

11. For a Chinese version of the "catching-up modernization" model, see Wang Yalin: "Zhongguo de 'ganchaoxin xiandaihua'" [The "catching up type modernization" in China], in *Shehuixue Yanjiu* [Sociological studies], Beijing, No. 1, 1994, 19–29.

12. Leslie Sklair (1995), for example, used an interesting notion of "culture-ideology of consumerism" in his explanation of the globalized institutional changes.

13. To some Chinese scholars, the notion of "modernity" has ceased to be valid in social sciences since it is a concept derived from "Western culture" after the Renaissance. See Zhang Yiwu: "Xiandaixin de zhongjie – Yige wufa huibide keti" [The end of "modernity" – An inevitable issue], in *Zhanglui yu guangli* [Strategy and management], Beijing, No. 3, 1994, 104–9.

14. Daniel Little (1989, 3) called China "something akin to a laboratory for social science." Yet, as Elizabeth Perry (1989, 579) concluded, "the study of Chinese politics itself has not generated convincing theories for either China scholars or general comparativists."

15. Przeworski & Limongi concluded that "[d]emocracy is or is not established by political actors pursuing their goals" and "is not a by-product of economic development" or "a product of modernization" (1997, 177 & 159).

16. For more discussion on the functional undesirabilities and practical infeasibilities of a world market and a world government, see Wang 1995.

17. For a classic definition of human behavior, see Parsons 1951b, 53.

18. For a rather complicated discussion on the content and classification of human needs, see Henry A. Murray: "Towards a Classification of Interactions," in Parsons 1951b, 441–64.

19. For an in-depth examination of Karl Marx's concept of "need of the united individuals" and its central role in Marx's theorizing efforts, see Heller 1976.

20. Parsons 1951b, 5. An anonymous reviewer of the *Journal of Theoretical Politics* is gratefully acknowledged for bringing the limits of functionalism to the author's attention.
21. Needs and desires can sometimes be hard to distinguish, and can be scientifically studied together. An example is human sexual desires and related social behavior. According to evolutionary psychologists, the human needs/desires for genetic transmission explain much of human sexual behavior, including the various patterns of marriage (Robert Wright: "Our Cheating Hearts," in *Time*, August 15, 1994, 44–52).
22. Here, what Talcott Parson called "personality" and "culture system" of an individual matter significantly (1951a, 6).
23. For a summary of Durkheim's arguments on these points and on the notion of "institutionalized individualism," see Parsons 1967, 24–33.
24. This is almost common sense for social scientists now. For a political scientist's view, see Buzan et al. 1993, 7–9. The "constraining" role of the institutions naturally denotes "facilitation" as well.
25. For a discussion on the concept of institutionalization of organizations, see Parsons 1951a, 51–8 and Abrahamsson 1993, 89–90.
26. Douglass North: "Institutions and a Transaction-cost Theory of Exchange," in Alt & Shepsle ed. 1990, 182. And North 1981, 201–2.
27. Friedrich Kratochwil and John G. Ruggie: "International Organization: A State of the Art on an Art of the State" *International Organization*, 40 (1986), 753–75. Kratochwil and Mansfield ed. 1994; and Kratochwil 1989, chapter 4.
28. Reynold Koslowski & Friedrich Kratochwil: "Understanding Change in International Politics: the Soviet Empire's Demise and the International System" *International Organization*, 48(2), Spring 1994, 222.
29. For a classic discussion on the important role of socialization in linking "social systems" to the "personality system," see Parsons 1951b, 17–18.
30. Jürgen Habermas: "Toward a Reconstruction of Historical Materialism" in *Theory and Society*, 2, 1975, 287–300 and Habermas 1987.
31. For example, see Brugger & Reglar 1994; Pomeranz 1993; Jacob Landau's book review on *Israel: Polity, Society and Economy: 1882–1986* in *Middle Eastern Studies*, 26, (April) 1990, 268–270; Alasdair Bowie: *Crossing the Industrial Divide: State, Society, and the Politics of Economic Transformation in Malaysia.* New York, Columbia University Press, 1991; Gordon White: *The Chinese State in the Era of Economic Reform: the Road to Crisis.* London, Macmillan, 1991; Kazimierz Z. Poznanski ed.: *Constructing Capitalism: the Re-emergence of Civil Society and Liberal Economy in the Post-Communist World.* Boulder, CO, Westview Press, 1992; Michael Peter Smith: *City, State, and Market: the Political Economy of Urban Society.* Blackwell, 1988; and John E. Jackson ed.: *Institutions in American Society: Essays in Market, Political, and Social Organizations.* Ann Arbor, MI, University of Michigan Press, 1990.
32. William R. Clark contributed to the refinement of the ideas presented in this paragraph.
33. The attempt, for example, by N. Waltz (1979) and others to borrow a

microeconomics model to study international politics has been clearly unsatisfactory due to, among many other factors, the conceptual problems of finding an equivalent of money in international politics.

34. *New York Times*, October 12, 1994, C6 and Philip Elmer-Dewitt: "Battling for a Slice of Thin Air" in *Time*, November 7, 1994, 58–9.

35. Humans have long passed the time when one person can survive, let alone reproduce, on his/her own. Therefore, beyond reproduction, our basic needs can only be met by the collective effort of many more than two people. As a challenge to the linear approach in sciences, the chaos theorists argue that "the laws of complexity hold universally, caring not at all for the details of a system's atoms." (Gleick 1987, 304)

36. Lawson 1993, 584. For a semantic and historic examination of the notion of "nation," see Greenfield 1992, 4–9.

37. Here, the word "legitimacy" refers to the acceptance, *de jure* or *de facto*, of a particular human institution by a practically meaningful majority of a human grouping.

38. Friedrich Kratochwil (1989, 53–4) made an interesting distinction between the "rule" and legitimacy of an institution or a regime. An effective regime may not always be legitimate, and vice versa.

39. Patrick McCarthy: "Legitimacy and IOs," a posting on the *IPE-Net*, an Internet publication. June 15, 1995.

40. Even culture can be cultivated in this way. In the mid-seventeenth century, when the Manchus conquered China, they forced every Chinese man to change his hair style literally overnight, with death penalties for noncompliance. After a few generations, the infamous pigtail male hair style became a much treasured part of "Chinese culture."

41. As some have concluded, the "consolidation" of the modernized institutional framework took 183 years in England, 89 years in the United States, and an average of 72 years for most European nations. See Black 1966, 90–4, also in Huntington 1968, 45–7.

42. *Webster's New World Dictionary*, Cleveland, OII, William Collins. 1992, 868.

43. See, for example, Adam Przeworski: "Could We Feed Everyone? The Irrationality of Capitalism and the Infeasibility of Socialism," in *Politics and Society*, March 1991, 1–38 and Przeworski 1991.

44. "Liberal" economists like Milton Friedman may argue differently. A close look at their works (for example, Milton & Rose Friedman: *Free to Choose*, New York, Avon Books, 1979) may reveal, however, that all the believers in the market institution, starting with Adam Smith, have actually assumed the indispensable role of social and political institutions before enthusiastically promoting the market institution.

45. The damaging role played by monopoly on the market is clearly understated by some in their argument for the "advantages" of coordination and "savings" of transaction cost (Paul Milgrom & John Roberts: "Bargaining Cost, Influence Cost, and the Organization of Economic Activity," in Alt & Shepsle ed. 1990, 58–60).

46. The public stock company system may abate this concentration trend by separating the ownership from managerial authority. But it does

not stop the process. A relatively "autonomous" management of the firms may actually cause more distortion of the market through corruption and waste since the managers do not necessarily always pursue the maximum efficiency for the firms.

47. Economists such as Paul Samuelson and Francis Bator listed negative externalities under transaction cost and the inability of providing public goods as the sources of market failure. See their articles collected in Cowen ed. 1988.

48. Conversely, for a genuine market to survive, the individuals and the firms must have a "sovereignty" type of decision-making independence despite their property ownership, which may be otherwise.

49. In this book, the term "international market" is used to describe the existing market institution that governs the economic interactions among nations, nationally based firms and individuals. The term "world market" refers to an ideal concept of a unified single marketplace that governs not only international economic interactions but also the domestic economic activities of most, if not all, nations. Similarly, the term "world economy" refers to the economic activities, international and domestic, of all nations, while the term "international economy" primarily refers to economic interactions across national boundaries.

50. Robert K. Merton: *Social Theory and Social Structure*, rev. ed., Glencoe, IL., Free Press. 1957. Cited in Palmer 1980, 34.

51. Quoted in Keane, 1988b, 18.

52. Palmer 1980, 22–3, and Parsons, quoted in Gold 1986, 11.

53. Cohen, quoted in Keane 1988b, 65. For similar descriptions, see Palmer 1989, 22–3; Gold 1986, 11; Keane, ed. 1988a, 19 & 1988b, 31–6; Black 1966; and Istvan Hont & Michael Ignatieff eds *Wealth and Virtue. The Shaping of Political Economy in the Scottish Enlightenment.* Cambridge, Cambridge University Press, 1983.

54. Also see John Keane and Norberto Bobbio in Keane 1988a, and Keane 1988, 31–36.

55. Some Chinese scholars recently argued that civil society should be viewed as the "fundamental social conditions of a market economy." See Jia Dongqiao: "Gongmin shehui: Jianli shichangjingji tizhi de shehui jicu" ["Civil society: The social basis for the establishment of a market economic system"], in *Shehui kexue yangjiu* [Studies of social sciences], Chengdu, No. 6, 1994, 25–9.

56. For a strong Chinese argument that the notion of civil society is historically and culturally a "product of the West," see Fang Zhaohui: "Shimin shehui de niange chuantong jiqi zha xiangdai de huihe" ["The two traditions of civil society and their modern convergence"], in *Zhongguo shehui kwxue* [Chinese social sciences], Beijing, No. 5, 1994, 82–102.

57. Max Weber: *The Theory of Social and Economic Organization,* New York, Free Press, 1964. Cited in Migdal 1988, 19.

58. Badie and Birnbaum: *The Sociology of the State,* Chicago, University of Chicago Press, 1983, 35. Cited in Migdal 1988, xiii.

59. This is the most widely accepted definition of the state. Cf. V.I. Lenin: *State and Revolution* (1917) for a similar Marxist argument.

60. This type of polity represents a unique type of social system to Talcott Parsons (1951a, 178).
61. Elizabeth Gleick: "Rich Justice, Poor Justice," *Time*, June 19, 1995, 41.
62. See the illustrative article "The Evolution of Despair" by Robert Wright, *Time*, August 22, 1995, 50–7.
63. A highly hailed work on the institutional performance of local governments in Italy concluded that market economy and the state need the companion of a particular social life to function well. The "building of social capital" or the formation of "civic communities" is thus believed to be the key to not only economic development but also "making democracy work" (Putnam 1993, 181–5).
64. The reason may be that social life is by nature a less coherent, less forceful, and less expansionist human institution that lacks the sustained and sufficient driving ability needed for institutional changes towards modernity.
65. Of course, as the Western Europe–North American experience demonstrates, a market-driven modernization *does* require certain facilitation or "permission" by the state, and a state-led modernization clearly *does not* rule out the role of spontaneous market-oriented economic activities.
66. This process took place first in Italy in the fifteenth century and then shifted its center to the Atlantic Coast of Europe in the sixteenth and seventeenth centuries.
67. Agnes Heller (1988) maintains that a relatively independent, free, and not completely capitalist civil society is crucial to a real or "formal democracy," and that there has to be an intimate connection between normative pluralism and the institutional division between civil society and the state (Keane, 1988b). Similar arguments also in Habermas 1989.
68. To a lesser extent, what happened in many other places, such as Chile, Brazil, Argentina, and Mexico, can be categorized as variations of state-led modernization (for example, Lustig 1992). Here, both Peter Evans's (1979) model of "underdevelopment" and Guillermo O'Donnell's (1979) "bureaucratic authoritarian pattern" are in fact descriptions of the international and political aspects of variations of state-led modernization.
69. For discussions on the concept of "strong" or "hard" state in the developing countries, see, for example, Myrdal 1968. Migdal (1988, 269–75) produced an exhaustive list of the necessary condition – a great social dislocation – and four sufficient conditions for a strong state to emerge in the Third World.
70. "Contextual conditions" refers to the general social, legal and political environment in which a market can function (a certain new consensus of social values; new legal norms, property rights, and tax system; and a sympathetic administrative management, and so on). A distinctive and interactive relationship emerges between the economy and the sociopolitical complex even though the relationship between the state and social life is still poorly differentiated. Thomas Callaghy and Fritz Kratochwil are acknowledged for these points.

71. Robert Wade: "East Asia's Economic Success," *World Politics,* January 1992, 318–19. For a more empirical investigation of such a state guidance of the market, see Haggard 1990.
72. Interestingly enough, a great variety of people share this same "classic" point of view. From the "classic" and "neoclassic" economists to the majority leaders in the developing countries, economic development *per se* is usually interpreted as modernization (Cf. the summary in Tipps 1973 and in Huntington 1968).
73. For instance, Daniel Lerner insists that all the major aspects of modernization "had to go together" (1958, 438). To a lesser extent, a similar argument can be found in Palmer 1980, 3.
74. Thomas Gold described a "Taiwan miracle" that illustrated such a "non-market-driven" modernization. He also demonstrated the unique role of the state in Taiwanese modernization by analyzing the patterns of changes in the Taiwanese state-society relationship in general (1986, 3, 19, 20, 128–9).
75. It is theoretically interesting to note that these NICs all eventually experienced another side of the story: the interaction between a "changed" or a "modernized" economy and a rather authoritarian political system that basically unifies the state and social life in a "traditional" way. As a result, we have witnessed political unrest and sometimes painful social transitions in the NICs and even in Japan. This fascinating and significant "time lag" calls urgently for further studies on the state-led road of modernization.
76. Parnell (1994). Katzenstein (1985) has a classic analysis of the peculiar domestic organizational structure ("corporatist democracies") and its very noticeable performance in the small European countries.
77. For example, half of the US population – the women – did not have political participation in the American modernity until 1920, some 130 years after the creation of the US Constitution. Similar institutional exclusion of women from political participation has been found in almost all other "modernized" nations. Swiss women, for instance, did not have voting rights until as late as 1971. See the "Chronicles" column of *Time*, August 28, 1995, 25.
78. For an interesting discussion on the emergence of a "new service proletariat" in the "post-industrial societies," see Esping-Andersen (1993).
79. The factor of timing explains conceptually the contrast between the so-called "modernization from within and modernization from without," as some have argued forcefully (Kautsky 1980, 17–19, 44–9). It is also a better way to describe the differences between "the modernization of Europe and North America" and the contemporary modernization processes in the non-Western environments (Huntington 1968, 46).
80. A number of works have examined this question empirically. Xiaonong Cheng argued that political democratization will inevitably happen in China because of market-oriented economic reform ("Dilemmas of Economic Reform in China – Voices of Dissent: The Democratic Revolution in China," in *World Affairs.* vol. 154, Spring, 1992, 155–9). Suzanne Ogden believes that an authoritarian regime of the CCP is

necessary for the eventual development of a market economy and social liberalization in China ("The Chinese Communist Party: Key to Pluralism and a Market Economy?" in *SAIS Review*, 13, Summer/Fall, 1993, 107–26). Paribatra Sukhumbhand concluded that social liberalization has taken place in Thailand in the absence of democracy ("State and Society in Thailand: How Fragile the Democracy?" in *Asian Survey*, vol. 33, September 1993, 879–94). Igor Klyamkin discussed the issue in the Russian context ("Russians Pine for a Firm (Socialist) Hand: Thatcher, Pinochet or Andropov?" in *The Current Digest of the Post-Soviet Press*, vol. 45, December 8, 1993, 19–21).

81. Cardoso & Faletto 1979; Amin 1974; Evans 1979; and Theotonid Dos Santos: "The Structure of Dependence," in *American Economic Review*, vol. 16, 1970. More general argument can be found in Wallerstein 1980.

82. Samuel Huntington classically analyzed the destabilizing effect of modernization (1968).

83. The functional justification for effective institutional exclusions in promoting economic development and modernization can be significantly more extensive. This book, however, is not planned to exhaust that argument.

84. Keleinberg (1990) found that this is the case in China's "opening" strategy.

85. Japan, for example, has for a long time been labeled "Japan Inc.," referring to its effective state role in its international economic activities. Stephan Krasner (1985) analyzed this issue, examining the state's role in the developing countries' civil aviation industry.

2 The Indicators: A Theory on Labor Allocation Patterns

To have a conceptual framework is only the first step towards an institutional analysis of modernization. A crucial question remains: how can we recognize, record and thus study a nation's domestic organizational structure and its changes? One needs to have reliable indicators demonstrating the relationships among polity, economy, and social life. As a methodological innovation, this book proposes labor allocation patterns (LAPs) as a set of indicators that are representative but certain and uncomplicated.

Labor[1] allocation is considered a major element of a nation's domestic organizational structure; thus LAPs reflect well the relative positions, links, and interactions among the institutions of polity, economy, and social life, as well as shedding light on the internal organization of each of those institutions. LAPs are part of the basic fabric of a nation's domestic organizational structure. There are two central issues for an analysis of LAPs: (1) how the working ability of people, as a major economic resource, is allocated and utilized; and (2) how the carriers of this economic resource, the people, are treated politically and socially. The answer to these two questions precisely demonstrates how the three institutions are organized. Even internal structures of the three institutions can be observed through the prism of LAPs. Namely, one can read from the LAPs whether the state is autonomous, effective and participatory; whether the economy is market-oriented; and whether there is a civil society featuring functional families, voluntary associations and individual rights. LAPs, especially changes in them, also indicate the mechanisms, channels, and driving forces responsible for the endurance and alteration of a country's domestic organizational structure. As a work on American political changes concluded:

> History and theory merge in the assertion that employment, with its characteristics of subordination, compensation, and discharge, is a model on which societies have historically organized purposeful

58

activities of all kinds and at all levels. This suggests that labor relations are definitely various and that their description will offer a full and comparable picture of political institutions, in time and over time.[2]

A theorizing attempt aiming at developing a set of institutional indicators of LAPs is, therefore, presented in this chapter. Section I discusses the concept of LAPs and their revealing function of a nation's institutional arrangement and institutional changes – the process of modernization. Section II examines analytically three historical types of LAPs and attempts to ascertain their relative institutional implications to a nation's domestic organizational structure. They can be used as reference points. Section III is a summary.

I. LABOR ALLOCATION PATTERNS: THE NOTION

A LAP is defined as the way in which the division of labor[3] is realized, maintained, reproduced, and transformed. LAP refers to the patterns and the norms that guide the organization of labor in production, that is, the allocation and the reallocation of labor force across the boundaries of industry, institution, rank and profession, and geography. The fundamental importance of the division of labor to human civilization has been ascertained at least since Adam Smith ([1776] 1983, 109). Kenneth Arrow (1979, 163–4) concluded his discussion of the division of labor in economy, polity, and social life with the following words:

> The pressure for efficiency in the broadest sense and the pressure to get the most out of ourselves and our resources (not merely economic but also political and social) lead to the division of labor and, in particular, specialization of knowledge.

Labor, or more precisely the working ability of the laborers, is a major resource and must be allocated in certain ways for an efficient utilization. The development of technology for better meeting human needs and satisfying human desires has been a major driving force of the formation and changes of LAPs. LAPs or the ways in which the division of labor is brought about are therefore self-evidently crucial to the production, reproduction, and the transformation of any human civilization. Since it is usually difficult to separate people from their "working abilities," the pattern of allocating labor relates not only to the mere economic consideration of efficiency or productivity, but also frequently to many other social and political concerns and imperatives that are the basic components of the needs and desires that ignite human behaviors. The very existence and well-being of labor are themselves the purpose of those goal-oriented behaviors. A clear resource/purpose "duality" of labor makes the allocation and arrangement of this "resource" a basic institutional structure of any human grouping. LAPs thus reflect the conceptual considerations of both economic development, namely the combination of the human resource with other production resources ("production mode" in Marxian terms),[4] and sociopolitical changes.

Institutionally, the LAP is clearly a major overlapping area among polity, economy, and social life. It constitutes a major part of the basic framework in which people interact with nature and with each other. To put it simply, social, political and economic changes – modernization and development – can be viewed reliably through the prism of a LAP. Any important changes in LAPs inevitably cause changes in the relative positions of the economy, polity, and social life. Any significant adjustment of the relative positions as well as the internal structure of the three institutions will inevitably be expressed by changes in labor allocation. For example, only when a certain LAP (that is, a market-oriented allocation of the working abilities of labor) is established can a real market emerge, distinguishing the economy from politics and social activities. Only when a certain LAP (under which laborers enjoy social mobility and equality, comprehensive political participation and substantial economic security) is established can a civil society and democratic polity exist. Therefore, a study of LAPs becomes a reliable way to analyze social, political, and economic issues and their changes. Unfortunately, such an approach has been greatly underutilized, if not overlooked, by students in the field.[5]

II. THE HISTORICAL TYPES OF LAP

Labor has historically been allocated by the combined force of knowledge or technology bounded and "spontaneous" economic activities (Hayek 1990, 6–8) and the political governing power. The LAP in a nation, or even across nations, is shaped, maintained, and altered through a combination of the forces of economic and political institutions, aided by a less visible but at times powerful third force of social institutions such as families. The internalized institutions of a human grouping (the group or national culture) are also influential: traditional belief, religion, circumstantial convenience, moral values, codes of conduct, and customs.[6] A fourth shaping force is the interaction between the nation's domestic organizational structure and the international environment. Foreign direct investment, for example, has been a major avenue for such interaction. The presence, function, and intensity of those forces are results of numerous interacting variables varying from case to case and setting to setting. Good empirical studies are naturally needed to specify those variables adequately.

Empirically, there have been three major categories or "ideal types" of LAP: the traditional LAP, that features personal dependence of laborers based on social or political institutions; the labor market, with personal freedom and mobility of the laborers; and an authoritarian political (state) allocation of labor, which actually can be viewed as an extremist version of the traditional LAP by the combined forces of the state and communist ideology. They reflect distinctively different types of domestic organizational structure – different types of relationships among the economy, polity, and social life.

For "premodern" nations, developing and socialist alike, their domestic organizational structures – their economy-polity-social life relationship, as demonstrated by their LAPs – are undifferentiated. Those nations generally have societal or political LAPs that allocate labor by social (mainly the family) or political (mainly the state) forces. Their economies are nonmarket, and thus are not independent from the political and social institutions – they have either a moral economy or a central planning system. The states in those nations are not distant from social institutions; they are either "weak" or authoritarian or even totalitarian states. Fulfillment of human needs is poorly achieved under premodernity. Economic development and technological innovations tend to have an underoptimal performance and speed. Economic poverty, social decay and political repression or chaos are some of the hallmarks of a premodern nation.

The Traditional LAP

The traditional LAP has dominated most of human history. It features an undifferentiation of the working abilities of the laborers from their physical being – both are "properties" subject to full allocation and utilization by heads of families, masters or political rulers.[7] The family-based handicraft workshops and the "self-employed" land-holding peasants in nations like China belong to the traditional LAP. This LAP has two variations: a societal LAP and a political LAP. They differ primarily in their institutional basis and the social status of the laborers.

Family-based LAP
The traditional societal LAP is primarily family-based or clan/community-based. Social institutions such as kinship are the institutional basis for this type of LAP and social concerns (reproduction-centered) of *everyone* including the laborers in the social group, not economic reasoning, are the primary concerns in the allocation and utilization of labor. Laborers are confined to their social institutions – families or communities. Labor organization is clearly hierarchically structured. Personal and even family dependence is the norm. Labor mobility is very low and the differentiation of the working ability of the laborers and the laborers themselves is generally undeveloped. This societal variation was the major component of the traditional LAP in history.

A labor allocation pattern based on the family institution typically reflects the economic and political role of the family: an undifferentiated economy-polity-social life arrangement a family institution represents. Therefore, this book suggests that, the degree to which a family-based LAP exists in a human grouping demonstrates the depth of the institutional premodernity in that grouping. A dominant presence of a family-based LAP thus labels that human grouping as premodern, since that nation's domestic organizational structure is an undifferentiated one.

As one of the "modes" of LAP, a family-based traditional LAP is conceptually distinguishable from, and empirically identifiable among, other patterns.

1. The dominance of noneconomic, mainly social, rationales in allocating labor. The division of labor under a family-based LAP is based primarily on social values rather than economic ones,

and seeking profit is generally secondary to the goal of "feeding" everyone in the human grouping. Recruitment, pay, promotion, penalties, and dismissal are generally based on noneconomic concerns such as social harmony, personal relationship, ideological interests, and kinship. Thus economically, the family-based LAP tends to be much less competitive and less innovative than a labor market.

2. Labor immobility. The laborers under a family-based LAP generally have a personal dependence on the employer, superior or head of the group, rather than merely economic ties. Almost everyone is assigned a basically fixed relational role, as in a family. As a result, labor mobility is low and laborers have very limited personal freedom and individual rights conditioned on their units.

3. Institutionalized inequality. Not only the economic status, but the social and political status of the laborers is lower than that of the employers, superiors or group heads. Labor contracting of "equal" parties is rare and "bargaining" is generally deemed "unnecessary" or "unacceptable." As a result, labor protection and labor rights are generally subject to the employer's good will or the social and political values an individual employer/ superior may have. A family-based LAP, therefore, is usually conducive to an authoritarian political system and a rigidly hierarchical social stratification.

4. Stability and low economic performance. Labor allocated under a family-based LAP tends to be generally small-scale and relatively stable over time. The job turnover rate is low, if not negligible. For small groups or enterprises and in certain industries, a family-based LAP can be rather effective and even efficient, as in family farms and some family craft shops. But for most economic activities and in most industrial enterprises which require complicated division of labor and almost constant innovation, the family-based LAP tends to perform very poorly due to low labor mobility and the heavy influence of noneconomic considerations.

Political LAP

The traditional political LAP is generally a slavery system organized along political institutions. Laborers, and usually their families and offspring, are virtually "owned" by their "employers" or masters. They have no meaningful geographical or occupational mobility, political rights, or social status. Labor is allocated by political decisions, often resulting from military actions such as conquest and war. Economic concerns such as productivity and innovation are important but by no means the primary concern; political needs generally prevail in allocating labor. Social concerns for the laborers were almost non-existent except for "breeding" the slaves. Family-owned slaves, even though they may be acquired via economic means, are a result of political allocation – it is the state or its equivalent that can legalize and maintain a slavery system for itself and for slave-owning families and communities. Serfdom, as a mild version of this traditional political LAP, is created by political decisions but gradually develops into more of a societal than a political LAP. Generally speaking, despite brutal treatment and exploitation, the traditional political LAP performs much poorer economically and tends to be much less stable structurally than the traditional societal or family-based LAP.

Traditional LAPs exist widely across nations and constitute a major part of the premodern domestic organizational structure under which the economy, polity, and social life are all organized in a giant undifferentiated complex. The two variations reflect the two types of a premodern domestic organizational structures (Figure 1.2) respectively: state dominance and social institution dominance.

The Labor Market

The second ideal type of LAP is the labor market, featuring personal freedom and mobility of the labor. Only the working ability of the laborers is traded on the market as a commodity at a price determined by supply and demand. Personal freedom and mobility of labor across geographical, occupational, and even national boundaries are institutionalized. "Equal" contracting rather than personal dependency is the norm between labor and employer (an individual or an organization) and there is a competitive rather than monopolized demand and supply of labor (Loveridge & Mok 1979, 27). An economist defines "labor market" as:

1. Employers and workers have fairly accurate knowledge about wages and job opportunities throughout the market.
2. Employers and workers are "rational" in the economic sense – that is, employers act to maximize profits and workers act to maximize satisfaction from real wages.
3. Each employer and worker represents such a small part of the total demand or supply for labor that their individual decisions have no influence on wages.

4. There are no obstacles to mobility of labor and other factors of production.

5. Workers and employers act individually and not in concert with other workers (through union) or employers (through association) in making wage and employment decisions.

6. Labor within a particular market is homogeneous and interchangeable. (Levitan et al. 1972, 201)

Labor market provides the very basis for a market economy to function. Naturally, it is by no means completely autonomous and is subject to several types of political and social influences. Political influences, for example, may be generated by policies adjusting the price of labor: wage control; adjusting the supply of labor through a change in the legal working age and/or a change of legal working hours; adjusting labor demand; and most important, adjusting labor mobility (De Neubourg 1988, 166). Empirically, we see that a market-oriented LAP in today's world is quite different from the pure theoretical model. There are powerful labor unions, collective (even "national") bargaining practices, and labor legislation. There are tremendous barriers to labor mobility, especially on the international level. There are even considerable "protected" or privileged labor allocation practices, such as public employees and government-assigned jobs. But generally, the majority of the labor force is allocated through a market pattern – though usually an imperfect market. The distortions of a labor market in a particular nation actually contains excellent information about the amount and effectiveness of interactions between the market economy and polity and between the market and social life in that nation.

Labor markets, especially national ones, emerged under capitalism[8] after the sixteenth and seventeenth centuries. By the nineteenth century, the labor market became the major LAP in the West.[9] Although there has been a close association between capitalism and the labor market, the labor market in the pure sense is not exclusively capitalist since it can exist even if the production means are owned by other than private owners. This book treats the labor market as a pattern of allocating labor in which the laborers trade their working ability/skills as their property with others, rather than making an ideological statement. The participants of a labor market are legally and politically "equal" and the trading is protected by law – at least in theory. Outside contractual arrangements, laborers, as well as employers, are free to move geographically and occupationally.

They can choose a job "freely" – though that is often difficult because of the transaction costs involved – and even "refuse" to work. Wages and other economic benefits are the only means through which the employer can control labor. A well-institutionalized national labor market is perhaps the largest integrated labor market. Functional labor markets tend to be nationally based because the nationally defined political and social institutions of the states tend to block the free flow of labor across their boundaries. Although certain market-oriented international labor allocation exists, an integrated world labor market is probably an ideal rather than a feasible institution. Since labor has perhaps the most significant political and social implications among all economic resources, established national labor markets tend to be much less free than national financial or commodity markets. Within a nation, there could be a clear presence of labor market segmentation in history. Labor market segmentation is the historical process whereby the LAP-shaping forces encourage the division of the labor market into separate, local submarkets, or segments, with varied market orientation or market distortion. A segmented labor market or, more precisely in the Chinese case, the community-based labor markets (Wang 1998, 163–220), may be viewed as the product of such a segmentation process. A market-oriented labor allocation may exist without a unified national labor market.

A national labor market: the features
Domestically, the uniqueness of labor as an economic resource – the difficulty of separating one's working ability as a marketable economic resource from one's physical human being – has made the labor market the most politically and socially distorted of all markets. Nationwide labor mobility, even if not very thorough, is perhaps the highest achievement of a labor market. By the end of the twentieth century, labor mobility beyond national boundaries is, as expected, still very low.[10] Facilitated mainly by the expansion of international economic activities, an international labor market grew alongside the integrating international financial and commodity markets. The now clearly visible but still very limited international labor market is exemplified by the controlled exchange of labor for fixed projects, and by legal and illegal international migrations. The international labor market, very influential on domestic labor allocation, is largely a supplement to national labor markets and other national LAPs that may not be market-oriented.

A national market generally has the following institutional features (Simai 1995, 73–6): First, the labor force of the nation has achieved a nationwide mobility. Workers are mobile vertically as well as horizontally across boundaries of geography, profession, and industry. Individuals can move from one community to another and change their jobs without political or social constraints except personal or family concerns. Except for contractual obligations and duties, workers are personally free from their employers. The employers have little control over the lives of their employees beyond the financial sphere. Aside from certain limitations against noncitizens,[11] no legal barriers prevent employers from hiring from every corner of the nation. Institutionalized or *de facto* national standardization of labor qualifications and performance is largely achieved. As a result, a national labor market, even with varied social and political distortions, tends to have the highest efficiency in allocating and utilizing the national labor resource.

Second, a national labor market, as the largest inclusive LAP, can nonetheless be very chaotic, disparate and even irrational at any given time and place. People with the same qualifications may at different times or in different places be treated or compensated in dramatically different ways. The transaction cost of information is responsible for the existence of such disparities. This micro chaos of the national labor market, just as in the markets for commodities and capital, yields the important advantage of flexibility in competition. The interesting point may be that the labor market tends to have much more of this disparity because it is usually much harder to compare two people than to compare two brands or two currencies. It is such a "natural" existence of chaos and disparity that provides the operational basis for the social and even political distortions of the labor market.

Third, pay is determined primarily by the national supply and demand of labor, as interpreted by the employer and the employee. Job information is generally available nationally to job-seekers. Negotiation and bargaining between the employer and the employee are very important in deciding on working conditions, workload, pay, and promotion. A common distortion of a national labor market is collective bargaining between employers and employees, especially those that are industrial or regionally based.

Fourth, unemployment is a natural result of a national labor market. Completely full employment, no matter how much political or social effort is devoted to promoting it, is impossible. In a mature national labor market, there should be a well-defined and effective national system of unemployment relief, labor insurance, retirement pensions, and job referral services. Underemployment has only an insignificant presence in a functional national labor market.

Fifth, workers' productivity and on-job performance are the main criteria for hiring, compensation, and promotion. The selection process is nationally open and competitive. "Inside" or secretive hiring is often deemed illegal or unethical. Personal attributes not directly related to job performance and noneconomic concerns are systematically ruled out of employment decisions. Discrimination based on noneconomic reasons, though a common distortion, has generally marginal impact in a well-established national labor market. The employer's financial situation is the basis for recruitment and dismissal. Social and political mechanisms have a very limited impact on the employer's employment decisions, especially hiring.

Finally, the labor contract and the above institutional features of a national labor market are protected primarily by the state and accepted by social institutions. Minimum working age, job safety, minimum wages and maximum working hours of employees are generally nationally enforced regulations. Many of the institutional features of a national market could be just accepted behavioral norms rather than legal rules. For the sake of convenience, therefore, a fairly complete national legal system legitimizing and regulating the labor market can be viewed as the birth of a national labor market.[12]

In reality, naturally, a national labor market tends to carry its own uniqueness imprinted by the nation's domestic organizational structure and culture. But, even in today's China, the above institutional features are generally considered the basis for any national labor market (Hu et al. 1993, 638–53).

Segmented or community-based labor markets
As a variation of labor market, the segmented or community-based labor markets (CLMs) have several institutional features that set them apart from the traditional LAP, the national labor market, and the authoritarian state LAP.

First, two essential indicators help us to identify a CLM or, more generically, a community-based LAP. One is that *every* member of the community is treated basically the same way concerning job opportunities, pay schedules, work-related benefits and protections, and job security. In the case of CLMs, every laborer in the community would be subject to the allocation and management of the community-confined and often socially distorted local labor market. Supply and demand fundamentally determine the allocation and utilization of labor, but only within the community. The other key indicator is that community members are systematically preferred over outsiders by the employers. An institutional discrimination is practiced against competition from outside laborers. Empirically in China, the *hukou* (household or residential registration) system has been an almost perfect tool for such labor discrimination by local communities.

Second, a CLM, by definition, is a market-oriented LAP practiced by a community within a nation. Depending on the size of the community, a CLM can be very small – as few as several hundred people – or as big as several million people, such as those in the cities in today's PRC. The cohesiveness of a CLM and the effectiveness of its institutional discrimination against outsiders, naturally, decrease as its size increases.

Third, CLMs are market-oriented LAPs and thus tend to be economically efficient and innovative. The labor allocated and managed by a CLM, within its particular community anyway, can achieve substantially high productivity. Due to the strong influence of social institutions, competition among laborers may not be as fierce and as motivated as that in a national labor market, but limited market mechanisms are often enough to reduce or even eliminate underemployment. This is especially true when the labor force in the concerned community is the appropriate size for an efficient scale of production of its particular industry or industries.

Fourth, CLMs demonstrate clear limits and rationales set by the social institutions of the community. A community that has a CLM generally has a clear emphasis on rough equality among its members. The employers are institutionally and culturally compelled to recruit community members first before even considering any outsiders, even those more qualified. When there is a need for payroll reduction, that order would be reversed. Unemployment relief, usually in hidden forms, is institutionally built in. A strong mechanism for income redistribution is therefore common for the CLMs. Those social distortions of the labor market, which stop at the boundaries of the communities, tend to reduce the efficiency of the community economies but greatly increase social harmony and stability. The redistribution scheme, however, usually does not cover outsiders who are working "temporarily" as supplements to the community labor force. Therefore, especially in prosperous communities which need outside labor and can afford it, a "mini" dual structure exists: a privileged and protected community labor force versus the outside workers, who accepted jobs with market-oriented terms but without the socially determined and community-based benefits. The bigger the difference, the clearer the community boundaries and the stronger the effort to maintain it.

Finally, a CLM may often act as single player in the marketplace or in a nonmarket national economy. Seen from the outside, a CLM is organized like a combination of the market institution with an enlarged family structure that includes unrelated community members. No matter how much distortion of the market exists within it, a CLM can engage in free-market style economic exchanges with other players as a unit. No matter how much of a market mechanism it has inside, a CLM can also survive well in a nonmarket national economy as long as the political authority of the state tolerates or at least restrains from "eliminating" the market institution in the local communities. The CLMs thus can preserve an authentic labor market with each other, or live in a nonmarket national economy on which they have only a limited and gradual, but perhaps persistent, eroding effect.

Authoritarian State Allocation

The third historical type of LAP, which may be becoming a thing of the past as a national phenomenon, is the sort of authoritarian state allocation practiced by the Leninist authoritarian regimes in centrally planned economies. (Berliner 1957, Jowitt 1983, Oi 1985, Walder 1986) As Alec Nove (1977) noted, labor in the former Soviet Union was regarded as noncommodity and was said to be allocated according to the principle of maximizing the obscure "social utility" through planning.

Under this LAP, the state allocates labor through administrative means according to various economic theories and plans and political decisions. There is a clear personal dependence of labor on the party-ruled state, economically, politically, and even socially. To a great extent, the authoritarian state LAP is like an enlarged traditional political LAP that is nationwide, agency-based, and administratively operated. Generically, an authoritarian state LAP has the following institutional features that separate it from the traditional family-based LAP and a labor market.

First, the state, as the central political authority of the nation, sets the basic rules and principles for labor allocation nationwide. The politicians and the state bureaucracy, rather than the supply and demand mechanism of the market, determine the criteria for recruitment, pay, punishment, promotion, and dismissal. Different states, naturally, have different levels of autonomy in their labor decisions. Some may consult with market-oriented forces, as in those "corporatist" regimes, while others, such as the Leninist-Stalinist regimes, are completely shielded from the market institution. Some states may use political authority and a thorough bureaucratic organization to allocate and manage labor directly, as in the cases of centrally planned economies, while others may just influence labor allocation through special legislation and fiscal and monetary policies, as commonly seen in the West.

Second, hierarchical structures and low labor mobility are some of the defining features of an authoritarian state LAP. Rank, compensation scales, benefits, promotion and demotion of workers are generally set nationally and routinely scheduled at a fixed pace. Job security tends to be high, as managers have few incentives for dismissing employees. Workers do not have much mobility as the flow of labor under an authoritarian state LAP is ordinarily regulated, in a variety of ways, by their superiors.

Third, political logic and the political rationales of the ruler, ruling group or party tend to determine the allocation and management of labor, usually at the expense of economic or technological rationales. Labor is not allocated and managed primarily as an economic resource. Workers' inherent quality and job performance are generally taken into consideration under an authoritarian state LAP, more so than in the family-based LAP. But political favoritism, obedience to authority, policy needs, political correctness and other political values and considerations are often more important. An authoritarian state LAP tends to swell in size constantly as a result of the political concern for "creating" jobs and attracting political support. It is relatively easy and rewarding for managers or supervisors under an authoritarian state LAP to hire, or strive to hire, more people. But it is much harder for them to reduce employees or contemplate discharges for fear of the political implications. Economic efficiency always plays a secondary role, because the state seems to have "unlimited" income from taxation as long as it can maintain its political authority – the monopoly of using force.

Fourth, much like the family-based LAP, the authoritarian state LAP has a clear trace of moral economy in its practice. Full employment or something close to it is the goal itself. Compared to a labor market, an authoritarian state LAP tends to provide significantly more labor protection and a certain degree of managerial participation to workers. Even under a dictatorship, such as Mao's, workers usually have a feeling (perhaps a false or empty one) of being the "masters" themselves. In this sense, an authoritarian state LAP may be viewed as an enlarged family-based traditional LAP – a state-dominated traditional LAP.

Finally, related to the above features, a typical authoritarian state LAP generally demonstrates significantly low economic efficiency in allocating and utilizing labor resources. Innovation is limited due to the low intensity of competition among the workers. Furthermore, political institutions and considerations, used by the managers or more often by the employees, tend to intervene, thus hindering efforts at serious improvement of productivity. It is, therefore, not unexpected to see that state-owned enterprises almost always perform less efficiently than private enterprises in almost every nation.[13]

The authoritarian LAP organizes labor according to political logics and political organizational principles. It is the basis for the centrally planned economy. It demonstrates the nature of a socialist domestic organizational structure: a giant, undifferentiated complex founded on a specific political institution – the Leninist and Stalinist "proletarian dictatorship," in which the party-ruled state tightly controls both the economy and social life.

III. SUMMARY

In this chapter, labor allocation patterns have been theorized as a set of indicators for us to observe a nation's domestic organizational structure and its changes. The three historical types of LAP have their distinctive institutional marks concerning the domestic organizational structures of the nations. Each historical type of LAPs reflects a specific type of institutional arrangement of the state versus the economy and social life. The dominance of a family-based traditional LAP would indicate the premodern, or undifferentiated, nature of a nation's domestic organizational structure. A well institutionalized labor market would signal the completion of a marketization of a nation's economy and the differentiation of the economy from polity and social life. A well-developed national labor market generally indicates a differentiation and even interaction among the economy, polity, and social life. The operational mechanisms of a particular labor market may further demonstrate the arrival of modernity in that human grouping (nation). An authoritarian state LAP represented a premodernity pushed to the extreme under Communist ideology in the nations like the former Soviet Bloc and China mainly before the 1980s.

In reality, of course, there are complicated variations, distortions, and exceptions. From an academic point of view, those distortions and variations contain enormously rich information about a particular nation's domestic organizational structure. One particular nation may have only one type of LAP. More often, however, nations tend to have more than one LAP, with one of them dominant and the others marginal supplements.[14] More interestingly, in nations like contemporary China, there could be several major LAPs, each allocating and managing significant numbers of laborers. An examination of LAPs has now been proposed to be useful and sufficiently illuminative for our analysis of modernization from an institutional perspective.

NOTES

1. International Labor Office (ILO) defines "labor" or "labor force" as the "economically active population" comprising all persons above 10–15 years of age, who furnish the supply of labor for the production of economic goods and services. It consists three parts: employed, unemployed, and underemployed (ILO 1987, 35; De Neubourg 1988, 193–201).
2. Karen Orren: "The Primacy of Labor In American Constitutional Development," in *American Political Science Review*, vol. 89(2), June 1995, 386.
3. "Division of labor" or "specialization" of skills, practice, and information, "is a basic structural aspect, not merely of the economic world, but of all other social worlds" (Arrow 1979, 154, 156).
4. The understanding of LAP's role is inspired by Marx's argument of "Production Mode." However, Marx apparently overemphasized, for one thing, the importance of the ownership of "production means" in his theory.
5. For a while, labor and the implication of LAP seem to be somehow "exclusive" subjects for Marxian scholars (Cox 1987). Max Weber,

among others, touched on the LAP logic in his analysis of the state-society relationship (1978). Similarly, Karl Polanyi (1957) emphasized the creation of the labor market in Western Europe as instrumental in the "great transformation" from the Middle Ages to the modern capitalist world.

6. The debate of "moral peasants" (Scott 1976, and others) vis-à-vis "rational peasants" (Popkin 1979, and others) is a good example to explain how those three forces can work together to determine the preference of the peasants and the outcome of certain ways of organizing the labor force in a rural economy. (For a summary of this debate, see Parish 1985, 13–20.)

7. This LAP alienates people differently from the one in the capitalist system described by Marx. This kind of alienation goes beyond "economic bondage" and is carried out mainly through noneconomic means.

8. "Capitalism" in this study refers to an economic system "in which (1) the optimal division of labor is so advanced that most people produce for the needs of others, (2) the means of production and the capacity to work are owned privately, and (3) there are markets in both" (Przeworski 1991, 2). "Capitalism means private ownership and the use of the market for resource allocation" (Cui 1991, 60).

9. The repeal of the Corn Laws in Britain in the 1840s can be viewed as a major landmark of the birth of a national labor market. For a multinational study of the national labor markets in the West, see Simai 1995.

10. In some regions and at some times, some nations may have substantial labor mobility among themselves. A current prototype of such a selective and controlled international labor mobility is the European Union which, if all goes as planned, will become a single state (or nation?) soon.

11. It is here certain overlapping of a national labor market and the international labor market can develop. Despite powerful political and social concerns, an employer generally is inclined to hire *anybody* who is productive. The issue of illegal immigrants is thus born.

12. One must distinguish the "laws" on paper from the actual institutional settings in a nation regarding the labor market. Law enforcement has commonly been a major problem in premodern nations like China.

13. To some, this LAP largely explains the low efficiency of the Chinese state-owned enterprises. See Elliott Parker: "Prospects of the State-owned Enterprises in China's Socialist Market Economy," in *Asian Perspective*, Seoul, Korea, vol. 19(1), Spring-Summer 1995, 14–16.

14. Even in the United States, where a national labor market has become the dominant LAP, for example, a family-based traditional LAP exists marginally in both rural and urban areas. Even a quasi-slavery LAP can be found in the form of some slave-like seasonal workers in the agriculture industry, despite the 1984 U.S. "Migrate Seasonal Agriculture Worker Protection Act." See CNN (Cable News Network): "Faces of Slavery," a *CNN Presents* program, Atlanta, July 23, 1995.

3 A Historical Review of the Chinese Domestic Organizational Structure: A Peculiar Premodernity

Observation-based social sciences rely heavily on history. Human desires, knowledge, capabilities and institutions are all historical phenomena that leave clear and deep traces; thus history not only records but also teaches and explains. Institutions and institutional changes in a particular human grouping, a nation, must be examined within a framework of history, even though the notion of "modernity" may be somehow objective and less time-specific. History actually provides the main clues to our understanding of human institutions, since many of the leading features of a particular set of institutions can be forged only gradually. The all-important legitimacy of institutions can be accumulated only over time. Only a historical review can reveal the inertia that makes many institutions live far beyond their utility, and the internalization of institutions – the formation of cultures. The consequential relative timing of a modernization process, can only be understood through a historical examination of the external conditions of a particular nation. A historical review is even indispensable to study institutional changes of a nation like China that has had a long civilization.

The study of China
As signified by its totem of dragon, China is a combination of many characteristics and has fascinated many with its complexity, elasticity, continuity, innovations, cultural sophistication, long stagnation, and survival ability.[1] To students, China "represents something akin to a laboratory for social science." "By focusing on China, it is possible to raise and discuss virtually any problem of social inquiry and to discover extensive empirical data on the basis of which to evaluate hypotheses" (Little 1989, 3). To political scientists, China offers a very "fertile ground for an important breakthrough in comparative political theory." Nevertheless, in spite of the obvious

potential, the study of China has long suffered from a lack of theoretical analysis. Despite the impressive scholarship already produced,[2] scholars have for generations observed an "immaturity" and underdevelopment in China studies (Tang Tsou 1967, Harding 1984, Perry 1989, Goldstein 1989). Most "borrowed" analytical models have been largely unsatisfactory in "capturing the peculiarities of the Chinese case, but the study of Chinese politics itself has not generated convincing theories for either China scholars or general comparativists" (Perry 1989, 585, 579).

Viewed through the lenses of this book, the problem of China studies perhaps lay in a lack of proper understanding of China's domestic organizational structure. Despite all the massive foreign invasions, bloody civil wars, and "earthshaking" revolutions,[3] the relationship among the three human institutions – economy, polity, and social life – has remained essentially the same for at least two thousand years in China. Contemporary China has a unique but rather traditional, or premodern, domestic organizational structure that determines much of its alleged peculiarities. An examination of the historical evolution of the Chinese labor allocation patterns (LAPs) may provide a firm ground for us to grasp the continuity of the Chinese domestic organizational structure. Not surprisingly, external forces became crucial to the alteration of the Chinese domestic structure, as illustrated by the emergence of the new patterns of labor allocation during the period of 1840 to 1949. The Chinese communists, however, forcefully reversed that trend after 1949. Under Mao's leadership, China was once again organized by an undifferentiated domestic organizational structure, and its premodernity continued.

To start our inquiry into the premodernity and modernization of China, this chapter reviews the history of Chinese domestic organizational structure from the Qin dynasty (third century BC) to the 1980s, through examining the history of the Chinese LAPs. A remarkable continuity of a family-based traditional LAP is found to have constituted a peculiar institutional premodernity of the Chinese domestic organizational structure. China, at least prior to the 1980s, appeared to have been always an institutionally premodern nation. The Chinese state, despite all its bureaucratic sophistication and administrative innovation, was generally undifferentiated from social institutions such as family and consanguinity. A "familism" type institutional arrangement deeply colored Chinese premodernity.[4] Not only was the internal structure of polity similar to that of the social life centered on the family, the values and contents were roughly the same. The Chinese economy was basically undifferentiated from this gigantic sociopolitical complex; thus economic values were hardly optimized.

Despite some visible "spontaneous" commercialization of the Chinese economy at times in history, even earlier than the Western European nations, the market was never a dominant economic institution that separated people's economic behavior from their political and social ones. The suffocating forces generated by the sociopolitical complex, magnified by its internalized version – Chinese culture – and the lack of external influences were responsible for the underdevelopment of the economy despite the accumulation of significant scientific knowledge. A market-driven modernization could not take place in such a premodernity that is isolated from the rest of the world. A state-led modernization would not happen until and unless the state was forced to alter the politically "comfortable" Chinese premodernity.

This centuries-old Chinese premodernity, so complete and so stable, is a unique historical phenomenon that has attracted tremendous attention and led to impressive scholarship (for example, Sun 1956, Hu 1979, Fairbank 1983 & 1986, Philip Huang 1990, Spence 1990, Zhang 1990, and Friedman et al. 1991). This chapter seeks to advance our knowledge on this issue by revealing and analyzing the continuation of Chinese premodernity. It also describes the institutional preconditions facing the Chinese modernization effort. Section I briefly reviews the domestic organizational structure from Qin to Qing through an examination of the LAPs in that period. A family-based traditional LAP is identified as the dominant LAP for these twenty centuries. Section II continues such examination on the century between the 1840s and 1949. New LAPs and institutional changes of the Chinese domestic organizational structure are described and discussed. Section III briefly analyzes the institutional history of the PRC from 1949 to the end of the 1970s. Maoist domestic organizational stricture is viewed as a giant "leaping forward to the past." A powerful authoritarian state, dominated by one party and ideologically radical, replaced the traditional family-like[5] sociopolitical complex as *the institution* for the Chinese politics, economic activities, and social life. Section IV further discusses five major observations of this historical survey to reveal the institutional background of the Chinese modernization. Section V is the summary.

I. LABOR ALLOCATION IN CHINA: FROM QIN TO QING (THIRD CENTURY BC–NINETEENTH CENTURY AD)

Chinese historians tend to agree that the establishment of the Qin dynasty by military conquers was a major turning-point in Chinese history and Chinese nation-building (Guo et al. 1956, Fan 1957, vol. 1, Hu 1979, and Jian 1984). The Qin government established direct rule over the country by using a *"junxian"* (prefecture and county) system instead of indirect rule through feudal lords.[6] All political and administrative power rested with the imperial court and its officials, all appointed, down to the level of counties (Twitchett & Loewe 1986, 463–90; Jian 1984). The emperor, therefore, acquired direct control of the people, although that control was routinely compromised by local officials and the gentry class due to the technical and logistic impossibility of complete direct rule. The Chinese domestic organizational structure, therefore, was largely an enlarged family structure where the father (the emperor) had all the authority and power to control not only people's economic and political activities but also their social life. There was no institutional differentiation among polity, economy, and social life. There were no institutional barriers between the people and the emperor, thus variety and experimentation of human behavior became structurally very difficult, if not impossible.[7] Over time, with modifications and sophistication, this basic organizational structure of China acquired a remarkably deep legitimacy despite the numerous changes of the "father;" that is, the ruling family of a particular dynasty. It continued until the late twentieth century.

Several innovations were important for the continuity of the premodern Chinese domestic organizational structure. Starting with one of the Warring States, Qin, which later united the country, Chinese rulers adopted a legalist political culture (*fajia*) characterized by the use of harsh and authoritarian political power based on a rigid authority structure, strict, often ruthless, rules and cunning manipulation of subordinates.[8] By the first century BC, Confucianism (*rujia*), a quasi-religious, order-conscious, family-based ideology that emphasizes the moral values of hierarchy and "appropriateness," was adopted as the official ideology by the Han rulers (Fan 1957, vol. 1, 50). This official ideology was upheld and interpreted with increasing policy relevance and theoretical sophistication by subsequent Chinese rulers. In practice, the Confucian political ideology of the state became a great cover for the savageness of the legalist politics most Chinese rulers continued to use until today. It became the backbone of Chinese culture that reinforced the premodern Chinese domestic organizational structure for centuries. At the same time, the imperial court decided to monopolize the most profitable and crucial industries of iron, salt, and mint or coinage.[9] By the time of the fifth to seventh centuries, the Chinese abolished their weak primogeniture system (Hu 1979, 45) and the imperial examination system was institutionalized to select able servants for the imperial court (Twitchett 1979, 8–21). This profound innovation, with subsequent improvement and modifications, served several important functions: to provide the means for the emperor to select capable officials, and to pre-empt the growth of meaningful opposition by providing a highly regulated upward mobility for the talented and the brave, thus "trapping all the heroes under the sun."[10]

Chinese political history was characterized by a highly centralized political power, a rather sophisticated and capable administrative system, a clearly defined and maintained hierarchy with an orderly mobility, a singular political ideology emphasizing traditional "family values," and a relatively isolated international environment. No autonomous economic institutions (the market) developed meaningfully in China, and both political activities and social life were essentially combined. The basic units of the human institution in China, the families and the state, were all undifferentiated institutions that constrained people's economic, political, and social behaviors in essentially the same way.

The self-sustaining Chinese premodernity reached its highest maturity by the Tang dynasty (seventh to tenth centuries). A "super-stability" of the Chinese domestic organizational structure hence became a distinguishing feature (Jin 1987). Since then, the only realistic chance for significant alteration of this super-stable premodernity lay in external factors: foreign invasion or foreign investment. Internal stagnation and the inevitable eruption of conflict after long periods of peace led to changes of dynasties. The fall of great dynasties such as Tang, Song, Ming, and Qing, however, was directly related to Chinese interactions with "outsiders" who were not necessarily firm believers of Confucianism, the internalized Chinese domestic organizational structure. With the exception of Western influence during the Qing dynasty, however, all those foreign invaders were generally less sophisticated culturally than the country they conquered. They were inevitably Sinicized quickly and thoroughly. Therefore, the fall of "Chinese" dynasties in the hands of the rebellious heroes or "barbarians" did not change Chinese premodernity much; the new regimes usually had little new to offer, and fell back on a quick restoration of the old domestic organizational structure. The dynasty cycles, institutionally almost meaningless, ended only in the twentieth century, primarily due to external forces.

A brief look into the history of Chinese labor allocation demonstrates and explains the unique and profound institutional continuation of Chinese premodernity. This angle of observation aspires to be an innovative way to examine Chinese history.[11] Through this long history, as a result and a cause of the super-stability of its premodern domestic organizational structure, China had basically a single pattern of labor allocation, one that fits the description of a traditional societal LAP discussed in Chapter 2. Labor was essentially personally immobile across geographic or professional boundaries. Slavery existed in China until the twentieth century with varied scope at different times; the sale of people, especially as domestic servants, was legal until 1949. Still, the traditional Chinese LAP was mainly a system of family-based or local community (clan-based villages) allocation of labor. This is especially the case after the failure of the Wang Anshi (1021–86) Reform during the North Song dynasty, which aimed at a more political organization of the peasants. Substantial commercialization of the economy took place at times and in several areas, often including the national capital cities (Lishisuo 1963–5; Ye Yaojun 1988). Accordingly, a certain amount of development of local labor markets occurred, especially after the fourteenth century. But both the commercialization and local labor markets failed to sustain and to expand (Huang 1990, 93–143). They were basically useful supplements to the dominant family/clan-based traditional LAP.

Serfdom and slavery were basically supplemental thus institutionally marginal. Personal dependence developed along social institutions that constituted the basic framework for an undifferentiated domestic organizational structure. The centralized and powerful imperial administration was, therefore, organized like a paternal family or clan. The negatives of this premodernity – its labor immobility, economic inefficiency, and steady growth of population – led to the inevitable breakdown of the moralistic economic system. Technological and organizational innovations as well as exploration abroad were institutionally discouraged. The grain productivity per *mu*

(0.1647 acre) rose only 100–115 percent from the Han (third century BC to third century AD) to the Qing (seventeenth to twentieth centuries) dynasties (Huang 1986, 17). Population, however, grew rapidly, despite the wars and famines that caused periodic decreases. Actual income of the Chinese agrarian laborers, *diannongs* (tenant peasants) and *gunongs* (hired farm laborers), stagnated for centuries and began to decline significantly by the eighteenth century, when population had a major explosion in growth. Archives reveal that, from the first century to the twelfth century, Chinese rural laborers' average income stayed roughly the same. By the eighteenth and nineteenth centuries, this figure had declined by more than half.[12] Over time, economic disasters and famines became increasingly frequent in China.[13] Excessive taxation, war or natural disasters were only the fuses to ignite the explosions. Peasant revolutions and wars were the natural, sometimes the only, outlets to solve problems. The super-stable domestic organizational structure, however, could not be changed by those explosive political struggles since no new LAP or culture was available. The result was generally the artificial reduction of population and a change of the imperial rulers. The new dynasty usually started its rule by reallocating the land and labor, thus restoring the politically stabilizing family/village-based LAP with some economic viability. The corrosive forces of economic commercialization were generally treated by the rulers with suspicion and suppression, as evinced by the low social and political status of merchants and craftsmen. The continuity of a dominant LAP in the history of China thus tends to confirm the "super-stability" of the premodern Chinese domestic organizational structure. It was super-stable primarily because its institutional basis was families, the first and perhaps most natural and thus most stable human institution of all.

Family-based LAP

A distinctive difference between the Chinese "feudal" system and the feudal system in Western Europe was that, in China, a substantial amount of land was transferable among private owners, and the owners usually did not have political authority over the farmers working on the land.[14] Landholding people included feudal noblemen, officials or generals, merchants and small farmers (Huang 1986, 26–7). A major consequence of this was the "massive existence of *zigengnong* (landholding farmers)" (Hu 1979, 44–56;

Lin 1983, 12–14).[15] On the one hand, the instability of feudal land ownership in China, caused predominantly by the lack of a primogeniture system (Fairbank & Liu 1980, 14) and presence of the *junxian* administrative system, tended to break up large landholding manors, thus producing small land-owning farmers over generations. On the other hand, political power was often used to create those family-based *zigengnong*s for the purpose of consolidating the rule of the imperial court.

The inevitable concentration of land-ownership over time, as a result of the economic vulnerability of small land-owning farmers[16] and the "legal" transfer of land, produced powerful, large landlords who could become real contenders for power with the imperial court. The production of *diannong*, *gunong* and unemployed peasants, as a consequence of the concentration of land-ownership, also greatly threatened the stability of imperial rule, which was a family-like institution. Thus, especially after the Sui Dynasty (sixth century), the Chinese imperial rulers often used force to reallocate land to create millions of small land-owning farmers to restore the premodern but "super-stable" domestic organizational structure.[17] The creation of *zigengnong* and the concentration of land-ownership constituted a major mechanism that determined the health or decline of a family-based labor allocation. Only a family-based LAP can provide the institutional fabric for the family-centered Chinese premodernity to continue. Therefore, it is not surprising to see the dynastic cycles in China coincide with the cycles in the family-based LAP – "*juntian*" (equally sharing land)[18] at the beginning of a new dynasty and the massive "*liumin*" (migrating landless and unemployed peasants) at the end.[19]

The family-based labor allocation, the *zigengnong* institution, will therefore be viewed, structurally and functionally, as the predominant type of traditional LAP in China from Qin to Qing.[20] As late as the last decades of the nineteenth century, *zigengnong*s still owned 40 to 70 percent of the land (Huang 1986, 123). The internal structure of this LAP varied over time and location. Basically, it organized the peasants according to their blood or kinship relationships or, less importantly, by their geographic location. The division of labor was decided by the family head or clan leader according to male/female differences and seasonal needs in a predominantly agrarian economy. No preset pay structure or working hours were involved. The income of the unit, family or a clan, was generally shared among the laborers and their dependents, decided by the family/clan heads based on the perceived "needs" of every member of the unit. Social norms were extremely important and moralistic considerations like fairness and harmony prevailed over economic concerns such as efficiency and expansion. Senior members of the unit, drawing on the legitimacy of family seniority, example-setting and their accumulated knowledge, had decision-making power and commanding authority. The division of labor and the individual's productivity was often maintained through noneconomic instruments and incentives. Quasi-religious behaviors like ancestor worship were very important to the legitimacy and continuation of this LAP. The mobility of individual laborers was not high, although the whole family had substantial mobility especially in comparison to other types of traditional LAP such as slavery and serfdom. In practice, however, the mobility of the families, constrained by the location of the land, was sufficiently low to make this LAP a fairly stable one. Family members, of course, could work outside the family to supplement its income.

Another major group of Chinese labor was the *diannong*. Combined with *zigengnong*, the two constitute the overwhelming majority of Chinese peasantry after the Qin dynasty (Hu 1979, 133). Besides paying rent to the imperial court, the ultimate owner of all the land, the *diannong*s had to pay rent to landlords for the right to work the land.[21] Their economic status was generally lower than that of the *zigengnong*s, although often their rent to the state was lower due to the help of the powerful landlord in evading taxes (Hua 1982, 6–10). The *diannong*s had basically the same type of family-based labor allocation pattern as the *zigengnong*s. The main difference is that the *diannong*s generally had more personal dependence on the landlord, thus an even more reduced labor mobility. At times, as between the East Han and Sui dynasties (third to sixth centuries), *diannong*s were treated as semi-serfs, or even semi-slaves, by their landlords. The landlord occasionally interfered with family labor allocation decisions by overruling the family head. However, the personal dependence of *diannong*s on the landlord varied in its rigidity and intensity, with a general trend of relaxation.

By the time of Qing, *diannong*s acquired much the same type of personal mobility and social status as *zigengnong*s (Huang 1986, 29–37 & 47–48). A *yongdianzhi* (permanent tenant system) that gradually became popular made *diannong*s virtually the same as the *zigengnong*s.[22] More economic concerns from the landlord's point of view played a role in the labor allocation in the *diannong* families.

Family members of *diannongs* were frequently exploited by the landlord beyond rent payment. Domestic service and other noneconomic duties were common burdens.[23] But institutionally, this was still a family-based traditional LAP. The rental contract between the landlord and the *diannong* was usually not written and could last for generations. In more than a few cases, the landlord and the *diannong* formed a quasi-family structure between them. Many landlords actually provided a better living standard and more stability to their *diannongs* than the *zigengnongs* could have. Many *zigengnongs* also needed to rent some land to have a meaningful scale of production to sustain themselves.

Frequently, Chinese peasants, *zigengnong* or *diannong*, were organized by villages, many of which were often extended families or *zhu* (clan).[24] The most senior family head usually enjoyed the highest respect and the most power in such a unit. Their authority and position were often formalized as *zhuzhang* (clan leader) and the villages usually had a set-aside source of income to maintain the "public" functions of the village, including ancestor-worshipping ceremonies. The unit of labor organization, the family or the village, functioned as an undifferentiated institution that governed people's economic, political, and social behaviors. Economic rationality, political logic, and social norms were, therefore, generally mixed together; this necessarily led to overemphasis on one of them and the sacrifice of others. Clearly, sociopolitical values such as order and authority structure were often overemphasized at the expense of economic efficiency, innovation, individuality, and equality. Economic rationality, such as seasonal needs and profit considerations, did play a role but was generally secondary to the logic of the social and political institutions represented by the family.

In fact, the Chinese were organized on the national level as a gigantic paternal family, as conveyed by the term *"guojia"* (country/nation/state-family). The imperial court, like the head of the family or the senior family of the clan, lived on the tribute of the peasant families in the form of taxation and conscripted labor of the "free" *zigengnongs*. In return, the imperial state was supposed to behave like a benevolent father to the peasants. Over time, the super-stable political institutions and the traditional LAP reinforced each other, and both accumulated almost unbreakable legitimacy. Chinese culture, the internalized Chinese institutions, in turn nourished and protected such a premodern domestic organizational structure. It is no wonder, therefore, that Chinese political élites always feared the destruction of *zigengnong* and *diannong,* the foundation of the family-based LAP.[25]

Serfdom and Slavery

At the early stages of this period, before the Wei Jin and the Southern-Northern dynasties era (fourth to sixth centuries), serfdom was common in China, although was hardly the dominant institution. Under this system, the peasants were fixed to a particular piece of land and owned by the imperial state or big landlords. The peasants could be transferred, together with the land they were attached to. The sale of peasants and their families, together with the land they worked on, was outlawed at roughly the same time as the primogeniture system was abolished. Serfs thus largely moved into five categories: small landlords, *zigengnong* who managed to have a sufficient size of arable land, *diannong* who leased their land from the landlords, *gunong* who were hired by landlords and *zigengnongs* on seasonal or long-term basis, and *liumin* (migrating unemployed peasants) who tended to become the main source of slaves, urban laborers, bandits, and even rebels. *Diannong* were no longer serfs, in the sense that they were not directly dependent upon landlords, although in reality contract sales of family members with fixed terms as a payment for rent were common. They had gained some mobility, certainly more than the serfs in a qualitative sense. In practice, serfdom nonetheless existed throughout Chinese history until the nineteenth century, with diminishing significance except in certain areas like Tibet and some southwestern provinces such as Yunnan. The major source of serfs was peasants turned into serfs by royal decrees or by war. The serfdom type of traditional labor allocation was not a major LAP in Chinese history.

Slavery was an important way of allocating labor, especially after a major war or a big change of dynasty. The practice was common even during the nineteenth century, although on a very small scale. Due to the family-based overall institutional setting, slavery in China was never fully developed.[26] Other than domestic slaves and servants, the areas with relatively high concentrations of slave labor were the state-owned industrial enterprises such as mining, porcelain manufacture, the arsenal and the mint that were established as early as before the Qin dynasty (Zhu 1988, 3, 39–40). There are only sporadic records of the existence of slave markets in the history of China. Many governments used prison inmates and prisoners of war to work on projects such as tomb-building, hydro-facilities, and palace construction. This type of labor allocation, therefore, though lasting, was generally only a supplement to the family-based LAP.[27]

Commercialization, Handicraft Industries and Local Labor Markets

For most of Chinese history until the twentieth century, the imperial state ran many handicraft industries such as iron, salt, mining, coinage, weapons, silk and porcelain, often in a monopoly fashion. This type of state monopoly functioned primarily for revenue collection, stabilizing the family-based agrarian economy, and supplying the imperial court with goods and weaponry. The scale of production of those state-owned enterprises reached very high levels by the Yuan, Ming, and Qing dynasties. Privately owned handicraft workshops replaced the "dominant position" of the state-owned shops only gradually after the eighteenth century (Zhu 1988, 38–43, 985). Despite the very high level of technology achieved,[28] the Chinese handicraft workshops, state-run or privately owned, were basically a supplement to the agrarian economy and had only marginal political and cultural significance in Chinese history.

The workers in those state-owned enterprises were largely state slaves or forcibly registered craftsman families. The craftsmen families generally practiced a family-based traditional LAP virtually the same as the family-based LAP practiced by peasants. The state-slavery LAP gradually became a type of authoritarian state employment with varied personal dependence and limited labor mobility.[29] Despite steady growth, craftsmen were strictly controlled and considered a lower class than peasants. They usually did not get a piece of land at the *juntian* (sharing the land) times (Zhu 1988, 41). Craftsmen were generally prevented from participating in the imperial exams that provided the peasants with institutional access to officialdom – the main avenue of social, political, and economic upward mobility in the family-like Chinese premodernity. Thus the craftsmen could not substantially expand their operations beyond the limits maintained by the imperial rulers. Their employment largely resembled the family-based LAP of the peasantry, with perhaps more personal dependence and less professional and geographic mobility.

Rich craftsmen or successful merchants, therefore, usually had a natural tendency to exploit the fact that land can be transferred among landlords. They tended to purchase land to become land-lords, and thus to elevate their social and political status – to re-turn to "the roots to guard [their] wealth"[30] – despite the fact that the rent from the land was usually much less than the returns from commercial and handicraft industries (Hu 1979, 56–8). This con-version of industrial and commercial capital to land-ownership was a significant consequence of the unique Chinese premodern dom-estic organizational structure. Even during the heyday of "capital-ist sprouts" at the end of the Ming dynasty, this trend continued.[31] As a result, development of handicraft industry and commerce in ancient China failed to create a market institution leading to auton-omy of the economy. The super-stable Chinese premodernity thus was safe from the challenge of spontaneous commercial activities. The unique institutional arrangement of Chinese handicraft indus-tries was very important to the continuation of the Chinese premodernity while providing the ruling élites with access to in-dustrial goods and commercial revenue. This historical "lesson" was not forgotten by the later rulers of China.

Some commercialization of labor allocation occurred in China, at least during the Ming and Qing dynasties (fourteenth to nine-teenth century) (Hu 1979, 173–206), although it can be traced back to much earlier years (Ye 1988). In places like southern Jiangsu and Zhejiang, hired labor was a major means of labor allocation to several industries such as construction, transportation and tex-tiles. Considerably formalized labor markets existed in many rural and urban communities throughout China. (Huang 1986, 49). This was a result of the increasing labor surplus in rural areas, and was a necessary condition for the development of craftsmanship and commercialization of the economy. But, an "involutionary commer-cialization" of the allocation of certain resources in China did not reach the point of creating a market institution. The "labor mar-kets" that existed in many areas of China, mainly the southeast, were essentially for seasonal labor allocation, an often necessary supplement to the traditional family-based or community-based labor allocation (Huang 1990, 110). Furthermore, most of the industrial employers were still family-based craft workshops that divided labor along the lines of families (Zhu 1988, 54–5). Local labor markets and commodity markets existed several times throughout the Chi-nese history; however, the market as an economic institution never developed as the main indicator, the labor market never became a meaningful LAP. Thus, although "a money economy had long existed in China" (Moore 1967, 218), China never had a market economy in its history until the nineteenth century.

II. THE ERA OF CHANGES (1840–1949)

Acceleration of the concentration of land-ownership and the bankruptcy of millions of *zigengnong* and *diannong* was a cyclic phenomenon of the Chinese political economy that had served as a major driving force for rebellions and dynastic changes in the past. History was about to produce another such bloody yet "necessary" dynasty cycle by the mid-nineteenth century. Increasing foreign factors, represented by European colonialism and its aftereffects, however, altered the historical perpetuation of the super-stable Chinese premodernity. The polarization of Chinese peasants worsened dramatically under the pressure of the exhaustive taxation system of the dying Qing dynasty (Huang 1986, 125–7) and increasing commercialization caused by foreign influence, assisted by the rapid decline of Beijing's political leadership and administrative ability. Huge numbers of unemployed peasants (*liumin*) began to flood the country, providing sufficient fuel to revolutionary causes and to alternative new LAPs. The inevitable collapse of the rotten Qing regime was accompanied by the emergence of new institutional arrangements such as concessions in some major cities under foreign control, the weakening of the family-centered sociopolitical structure, and the development of local autonomous regimes throughout China. The centuries-old culture was deeply discredited by a new generation of Chinese intellectuals.[32] The subsequent Republican Era (1911–49) featured continuous foreign aggressions and a weak central government that perpetuated much of the dreadful incompetence and illegitimacy of the Qing dynasty. The collapse of many of the old institutions, generally relaxed political control, plus heavy foreign influence caused some of the deepest changes in the Chinese domestic organizational structure,[33] reflected by the fact that Chinese labor began to be allocated in some new ways.

Labor Market and Some Profound Distortions

The same family-based traditional LAP still dominated Chinese labor allocation, especially in the countryside where the majority of Chinese lived. *Zigengnong*, *diannong*, and *gunong* continued to be the major patterns of allocating the rural laborers. Many urban shops and enterprises employed their workers in roughly the same way. Meaningful alternative LAPs, however, began to develop after the mid-nineteenth century.

The most significant change in Chinese labor allocation during this period of history was the emergence of a market-oriented LAP, brought in primarily by foreigners. A quasi-market allocation of labor grew in the coastal urban areas and began to acquire legitimacy from the weakening central government. In the 1840s and 1850s, the first generation of industrial labor emerged in foreign invested enterprises. The first of these were in Guangzhou in 1845 and soon afterward in Shanghai.[34] By 1894, the number of modern industrial employees of China reached at least 100,000 with nearly 40 percent in more than 100 foreign-invested enterprises and about 25 percent in Chinese private enterprises.[35] In the 1920s, it was estimated that China had about 3.8 million industrial workers, with more than half of them employed in a market-oriented fashion.[36] Among these two million or more market-allocated workers, about 20 percent were employed by foreign invested enterprises (Wang et al. 1987, 9). By the late 1940s, an estimated eight to ten million industrial workers were employed by a variety of enterprises (Yue 1989, 20 & Wang et al. 1987, 315).

Besides active foreign enterprises and a growing number of private employers, a consequential new development was the development of employment in state-owned enterprises (*guanying* or *guanshang*). Started by some reform-minded Qing officials, the *yangwupai*, in the late nineteenth century, sizable state-owned enterprises developed primarily for the purpose of enhancing China's national defense. Famous industrial giants of today's China such as the shipyards in Shanghai and heavy industries in cities like Wuhan, Nanjing, and Chongqing were built by the Qing or the Republic governments. Some of them later began to absorb considerable private investment (Gai 1988, 2). After World War II, this type of state-owned employment became very important (see Table 3.1). Labor in those enterprises consisted basically of two tiers: a largely market-oriented allocation of blue-collar and some white-collar workers, and a mostly state allocation of most of the white-collar workers including managerial and technical personnel. The latter was a distorted labor market that featured strong noneconomic considerations in allocating and managing labor. Personal and kinship connections, the so-called "petticoat influence," and political favoritism were the norm for this type of LAP. In a way, it was midway between a rather crude market-oriented LAP and the centuries-old, warm, family-based traditional LAP. It covered a very small but important portion of the Chinese labor force, and thus deserves our attention. Later, it apparently provided the historical precedent for the PRC government to allocate its administrative and technical cadres, even its entire industrial labor force, as state employees.

Table 3.1   Industrial structure in China (1936 and 1946)[37]

Year	1936 (percent)	1946 (percent)
Foreign Enterprises	61.3	32.8
Native Capital	38.7	67.2
Among the Native Capital:		
State-Owned Industrial Capital	15.0	67.3
Private Enterprises	85.0	32.7

Though still small, the market-oriented LAP developed in China for nearly one century and produced visible institutional impacts on the domestic organizational structure. This new LAP differed from the old "labor markets" that existed for centuries in two important ways. First, the workers employed and managed under this LAP were usually permanent workers, although many of them had a strong desire to retire to their old villages – a dream that was gradually broken. Second, despite the widespread existence of ultra-economic ties between the workers and their employers, economic considerations were generally the main concern of both. The workers generally had personal freedom and professional mobility, though economic needs and political constraints often limited their exercise of these rights. Societal concerns played a diminishing role to job-seekers and employers. Economic efficiency was the main criterion and the old family-based organizational structure became less important everyday. This new LAP covered essentially all of modern Chinese industry and contributed significantly to the urban development of the economy. A whole new class of modern workers, the Chinese "proletarian class," emerged, as well as a sizable capitalist class and professionals. Even many rural areas, mainly those near major industrial centers like Shanghai, Tianjin and Guangzhou, were greatly affected by the market institution that was symbolized by the market-oriented LAP (Huang 1990, 115–43). Clearly, the economic successes today of the so-called Sunan Model in southern Jiangsu province, the Wenzhou Model in Zhejiang province, and the Dacuzhuan Model near Tianjin have their deep roots in the early market development before the PRC era.

Industrial employment in foreign-invested enterprises and in native private enterprises, though basically market-based, had some strong "Chinese" characteristics. It was distributed very unevenly with a very heavy concentration in the coastal cities, under strong foreign influence. In 1936, the peak year of Chinese native capitalism, seven coastal cities had over 94 percent of China's industrial production (excluding the Northeast, which was then occupied by the Japanese) (Wang et al. 1986, 20). The native enterprises tend to be very small. For example, in flour milling, the most developed Chinese native industry, one employer employed 25.9 to 92 workers.[38] Technological innovation was minimal. From 1911 to 1936, patent applications filed in China totaled only 275. Productivity of the native textile industry was significantly – as much as 1.6 times – lower than that of foreign invested textile factories. The worst were the state-owned enterprises. The productivity of some state-owned light bulb factories was only 15 percent of that of similar private enterprises (Wang et al. 1986, 23). One can conclude that the Chinese labor market at this time was fairly underdeveloped, with heavy distortions.

More important regarding labor allocation, the Chinese market-oriented LAP was rather crude. Several unique labor practices were notoriously exploitative. The infamous *baogongzhi* (contracting) made sweatshops standard practice in China. *Yangchengongzhi* or *haoshengongzhi* (indentured labor) legalized child labor and made the apprentice system in Chinese industry synonymous with hardship and naked exploitation (Gai 1988, 9–13, Wang et al. 1987, 23–4, 148–9). The miserable position of Chinese workers, especially compared to that under the "tender" family-based traditional LAP, undoubtedly contributed to the relatively high political belligerence of the Chinese industrial labor (Wang et al. 1987). Mao Zedong thus called the Chinese industrial workers "especially capable of fighting."[39]

In short, by the mid-twentieth century, Chinese labor allocation continued to be a largely family-based traditional LAP. But new patterns emerged. The most important development was the advancement of a labor market in the major cities and in some rural areas. Several profound distortions of the developing labor market were also identifiable. The serious problem of unemployment was not solved since there was no "*juntian*" or land reform to restore a stable family-based LAP for millions of unemployed peasants. From the 1920s to 1940s, the urban unemployment rate was as high as 55 percent for males and nearly 80 percent for females (Wang et al. 1987, 149–50). The addition of hyperinflation from 1937 to 1949 (a 368 trillion times rise in the consumer price index)[40] gave the former peasants who were used to the tender family-based traditional LAP enough reason and motivation to fight for changes against the existing domestic organizational structure including, ironically, the newly emerged labor market.

The history of LAP during this period provides illustrative information about the cracking premodern Chinese domestic organizational structure. The traditional LAP was still the main LAP, especially in rural areas, while conditions became less and less conducive for sustaining it peacefully. New LAPs began to develop. But the heavy human toll and distortions caused by China's weak international status and its chaotic political situation implied an ill fate for the emerging market-oriented LAP. The overall institutional arrangement among the Chinese economy, polity, and social life remained basically a premodern one, with a clear dominance of the traditional political structure – family-like – and an undifferentiated social-economic political complex. The market, an "imported" institution, began to advance as a new economic institution, as indicated by the development of a market-oriented LAP. The formidable and penetrating influence of external forces, the foreigners, was evident. The newly emerged state allocation, practiced by both the Republican State and the opposing CCP in its "revolutionary bases," demonstrated an interesting new LAP based on a mixture of traditional practices with some market mechanisms. All these pointed to the alterations of the Chinese domestic organizational structure. The outcome of the Great Chinese Revolution (1911–49), however, powerfully twisted the institutional changes and ironically reversed many of these new institutional developments. A popular restoration of traditional institutions was accomplished in the name of new ideologies. When foreign forces were kept away, the historical trajectory of China almost predestined the emergence of a new dynasty that would restore the institutional foundations of the Chinese imperial regimes: the super-stable and premodern Chinese domestic organizational structure reflected by a family-based traditional LAP and its extremist version: an authoritarian state LAP.

III. "LEAPING FORWARD" TO THE PAST (1949–78)

Mao Zedong and his comrades won the three-year civil war against the KMT (Kuomintang) regime in 1949 after their legendary two-decade struggle conducted primarily in the rural areas. Much like the dynasty-founding emperors before him, Mao needed to restore order and unity to China and thus to consolidate his rule. The institutional development of the PRC (People's Republic of China) shocked many as a seemingly dramatic departure from the patterns set by Chinese history. A closer look at labor allocation patterns, however, reveals that the traditional domestic organizational structure, the Chinese premodernity, did not change for another three decades under Mao. The CCP regime first restored the traditional family-based LAP in the countryside. In the cities, for only four short years, Beijing sought to allow some market-oriented economic activities by establishing a "state capitalism" system (Wang et al. 1986, 124). Very soon, however, and at a dizzying speed, Mao used his sweeping political power to launch "socialist reform" campaigns throughout China that culminated in the disastrous "Great Leap Forward" (1958–61).[41] As historians now conclude, the "leap forward" was actually a giant economic crash that set back Chinese economic development many years. More important, the PRC regime managed to return to and reinforce the Chinese premodernity by establishing a family-like party-state as *the institution* for Chinese economy, polity, and social life. The establishment of a singular authoritarian state LAP, explains how the Chinese premodernity continued in a "socialist" or "communist" PRC. The institutional evolution of the Chinese LAP and the overall Chinese domestic organizational structure, based on a comprehensive study of labor allocation patterns in contemporary China in the sister volume of this book, Wang 1998, is outlined below.

Land Reform, Collectivization, and the Communes

To address one of the major social and economic problems in the vast Chinese countryside, the chronic decay of the *zigengnongs*, the CCP launched its *tugai* (land reform) campaigns through reallocating violently confiscated land and restricting rent (Bianco 1971, 150–1). In 1947, the CCP proclaimed its *tugai* guidance in the *General Outline of Chinese Land Law* (Huang 1986, 366–9). Unlike the failed reformers who advocated "rural construction" and "rural rejuvenation through education" before,[42] the CCP's land reform was received by the peasants with open arms and became a major source of its strength in its bloody struggle with the KMT for national political power. The historical logic of China once again proved to be extremely powerful. The restoration of family-based institutions to the Chinese rural areas effectively led to the establishment of a new political regime. Mao, the son of a Hunan *zigengnong*, knew this historical secret and applied it well.[43] By the spring of 1953, the land reform was basically finished. (Huang 1986, 378). After this *"fanshen"* (turnover) that touched almost every corner of China, millions of family-based farms were created and the ancient family-based LAP was restored on a massive scale. A honeymoon period started between the peasants and the CCP. The peasants, now mostly *zigengnongs*, were ready to embark on the familiar road of traditional agrarian economy to "develop household fortune" and to restore the traditional culture (Friedman et al. 1991, 112–15).

The new PRC *zigengnongs* were very small. On average, a peasant family owned 11.7 to 19 *mu* (1.93 to 3.13 acres) of land and a half to one farm animal.[44] The long-familiar bankruptcies of *zigengnongs* and covert land transfers, however, quickly began to reoccur. The political implications of this inevitable development deeply worried the CCP leadership. The ambitious industrialization plans of the party demanded much greater agricultural output, which could hardly be met by the small and inefficient farms or the scattered neighborhood cooperatives, despite increasingly heavy state taxation and the very exploitative *tonggou tongxiao* policy (state monopoly of the purchase and marketing of grains).[45] The CCP also had a burning desire to depart from the patterns of Chinese political history thus to escape from the dynasty cycles. The party was eager to proceed along the Soviet-style fast lane of socialism, at least for the goal of safeguarding Chinese independence. Something drastic had to be done.

The CCP decided to adopt the Soviet-style agriculture collectivization. Mao very quickly and very impatiently began in 1954–5 to alter the restored traditional family-based LAP and thus the overall Chinese organizational structure in the rural areas by launching "collectivization" campaigns among the peasants. With the exertion of tremendous political power, ideological agitation, and grassroots organization, the "instant" collectivization movement took off like wildfire (Friedman et al. 1991, 185). In literally a matter of months, five hundred million peasants were collectivized (Huang et al. 1989, 93). Originally planned as a ten-year process,[46] collectivization was completed in less than two years.

The village-based collectivized Chinese peasants were pushed further at a dazzling speed to form "people's communes" during the disastrous "Great Leap Forward" years. Only two months after the CCP Politburo adopted the "Resolution on Establishing People's Communes in the Countryside" in August 1958, over 99 percent of the peasants were organized in communes that are *"zhengshi heyi"* (integrating government administration and economic management) and *"gongnong bingxueshang xianjihe"* (combining industry, agriculture, military, learning, and commerce) (Huang 1986, 470–2). Property rights over land and other "means of production," even some consumer items, were defined on a commune (formerly *xian* or township) basis. Labor was also allocated in an authoritarian way by the communes instead of the village-based collectives.

Mao Zedong envisioned the communes as the basic cells of the PRC: self-containing and self-sustaining complexes performing the roles of industry, agriculture, commerce, education, military, and social life.[47] The new units often had forty thousand to fifty thousand people each. Labor was commonly organized in a quasi-military fashion, heavily and sometimes brutally exploited and wasted on many economically meaningless projects. A "miniature cultural revolution," or a "socialism and communism education," took place simultaneously to erase opposition (Friedman et al. 1991, 234–8 & Huang et al. 1989, 122). When the inevitable harvest failure and economic collapse came, the peasants faced the threat of a nationwide famine. Chinese agricultural production declined 13.6 percent in 1959 and 12.6 percent in 1960, while the state's grain purchase from the communes increased by 14.7 percent (Huang 1986, 478). Millions of peasants believed in climbing a "commune" ladder to reach the heaven of communism and thus to escape the age-old vicious cycle of rural poverty. In the end, the ladder proved to be just a mirage (Friedman et al. 1991, 216–43; Domenach 1995).

After the loss of twenty to thirty million lives,[48] the "super-stable" PRC regime adjusted its disastrous policy of "Great Leap Forward." The communes were kept, largely to save Mao's face. The "accounting units" were basically reduced to the level of the "production team" (a small village or part of a large village).[49] Mess halls were disbanded, privately owned livestock and small family plots of land were restored (Huang et al. 1989, 147, 158–60). In terms of value extraction and labor allocation, however, the communes and the "brigades" (a large village or a few small villages) still had tremendous authority until 1978–9. Numerous actions were taken to protect, strengthen, "purify" and institutionalize the communes and the subordinate brigades and production teams. The authoritarian LAP thus was maintained in the rural areas despite the economic disasters. During the decade of the "Cultural Revolution" (1966–76), the authoritarian LAP in the rural areas was further consolidated through numerous political campaigns.

The authoritarian state LAP in the Chinese countryside was a combination of the traditional community-based LAP and heavy authoritarianism and personal dependence. The peasants were all organized by geographic location and subject to the control of the cadres, some of them fellow peasants who were "developed" by the numerous "working teams" of the CCP organizations starting in the land reform era. Jobs, workload, rewards, and punishments were all decided through "democratic centralism"; that is, the cadres and a few "core" peasants made decisions after consultations (often rubber-stamp exercises) with every member of the unit, excluding "class enemies" such as the former landlords, "rich peasants" and other "criminals." In most cases, the institution worked like an extended family-based LAP in which the cadres served as the "father figure." Moralistic concerns, traditional values, kinship considerations, and community bonds were important factors. Pay depended on the total income of the unit, usually a production team. A laborer's work was recorded daily in points (*gongfen*) determined primarily by the cadres. Labor used by the communes and the brigades was recorded as points earned by the laborer, but paid later by his/her home production team – essentially a value extraction. At harvest time, after paying taxes, grain and other essentials were distributed on a per capita basis to meet everyone's basic needs. The remainder was then distributed according to points accumulated. Cash payment was generally a very small portion of the pay. For those who lost the ability to work and had no relatives to support them, the teams provided basic supply and service. The books were open but dishonesty, self-serving behavior and favoritism by the cadres were the norm. In many ways, the system looked more like a traditional community-based LAP with only a certain communist political "flavor."

The CCP-state tried to have more direct control over the peasants through the cadres in the communes and below. Promotions by the party, ideological indoctrination, the supply of rationed or subsidized materials, and credit lines were frequently used as leverage. Practically, however, local cadres, as high as the commune leaders, tended to resist the state demands considerably, especially in the case of dividing the harvest (Oi 1989).[50] Most of the local cadres, the new holders of the "father role" played previously by the local gentries, tended to be in power for life. They held on to power partially for political correctness in the eyes of CCP operatives, but more for their social status, moral or cultural power, connections, and family strength.[51]

To Establish the Urban Authoritarian State LAP

Half of the eight million Chinese urban workers were unemployed in 1949. New policies of the CCP such as banning certain service industries and bloody political campaigns known as the "Three Antis" and "Five Antis" also contributed to the unemployment problem. In less than four months in 1950, nearly 400,000 workers lost their jobs (Yuan 1987, 3–4). To consolidate its regime, the CCP used its political power to reshape the labor allocation institutions in the cities, hoping to eradicate the unemployment problem. Initially, the CCP attempted to use the rural economy as a reservoir by sending large number of urban workers to the countryside, to "return to their villages." That move proved to be rather unpopular and ineffective since land reform in the rural areas made the new *zigengnongs* reject additional people who would have to share their land. The rapid completion of the land reform made this policy useless very quickly. By 1952, the urban unemployment rate was still at 13.2 percent (Yuan 1990, 6).

As the new owner, the PRC assured full employment to all the employees of the confiscated KMT era state-owned enterprises. More than 750,000 workers in about 2,858 enterprises and many more former civil servants and public school teachers and professors were "taken care of" by the new regime. The CCP also adopted a realistic policy of allowing private industries to operate, thus to absorb substantial labor force. By 1950, China had more than 123,000 private enterprises generating 63.3 percent of its industrial production and employing more than 53.7 percent (1.64 million) of its industrial workers. In the commercial sector, 76 percent of wholesale and 85 percent of retail trade belonged to private shops.[52] Led by pragmatic leaders such as Liu Shaoqi, the CCP gave those private enterprises the same materials supply and market access as the state-owned enterprises.

Very soon, however, the honeymoon for private business passed. By the end of 1950, Beijing began to put a yoke on the labor allocation for private enterprises. Under a new policy, recruitment of new workers and temporary workers was strictly monitored. Any dismissal of workers had to be approved by the authorities. Surplus labor produced by the rise of productivity in state-owned and private enterprises "must not be dismissed." Rather, they should stay in the original unit, paid fully to "study" or merely wait to be "reallocated."[53] Overtime work was generally closely monitored and often prohibited. Hiring new workers from the rural areas had to be approved by the authorities, and the CCP launched campaigns to use its rural organizations to prevent surplus rural workers from leaving their own villages.

Beijing further adopted a combination of policies to curb urban unemployment. Together, those policies led to the establishment of a comprehensive authoritarian state LAP in China. First, there was the institutional separation of rural from urban by the device of the *hukou* (household registration) system. Every PRC citizen was required to have identification papers to have access to land, jobs, social welfare benefits, housing, education, party membership, good-character credentials, and numerous other opportunities. Without such *hukou* papers, a person was subject to the arrest and investigation by the police. A very important piece of information contained in the *hukou* papers was whether the holder was an urban or a rural resident. This provisional controlling measure was later built into a legal Great Wall between the majority rural population and the somewhat privileged urban dwellers. A striking dual economy was thus created in China (Xia and Dang, 1991, 148). The *hukou* system enabled the PRC government to control labor mobility geographically and created very rigid and very contrasting urban–rural dual economic and social structures. Market-oriented labor allocation became extremely difficult, if not impossible. All urban workers were effectively transformed to be state employees. Eventually, all college graduates, polytechnic school graduates, discharged and demobilized military personnel, high school graduates, and even released inmates – as long as they were urban *hukou* holders – were all guaranteed job assignment by the state (Yuan 1987, 19). Soon, there was only an increasing inflow of such permanent employees, and no meaningful outflow of unsuitable or unnecessary workers.

Second, micromechanisms such as *dangan* (personal dossiers) and the *danwei* (unit) were devised, leading to the establishment of an authoritarian state LAP nationwide. A *dangan* was set up for every state employee, required for job-seeking, promotion and advancement. Started as a CCP institution to keep track of its members, the system was adopted nationally by the mid-1950s to cover all urban workers and most rural cadres. Maintained by employers, it contained generally secret files that were not available to the employee and often could be accessed and modified only by the worker's supervisors. It contained basically the following items: personal history and credentials, supervisor's regular appraisals, examinations and assessments, political history and screenings, party membership and activities, records of awards or punishments, job information and promotion records, and other "suitable" information (Zhang et al. 1987, 133). Established during a citizen's middle/high school years, the *dangan* followed every state employee for life, and served as a major controlling mechanism for the state. To control one's *dangan* used to be the same as controlling one's destiny. Related to *hukou* and *dangan*, a *danwei* (unit) became a mini-PRC. A *danwei* could be a factory, shop, hospital, school, or an agency. It was a smaller version of an undifferentiated social-political-economic complex, performing functions in all three areas. Labor, production resources, and even consumer goods were primarily allocated, managed, and *de facto* owned by the *danweis*. Once assigned to a *danwei*, a worker was usually fixed to it for practically his/her entire life. To some extent, the bond between workers and their *danwei* rivaled those within the traditional Chinese family. Instead of having families as the cells of the domestic organizational structure, the PRC gradually established the *danweis* in that role. These enlarged and distorted "families" directly contributed to the preservation of the Chinese premodernity.

Third, the CCP quickly set up a labor management bureaucracy. In 1952, Beijing began to charge the labor bureaus with the responsibility and authority to monitor, allocate and assign labor in their respective regions. No recruitment was allowed without that approval. Cross-regional labor allocation had to be approved by a superior labor bureau overseeing the regions involved. Only the central government, through its Labor Ministry, had the authority to allocate labor beyond the provinces. By 1957, "the labor and wage authority was already centralized in the hands of the central (government)" (Yuan 1987, 15–16, 127).

Fourth, the CCP adopted a "Provisional Measure on Public-Private Joint-Management Enterprises" in 1954 and started the socialist reform campaign in urban areas. The law limited the stock dividends and private managers' salaries to no more than 25 percent of the profit of any joint-managed enterprise.[54] Like the swiftness of the rural collectivization movement, complete socialist reform of the private urban economy took less than two years. The PRC nationally set a 5 percent fixed rate of payment (*dingxi*) for seven years for private properties that were "socialized."[55] More than 810,000 *dingxi* payees were also assigned a job, mostly in the enterprises they formerly owned. Those "joint-managed" enterprises began to adopt all the institutional features of state-owned enterprises and soon were virtually identical to them.

Finally, at roughly the same time, urban handicraft shops and commercial industries were also collectivized into similar "public-private joint-managed" shops. Tolerated and even encouraged before 1954, elements of the private household economy such as craftsmen and individual shopkeepers were driven into extinction. There had been nine million such private household workers in the cities; by 1958, fewer than fifteen thousand were left (Yuan 1987, 19). The once active "labor referring" services all but vanished by 1958. Meanwhile, in the rural areas, the formerly active private handicraft shops and commercial shops were collectivized and became part and parcel of the collectives and, later, the communes. The authoritarian state LAP was, therefore, established as the dominant LAP in the Chinese urban areas.

Societal LAP: A compromise
From very early in the 1950s, even the almighty CCP realized that it could not directly manage millions of urban laborers; nor did it have enough resources to maintain an authoritarian state LAP for all the urban job-seekers. Despite the forceful exclusion against the hundreds of millions underemployed rural laborers, urban unemployment continued to be a major problem for the political stability of the CCP which, because of its "socialist construction plans" and its claim of being the "representatives of the Chinese working class," could hardly adopt the ancient but useful policy of the dynasties that limited and suppressed the urban population, especially industrial and commercial workers. The CCP was, therefore, caught in the middle, between a very inefficient urban economy under its socialist central planning that could not generate enough new jobs; and its burning desire to industrialize China to fulfill its political missions. The largely restored and strengthened Chinese premodern

domestic organizational structure offered very little hope for the regime to maintain its rather traditional family-like political dictatorship *and* to fulfill the economic development ambitions that were necessary for the survival of the CCP and the PRC during the Cold War.

Some remedies had to be found to compensate for the defects of Chinese premodernity and the flaws of the Soviet-style centrally planned industrialization. The CCP tried to give local authorities some flexibility in managing labor under the authoritarian state LAP. But the result was wild cyclical swings of *fangquan* (delegating power to the local authorities), which lead to the swelling of state employment, causing many of the serious unemployment and underemployment problems, and the subsequent *shouquan* (centralizing power), causing tremendous economic hardships throughout the years of the PRC (Yuan 1987, 25–26 & 134–137). To provide managerial flexibility and combat unemployment, a community-based societal pattern was introduced as a "socialist" but Chinese LAP, first in urban areas and then gradually in the countryside. Practiced primarily by the small urban collective enterprises and the rural CBEs (*shidui qiye* or commune-brigade enterprises)[56] which later became the TVEs (*xiangzhen qiye* or township-village enterprises), the societal LAP of the PRC allowed for certain labor mobility and competition within local communities.

Those collective enterprises only hired from among local job-seekers. As a small scale replica of the authoritarian state LAP, the community-based LAP allocated workers in a similarly authoritarian fashion but with little direct drain on the state budget for nationally provided job security, benefits, and sociopolitical status. The employees were contract workers and no permanent employment was guaranteed. Their pay was determined not by the state in a unified way but by the financial situation of their employers. This LAP was primarily a community-based societal LAP that combined strong social concerns of local welfare, political power and certain market mechanisms. Social institutions such as family, neighborhood, and local community were important factors affecting labor practices under this LAP. This supplementary LAP, as a compromise between the Maoist premodernity and the economic need of the PRC fighting domestic unemployment and international isolation, nonetheless developed rapidly in the PRC even under Mao. In areas like Sunan (southern Jiangsu province), successful CBEs began to contribute more to the income of the communes or brigades than agriculture even before the end of the 1970s. Later, in the 1980s–1990s, the societal LAP developed spectacularly into the very successful community-based labor markets.

In short, in just a few years (1954–7), the CCP regime completed a major transition from a multipattern labor allocation to the establishment of a centralized authoritarian state allocation as the dominant Chinese LAP in both urban and rural areas, at the expense of eliminating the market in the economy and personal freedom and mobility in social life. The CCP suppressed the existing market-oriented LAP and attempted to transplant an authoritarian allocation pattern from its longtime military operations. Universal political management of every urban worker was institutionalized at various levels. The state-allocated workers were guaranteed a lifetime job and related access to a variety of "socialist" benefits. In exchange, the workers became dependent on their superiors and lost most of their personal mobility and freedom. The incomes of the workers were also held stagnant at a low level. According to Premier Zhou Enlai, a "reasonably low wage system assures enough rice to most possible people; that is what we mean by saying 'letting five people share three people's rice'."[57] Economic efficiency was sacrificed for political concerns such as social stability, certain ambitious or even unrealistic development plans, or some leaders' brainstorms.

The new LAP worked to literally eradicate unemployment for a time. By the end of 1956, urban employed workers reached 24.51 million, triple the number in 1949 (Yuan 1987, 17). Rural labor was effectively controlled by the CCP through the collectives and so was no longer a threat to urban employment. The rural-urban dual structure was institutionalized and *danweis*, including the rural collectives, finally became the family-like cells of the PRC's domestic organizational structure. The new patterns of labor allocation that had emerged in the previous century were systematically and effectively abolished.

On the macro level, Mao managed to "rejuvenate" Chinese premodernity by nationally combining the economy, polity, and social life into one centralized institution – the CCP-dominated state that tended to adopt the centuries-old international isolationist posture. On the micro level, the traditional family-centered or community-based institutions were restored as the basis for the PRC state. The old Chinese premodernity was therefore forcefully restored and strengthened, despite the seemingly different ideological claims and labels. This domestic organizational structure had some inherent aspects that were seriously unfeasible, both technologically and practically, as well as undesirable economically and socially. The seemingly high achievement of political values – that is, order, tranquillity, and members' security – was therefore bound to be short-lived. This nation-based traditional LAP restored the premodern Chinese dom-estic organizational structure with a comprehensive and penetrating political power that was unprecedented for the central government, which behaved like a traditional Chinese father.[58]

The crisis of the Maoist premodernity
Starting in 1957, the political atmosphere was heated by Mao's dream of "jumping into communism." His "open plot" known as the "Anti-Rightist Movement" in 1957 cleared the way politically for the disastrous "Great Leap Forward" and demonstrated the great power which restored Chinese premodernity had given to an emperor-like dictator. This infamous "Anti-Rightist Movement" caused millions of people, most of them intellectuals who aspired only to limited freedom and rationality, to be labeled as "rightists" and thus to suffer as second-class citizens and class enemies for more than twenty years. A major theme in the movement was to consolidate the "unified" or "centralized" leadership of the CCP, through the state, over all aspects of the Chinese polity, economy, and social life, even people's minds. The "Leap," however, was a major economic disaster, leading to a nearly total collapse of the economy and widespread unemployment; it was a clear verdict on the incompetence and ineffectiveness of the Chinese premodernity in developing the nation's economy.[59]

Chronic shortages and the massive unemployment began to threaten the CCP regime. By 1961, Beijing was forced to cut the urban population through political measures. The CCP used forceful administrative means to send most of the 25 million new state employees back to their former villages, now the economically struggling communes, to reduce the burden of the state in supplying its swollen *danweis* (Huang 1989, 159). The political power of the CCP and the premodern domestic organizational structure were the keys to overcoming the resistance inherent in such a large-scale human tragedy. In the end, by mid-1963, more than 19.4 million state employees and 24 million urban *hukou* holders were relocated to the countryside. Chinese industrial labor declined from 16.6 percent of the total labor force in 1958 to only 6 percent in 1965

(Yuan 1989, 135–7). Those and other coercive policies, including further collection of agriculture taxes, saved the authoritarian state LAP and the CCP regime at the expense of the people, who paid dearly with millions of lives. The remaining urban population and especially state employees now truly became a privileged minority of China.

The monolithic and encompassing state LAP in the urban and the rural areas could not accommodate the new growth of the labor force even in an inefficient way. Millions became unemployed in the cities, and millions more in the countryside became underemployed and ready to flood the cities at any time. Mao and his "leftist" followers, including his wife, Jiang Qing, relying on the political power generated by the Chinese premodernity, hoped to use the collectivized rural areas as the outlet for surplus urban labor. A national campaign of sending high school and middle school graduates to the countryside to be "re-educated by the poor and lower-middle-class peasants" was thus launched, and millions of human tragedies occurred. More than fifteen million young urban dwellers were sent to the rural areas between 1967 and 1977. This policy, however, hardly prevented the worsening situation of the authoritarian state LAP in the cities because nearly thirteen million rural workers were recruited by the state-owned enterprises in the urban areas through numerous channels (Yuan 1989, 102–204). The aggravated inefficiency and increasingly unbearable burden on the state reached the point of general crisis. When the former urban youth returned to the cities, gradually at first but then massively after Mao's death in 1976, unemployment in the Chinese cities exploded, with deep political implications. The monolithic authoritarian state LAP reached its end in the Chinese cities by the end of the 1970s, while its rural version was at the point of total collapse.

In short, after 1949, the emerging market-oriented LAP was deliberately and gradually abolished in the Chinese urban and rural areas, together with foreign-owned businesses. The new PRC regime, with a central political power among the strongest in China's history, attempted to reform the Chinese LAP once and for all. In the hope of making great leaps forward into the future world of communism, the CCP leadership under Mao Zedong actually attempted a general rejuvenation of the past. Facing serious problems of unemployment and a hostile external environment, Beijing used the totalitarian nature of the PRC political system to reshape the Chinese LAP quickly and comprehensively. During the 1950s

and 1960s, under the politically destabilizing pressures of high unemployment, the CCP regime established and institutionalized a
dominant LAP – the authoritarian state allocation – and a supplementary LAP – the community-based LAP (both are still largely in
existence today). These two LAPs, especially the dominant authoritarian state LAP, were essentially modified continuations of the
family-based Chinese traditional LAP and demonstrated the continuity of the premodern Chinese domestic organizational structure.
The institutionalization of the PRC along a Leninist-Stalinist road
was therefore twisted, delayed and even blocked substantially.[60]

The traditional family-based LAP that had proved capable of
supporting a super-stable imperial regime for a long time lost its
flexibility due to the gigantic scope – nationwide – of the authoritarian state LAP. In the past, individual families could go under
while the whole family-based LAP remained intact. But financial
difficulties of the PRC "family" meant the bankruptcy of the whole
authoritarian state LAP, threatening the restored Chinese premodernity and the political power of the CCP. Flexibility and efficiency were both lost and unemployment kept coming back. The
rural-urban dual LAP and economy further caused political problems for the CCP leadership. For the pressing needs and desires of
economic development and technological progress, this newly enhanced Chinese premodernity could spell only failure for the Chinese. The CCP regime, therefore, could hardly escape from political
turbulence, instability, and uncertainty. Chinese modernization was
then pushed forcefully into the incongruous direction of eliminating the market and reintegrating the economy, polity, and social
life. An unsatisfactory record of performance was thus inevitable.

IV. THE CHINESE PREMODERNITY: MESSAGES FROM THE READING OF HISTORY

Several interesting observations stand out in this brief review of
China's institutional history. Five of these observations are analyzed below to further the assertion that, at least until the 1980s,
China had basically been a premodern nation with a super-stable
and self-perpetuating undifferentiated social-political-economic complex based on the family structure. The powerful role of Chinese
culture, self-imposed international isolation, the lack of autonomous
social organizations or "civil society," and the legitimized existence

of an authoritarian political power culminated in the CCP-PRC regime – all point to the special timing (both absolute and relative) and thus the unique path of Chinese modernization. An internationally isolated Chinese premodernity made a market-driven modernization in China very difficult, if not impossible. The social-economic-political complex blocked the emergence of the market by undercutting some of the fundamental fabrics of a market economy. The strong and stable existence of nonexclusive property rights fundamentally limited the meaning of market transactions; the culturally sanctified traditional LAP prevented labor mobility and condemned labor commercialization; the moralistic objectives of economic activities made market-oriented economic activities difficult, disrespected, and even illegitimate. This social-political-economic complex thus hindered the development of a "spontaneous" market or a foreign-induced market in China.

A Stable Premodern Domestic Organizational Structure and Culture

The Chinese domestic organizational structure prior to the 1980s was basically the unchanged premodern institutional arrangement, illustrated by the persistence of a largely unchanged labor allocation pattern that relied on noneconomic institutions – family and/ or the state – to allocate labor. In this gigantic complex of an undifferentiated economy-polity-social life relationship, the economy was largely a nonmarket one – a traditional agrarian, or "moral," economy and/or a centrally planned command economy. This assertion of institutional continuity by no means denies the fact that the Chinese experienced countless economic, political, cultural and technological developments to make the Chinese civilization one of the most colorful and interesting achieved in human history. Yet, it maintains that, institutionally speaking, the Chinese domestic organizational structure remained essentially the same for centuries, explaining the historical stability and the lasting stagnation of that nation.

The Chinese economy had basically been an agrarian one for thousands of years. Even by the 1990s, close to three-quarters of the population lived in the countryside, though industrial output had surpassed agricultural output since the middle of the 1960s.[61] Typically, the Chinese agrarian economy was strongly family-based and community-confined, small scale, oriented to local exchange, basically subsistence-providing, and quite self-sufficient. All these fit well into the description of "moral economy" (Little 1989). The agrarian economy and its associated social institutions were characterized as a "honeycomb" social organization that perpetuated the segmented and parochial structure of Chinese politics.[62] The Great Chinese Revolution shook but did not alter the nature of this economy, or the nature of the Chinese domestic organizational structure. As a matter of fact, Maoist modernization strategy and revolutionary campaigns almost turned the whole country into *one* giant traditional family.

The Chinese domestic organizational structure, centered on a family/clan structure, gradually internalized itself among the people to form a unique, extremely stable and influential culture that powerfully legitimized Chinese premodernity.[63] The reinforcement of this culture and the undifferentiated Chinese domestic organizational structure made China remain, institutionally, essentially unchanged for millennia until the 1980s. Chinese scholars themselves have concluded that a "super-stability" and an "unchanged nature . . . [and] structure" are some of the most important characteristics of China's domestic organization and culture.[64] According to Zhang Mingyuan (1990, 4–5):

> Compared to other cultures, Chinese culture has a stronger historic heredity. The nature of the traditional rural society we can see today in China is not very different from the primitive culture of the tribal society that existed widely in China some five to six thousand years ago. They are the same family-based social organizations, the same small agrarian self-sufficient economies. . . . Family ethics/principles are above everything else; the incompletion of the political and legal system [led to] the expansion of the patriarchal lifestyle and made it the managerial model for the whole society and even the state.

As Max Weber noted long ago, there is not a single dominant religion in Chinese thinking.[65] The three major Chinese religions, Confucianism, Buddhism and Taoism, have competed with each other for thousands of years without eliminating any one of them. Political intervention by the father-emperor was important.[66] A "peaceful coexistence" among these religions is, therefore, visible in Chinese history, and may still be found in many well-known shrines today.[67] The lack of a unified and dominant religion, as a result of the family-like Chinese premodernity, resulted in the absence of a power-ful social force outside the state administrative structure. It con-tributed to the supreme position of the Chinese family as *the institution* not only for economy and polity, but also for social life including religion. The continuity of the family, and the associated ancestry worship, overcame the fear of death and thus addressed the religious question for most people (Tang 1991, 3).[68] The conti-nuity of the family-based traditional LAP in China, therefore, ex-plains the institutional bases of the Chinese culture. Stable dominance of a certain reformed or secularized religion, such as Calvinism, might have different impact on people's behavior concerning the development of the market economy. However, we may not want to overemphasize the role played by the Chinese religion (or the lack of certain kind of religion) in the hindrance of a market economy. The famous Weberian belief in the crucial role of Protestant reli-gion in facilitating capitalist entrepreneurship[69] may be overstated and may not preclude non-Protestant nations from engaging in equally aggressive capitalistic or market-oriented economic activities. Ap-plied to the typical Protestant environment of New England in the seventeenth century, for example, Weberian analysis actually was not accurate;[70] and it was in the Catholic Italian city-states in the fourteenth and fifteenth centuries that a capitalistic market economy first emerged.[71]

One of the three religions, Confucianism (more of a philosophy or ideology than a religion), had the greatest influence on Chinese politics and culture (Fairbank & Liu 1980, 313). Harboring ruth-less Legalist tactics after the Han dynasty (first century BC), Con-fucian culture highly valued the paternal family-like hierarchical structure in organizing human behavior. The "orthodox thinking of the Chinese historical and cultural traditions" stresses the prin-ciple of "retaining Heaven's principles and extinguishing the hu-man desires."[72] According to the core teachings of Confucian ethics, the so-called *sangang wucan* (three cardinal guides or heaven's prin-ciples – ruler, father, and husband – and five constant virtues or cardinal relationships), all Chinese human institutions were basi-cally modeled after relations in the traditionally paternal family, with a set of rather fixed duties and obligations for each of the members.[73] Trying to be "right," as judged mostly by one's superi-ors, was regarded as an extremely important virtue for everyone.[74] The "ten righteousnesses" governing the five cardinal relationships implied a reciprocal relationship between the two parties of each pair. For example, the benevolence of the ruler and the loyalty of the subjects were preconditions for each other.[75] Politically, Chinese culture strongly favored informal networking; personal patronage; unequal exchanges in an informal way and "behind the door"; a unitary and centralized authority structure; and mere obedience to those "in authority."[76] Historically, China has been a nation ruled by personal will rather than by law. The legal system is poorly developed and law enforcement is even worse. Face, status, and nominality are critical to those "in authority" and for maintaining order. Open contention among interest groups, the supremacy of man-made laws, as well as the notion of "the loyal opposition" are completely exotic ideas in the Chinese political culture.[77] A politically controversial Chinese scholar (He 1987) argues that:

> The value-system of [the traditional Chinese culture] is an ideology of politics, law and ethics centered on Confucianism. The economic basis of the traditional culture is the backward natural economy. The social structure of this culture is built upon a patriarchal clan system that centered on the three major principles of honoring the emperor – respecting the father – serving the family.... During the more than two thousand years, the basic structure and value-system of it have maintained a consistent continuity, despite some microevolution and progress.

A leading Chinese scholar on ethics wrote in the official press in 1995:

> The Chinese nation was historically organized along kinship fabrics and centered on the family. Thus cultivating one's moral characteristics, supporting the family and serving the state became the three levels of [our] ethics. The interest of the state is higher than that of the family and individuals.... The most fundamental requirements of [Chinese] ethics have been filial piety to the parents and loyalty to the state. If there is a conflict between the two, one must put loyalty to the state ahead of filial piety to the parents. For the loyalty to the state, one even has to put up with the risk of killing his parents.[78]

Alienation of the Chinese family-centered social values and ethics was thus completed to require everyone under Confucian culture to serve the state first, then the parents, and the self (and the nuclear family) last – the supremacy of "patriotism," a Chinese (especially

PRC) version of nationalism distilled from the family-like domestic organizational structure.

As an internalized premodern institution, Chinese culture has been used as a very mysterious, powerful and convenient "black box" in explaining China and Chinese behavior.[79] It is praised as the source of the "super-stability" of the social structure, or blamed as a major cause of the backwardness of the economy. Some, like the seventy-seventh lineal descendant of Confucius, believe that Confucianism contributed significantly to the economic success of the East Asian nations, including Japan.[80] Many Chinese take deep pride in their culture; others would try to modernize China with a total eradication of this culture.[81]

Chinese traditional culture nourishes human behaviors that are static, moralistic, harmony-valued; that despise commerce and profit; that are localistic, segmented, lethargic; that lack individuality and open competition; and that excessively depend on a "center" which is usually *in* authority rather than *having* it.[82] What Qiang Mu described as the ideal of the Chinese world outlook – "*datong* (大同, great harmony or largely identical) *xiaoyi* (小异, small differences)" – clearly reflects the centuries-old admiration for a traditional Chinese family, with smaller and slightly "different" generational units in it, as *the* human institution.[83] Starting with Dr Sun Yat-sen, the "father" of both the Republic of China and the People's Republic of China, the *datong* ideal based on family-like societal institutions was revitalized as the goal of Chinese revolution and construction.[84] Chiang Kai-shek stated very bluntly that the "fundamentals" of the Chinese family-like Confucian domestic organizational structure should and would never change.[85] According to *Liji-Liyuan pian* [The book of rites – Liyun section] which was drafted some twenty-four centuries ago, an ideal domestic organizational structure in China was described by Confucianism:

> When the Great Way (*dadao*) was practiced, the world was shared by all alike. The worthy and the able were promoted to office and men practiced good faith and lived in affection. Therefore they did not regard as parents only to their own parents, or as sons only to their own sons. The aged found a fitting close to their lives, the robust their proper employment; the young were provided with an upbringing and the widow and widower, the orphaned and the sick, with proper care. Men had their tasks and women their hearths. They hated to see goods lying about

in waste, yet they did not hoard them for themselves; they disliked the thought that their energies were not fully used, yet they use them not for private ends. Therefore all evil plotting was prevented and thieves and rebels did not arise, so that people could leave their outer gates unbolted. This was the age of Grand Unity (*datong*). (*Liji-Liyun pian*. English translation in De Bary 1960, 176)

The Importance of International Isolation in Chinese History

Very important to the historical perpetuation of the Chinese premodernity is the fact that China was for centuries isolated by choice or by location from interaction with the outside world. To the ancient Chinese, a world government had been established in the "central kingdom" (*zhongguo*) and the end of history had been reached long ago when the Qin dynasty unified the country in the third century BC. Cyclical dynastic changes as well as alternations between political unity and division were norms but only happened once every few centuries, and then everything would continue basically the same,[86] due to the super-stability of the Chinese domestic organizational structure. The super-stability of the Chinese premodernity, as mentioned earlier, was possible primarily because its institutional foundation was the family – the first and foremost, thus a very stable, human institution. The super-stability of Chinese premodernity was also clearly facilitated by the lack of international interactions, initially caused by geographical barriers such as deserts and high mountains to the west and south, the ocean to the east, and the Arctic weather to the north. The inherent structural stability of the premodern Chinese domestic organizational structure was thus basically immune from challenges by other human groupings. This was indeed profoundly different from the modern history of Europe.

An authoritarian or "absolutist" imperial ruler soon found the premodern organizational structure safe, reliable, stable, rewarding, easy to control and thus very desirable. With the centuries, China's political rulers learned this lesson and became forceful defenders of this undifferentiated social-economic-political complex. Besides actively maintaining the family-based agrarian economy and the family-based LAP, the ruler realized the great advantage of eliminating foreign influences, competition or aggressions. This is especially true in the case of the Ming (fourteenth to seventeenth centuries) and Qing (seventeenth to nineteenth centuries) dynasties when the traditional policies despising commerce and preventing land aristocracy were enhanced by a policy of "*haijing*" (ban on maritime intercourse). The collapse of the Yuan dynasty in 1368 had cut off land transportation between China and central Asia and Europe. The founder of Ming dynasty began a ban on foreign trade.[87] After a massive naval expedition that reached as far as East Africa, the Ming government finally proclaimed a total *haijing*.[88] The Qing government implemented the *haijing* with even more vigor. A stable imperial state and total control over the economy and social life, including ideology, were achieved. The Chinese, for most of their history after the Qin dynasty, did not have a notion of diplomacy. The "Chinese world order" was based on the traditional family institution where there can only be one father, one emperor.[89]

The price, however, was chronic economic and technological stagnation and poverty, the suffocation of primitive capitalistic developments that started in roughly the sixteenth century in south and southeast China, and the backwardness of the whole Chinese nation. China kept itself away from the worldwide revolutions of science and technology. The inevitable tensions and strains that accumulated released themselves as cyclical institutional explosions that led only to a repetition of the Chinese premodernity under a new royal name at the expense of millions of lost lives. Such a static, isolated, and self-centered political "paradise" for the Chinese rulers ended when the modernized Western powers came to China after the mid-nineteenth century. But, as our brief historical review of Chinese LAPs revealed above, foreign invaders started but did not finish the demolition of Chinese premodernity; it was restored, maintained and even reinforced under Mao. The lack of interactions with other "sovereign" nations contributed immensely to the superstability of the Chinese premodernity. Thus, as Immanuel Wallerstein (1980) argued, China lost a major condition for market-driven economic development.

Authoritarian Politics as the Norm

As the continuity of a family-based traditional LAP indicates, there has been a strong tradition of rigid hierarchy of authority and deep legitimacy of authoritarian regimes in China. The notion of the state (*guojia*) conveys much more than just "government" to the Chinese. It often resembles the concept of a family-like nation which is viewed as representing the highest interest of the people. Despite the Confucian value ranking of "people first, state second, and monarchy last,"[90] the Chinese normally had an order of state first, monarchy second, and people last. Mao Zedong promoted the Confucian notion by labeling almost everything under his regime with the term "People's." What actually happened in the PRC, however, has largely been the same "state first, rulers second, and people last" order. (At times, such as during the "Cultural Revolution," it was clearly "the rulers first" at the expense of not only the people but also the PRC state.) Since the establishment of the Qin dynasty, the Chinese state has basically enjoyed the status of authoritarian "absolutist state."[91] The ruler, helped by his ministers, has had ultimate power over every person and every piece of property in the country.[92] This ultimate power, however, has generally been defined along the principles of Confucian doctrines, limited by the administrative capacity of an agrarian economy, and carried out in a context of a sea of organizational cells of paternal families.

Usually, there has been a strong vertical connection between the central and local authorities. Power normally rested in the hands of the superiors, since the Imperial Court appointed every official all the way down to the level of counties. The exercise of political power over peasant households was assisted and conditioned, however, by the local gentry class in the villages.[93] Only when the central authority went too far beyond traditional Confucian teachings and beyond the surviving ability of the peasantry, especially the gentry class, to tolerate was this authority challenged. Then, the head of the authority changed and some slight adjustments of policy were made, followed by the all-important restoration of the family-based LAP as discussed before. The state, equipped with the most advanced bureaucratic system of its time,[94] continued its tight grasp on almost all aspects of the nation. The value system was such that a unified, centralized and stable state was most important, followed by the family. Individuals were the least important concern.[95]

In short, the Chinese state historically has been an unseparated part of the Chinese social-political-economic complex, organized as a paternal family, and has been in a position of controlling the whole nation, including its economy and social life. The PRC state inherited this institutional legacy. The fact that an authoritarian state LAP replaced the emerging market-oriented LAPs in the 1950s illustrates a strong effort by the CCP to further enhance the absolute position of the state versus the economy and social life in contemporary China.

Such a stable and strong state could easily suffocate the process of market-driven modernization, as it did for a long time in Chinese history. This is especially the case when the sovereign power of the state is not meaningfully paralleled or challenged by external political forces, as happened in Modern Europe. On the other hand, a strong and stable state may produce a state-led modernization by forcefully separating the economy from the bondage of a premodern domestic organizational structure, creating a market economy through the effective and constant effort of state administration, as happened in Germany in the nineteenth century and Japan after its Meiji Restoration in 1868. The feasibility of a state-led modernization is especially important to latecomers such as China, which may find that a state-led route is the only realistic pathway to modernity and all its associated benefits.

The Lack of a Civil Society

As indicated by the fact that China has had basically only one LAP in its long history, the notion of "civil society" has been problematic for the interpretation of China's domestic organizational structure. The undifferentiated social-political-economic complex dictates that there has been no such concept as "civil society," nor any distinction such as a state "independent" from social life. Rather, there has been only one basic human institution: the family and its concentration, the imperial state. The Chinese imperial state essentially functioned like a paternal family, with the emperor as the undisputed head of the family. It is quite inconceivable in Chinese thinking that anything, the economy or a "society," could be autonomous vis-à-vis the almighty family/state institution.

Formally and legally, there was supposedly nothing between the state and the peasant families except the bureaucratic system, assisted by the local gentry. As noted by Barrington Moore (1967, 417), at an early stage of its history "the Chinese polity had eliminated the problem of a turbulent aristocracy tied to the land," which had been "a decisive precondition for democracy" in Western Europe. In reality, some organized, even semi-autonomous, institutions have existed between the state and the families: temples, villages, gangs, underground or black societies, and neighborhoods. Those traditional social or interest groups, however, were generally very informally organized. Open contention among these groups was heavily disguised and distorted, poorly regulated, and sometimes banned as legitimate means for social and political activities.[96] Thus, "the framework of traditional Chinese society both encouraged rebellion and put severe limitations on what it could accomplish" (Moore 1967, 217). The gentry class and the Chinese societal organizations nonetheless played a meaningful role between the imperial state and the families. Societal or "quasi-societal" organizations have been responsible for many social activities including the needed local economic exchanges. They created local markets throughout China for a "moral" economy to function. Most religious, cultural, and educational activities have been conducted and organized by such nonstate organizations as well.

Ever since the Song dynasty (ninth to thirteenth centuries), the Chinese state has attempted to organize peasant families to gain direct control in the villages. An administrative system at the grassroots level, the *baojia* system, was implemented periodically until 1949, only to be replaced by the much more powerful political structure of the CCP's *hukou* system. Quite a few of those nonstate organizations even maintained military units serving as local police forces, especially during the warring periods. Nevertheless, none of those nonstate organizations have had legal autonomy or formal independence. Their *de facto* independent status has been determined mainly by the rise and fall of the imperial power, as indicated by the rise and fall of the community-based LAP and the serfdom LAP. Furthermore, Chinese societal organizations have been built upon the powerful family structure, headed by gentry families. They have not had any differentiation between their economic and social functions. Chinese social life, based on family structure, may be visibly distant from the imperial state, but by and large it has been "affiliated" to rather than "independent" of the latter.

Some Peculiarities of the PRC

After about one hundred years of turmoil, China was once again united by a powerfully centralized regime under a revolutionary political party in 1949. The history of labor allocation under Mao prompts the conclusion that the PRC was created and altered by Mao as a restoration of the authoritarian family-like and undifferentiated Chinese imperial state. Instead of Confucianism, which was largely discredited by the revolutionaries, "Mao Zedong Thought" – a version of Marxism revised by Mao with (not surprisingly) elements of

Confucianism and Legalism – was used to justify and legitimize the restored dynasty. This is interesting in two important ways. First, it demonstrates the depth and power of Chinese culture even for the most "revolutionary" Chinese politicians. Second, it may reveal a theoretically provocative link between Marxist political theories and premodern human institutions. Karl Marx, for example, appreciated the distinction between the state and society; while believing that the state is usually used by certain classes, he nevertheless believed that this distinction is a temporary and alienated phenomenon and will be inevitably abolished through a proletariat revolution to create a unified new society with a withering away of the state. Later, mainly due to Lenin's revision and Stalin's practice, Marx's original thought on the relationship between the state and society was "distorted into an ideology to legitimize a bureaucratic dictatorship which rules over society" (Nee & Mozingo 1983, 119). This distorted Marxist view undoubtedly had a great deal of influence over the Marxists in China as well as in many other countries. In a sense, this Leninist doctrine provides a powerful justification for the "traditional" Chinese view of having a unified polity-economy-social life relationship with a clear state dominance.

Armed with the allegedly "modern" and "scientific" ideology of Marxism, CCP forcefully strengthened the premodern relationship among the Chinese economy, polity, and social life at the price of literally millions of human lives. Given our analysis of the evolution of the Chinese LAPs in the 1950s, now we know why 1957 was a major turning point in PRC history (Tang Tsou in Nee & Mozingo 1983, 85–6). By then, the revolutionary and authoritarian CCP state had managed to twist the Chinese modernization impetus into a wrongheaded effort – eliminating rather than establishing the market, entirely for political goals that had been traditionally valuable. The solution was to built an authoritarian state LAP, modeled after the old family LAP, in both urban and rural areas. A spontaneous market-driven modernization was even less feasible under the CCP regime.

V. SUMMARY

The history of labor allocation in China demonstrates that there had been primarily one dominant LAP prior to the 1980s: a family-based traditional LAP and its Maoist national variation. The market

was not an important economic institution and the Chinese domestic organizational structure was largely an undifferentiated, family-like, state-centered social-political-economic complex. Mao's PRC strengthened the traditional Chinese premodernity and reversed the new trend of institutional changes exemplified by the emergence of alternative LAPs between 1840 and 1949. The PRC LAP was dominated by the 1980s by an authoritarian state allocation in the urban and rural areas. As a supplement, a small societal pattern of community-based labor allocation existed. The institutional arrangement of the PRC under Mao, therefore, was largely a restoration of the premodern Chinese domestic organizational structure. This "super-stable" Chinese domestic organizational structure made a market-driven modernization institutionally impossible. Once the externally-induced institutional changes were reversed, the only realistic hope for a Chinese modernization became, perhaps ironically, the authoritarian state which may start a state-led modernization utilizing again the "imported" institutional ideas and norms for its own political reasons.

NOTES

1. The dragon became the totem of the Chinese two thousand to three thousand years ago at the latest. The dragon, as the Chinese interpreted it, is an almighty, unpredictable, and eternal creature. It is not necessarily always bad-tempered, and is not an evil creature as Europeans might believe. In appearance, the dragon is a mixture of boar, deer, lion, snake, horse, lizard, and fish. It was especially associated with weather and precipitation, which are extremely important to an agrarian economy. It has been the exclusive symbol of male imperial rulers; in fact, almost all the good emperors in Chinese history were called "*zhenglong tianzi*" (genuine dragon as the son of the heaven).
2. For example, Barnett (1990), Eckstein (1966), Fairbank (1983), Friedman et al. (1991), Goldstein (1990), Harding (1987), P. Huang (1990), Little (1989), Oi (1985, 1989), Perkins (1984), Perry, Wong (1985), Perry (1989), Pye (1981, 1985), Shirk (1982, 1993), Shue (1988), Spence (1990), Vogel (1969, 1989) and Walder (1986).
3. The "institutional changes" after 1949 were often described by the CCP-PRC as *fantian fudi* ("flip over the heaven and the earth"). The scale and zeal of the changes might have been such, but the goal of the Maoist regime was primarily to rejuvenate the traditional Chinese domestic organizational structure, as will be analyzed later.
4. A similar view is in Parsons 1951a, 195–8.

5. We use "family-like" rather than the commonly used word "patriarchal" for two reasons. First, the term "family-like" primarily refers to a set of specific institutional arrangements, behavioral norms and goals essential to a family institution, rather than just a specific father-centered authority relationship. Secondly, the head of the family or family-like groups may or may not be a senior male. The "head" can even be a group of people selected through a variety of processes.
6. Si Maqian: *Shiji* [History]. *Qinshihuang benji*.
7. There were brief periods (such as Wei and Jin) when large land-based autocrats developed to form European style manors that reduced the family-based peasants to serfs and semi-serfs. Powerful large landlords and local gentry existed throughout the Chinese history. But they were largely controlled by the family-like centralized imperial state and tend to diminish quickly. After the Ming (established in fourteenth century), institutional barriers between the emperor and the peasant families were reduced to a minimum as the centralized Chinese despotism reached its peak.
8. The leading thinkers and practitioners of legalist tactics (Legalism) were Shang Yang (fourth century BC), Han Fei (280–33 BC), and his brilliant but tragic student Li Si who later became the first prime minister of the Qin dynasty.
9. Ben Gu: *Hanshu* [The history of Han] – *Shihou zhi*. This monopoly, however, was not implemented completely and was abolished a few times in later Chinese history. The notion of imperial ownership over most natural resources, including uncultivated land, minerals, open waters, and oceanic resources, lasted until the twentieth century.
10. Li Shimin, the Tang emperor who institutionalized the imperial examination system, claimed so. See *Xingtang shu* [New history of Tang] – *Taizhong benji*. An American educated economist believed that this imperial examination institution was largely responsible for the backwardness of science and technology in ancient China (Lin Yifu 1994, 271–2).
11. Despite countless works on Chinese history and the best-kept official historical records in the world, there is surprisingly scarce research on the allocation of labor in ancient China. The official historical records of China, the so-called "Twenty-five Books of History," have only sporadic mentions of labor allocation. Even the records of the Chinese population were very unscientific and inaccurate. See Gu Monyu: *Zhongguo renkou wenti lunji* [On the issues of Chinese population], Hong Kong, Yadong Society, 1965, 4–7.
12. Liu Yonchen & Zhao Gang: "18–19 shiji Zhongguo nongye gugong de shiji gongzi biandong qushi" [The changing trend of income of the Chinese agricultural laborers during the eighteenth and nineteenth centuries], in *Mingqing dangan yu lishi yianjiu* [Ming Qing records and historical research], The First National Archives, Beijing, Zhonghua Books, 1988, 874–5. A recent "reportage" asserted that in the Tang Dynasty (seventh to tenth centuries), the Chinese passed the peak of per capita cultivated land (12.6 *mu*) and per capita grain production (500 kilograms). See Ma Yuejun: "Huang tudi, he tudi" [Yellow land,

black land], in Liu Ying ed.: *Dangdai Zhongguo yeshenghuo – Dangdai Zhongguo redian xiezhen chongshu* [Night life in contemporary China – the series on the hot issues in contemporary China], Beijing, Huayi Press, 1993, 4–5.

13. A study called China "The Land of Famine." The frequency of famines increased over the centuries: There were about 69 during the first century, 171 in the second century, 263 by the eleventh century, 391 during the fourteenth century, and 504 in the sixteenth century (Deng [1937] 1984, 1, 61, 86–126).

14. Even the sometimes large estates in ancient China were institutionally different from those of the manorial system in Medieval Europe. See Sun Yutang, cited in Robert Barnett 1990, 56–9.

15. The Chinese imperial courts asserted ultimate rights over all the land. This was the basis on which the rulers collected rent nationwide from landlords and farmers. The transfer of land in ancient China was the transfer of the "user's right" rather than the exclusively defined property rights of the land. In practice, however, one can argue that the user's right was in most cases roughly the same as genuine property ownership.

16. Chinese scholars argued forcefully that Chinese *zigengnongs* were inherently unstable and easily bankrupted. Except for a small portion who became landlords, most of them tended to become *diannong* or unemployed peasants. (Hu 1979, 127–31)

17. The most often used policy is the *"juntian"* (equally sharing land) policy. For a typical *juntian* policy and its implementation in the early to mid-Tang dynasty, see Fan 1965, 200–6.

18. *Juntian* (均田) was used by the Sui and Tang dynasties. It had varied names at different times. In the Han dynasty, the imperial court adopted *tuntianzhi* (屯田). In the Jin and the Southern and Northern dynasties, it was called *zhantianzhi* (占田制). By the Ming dynasty, we see *kentianzhi* (垦田制). The Qing dynasty used *gengmingtian* (更名田).

19. Chinese historical records since *Shiji* have clearly documented the corelationship between political instability and the phenomenon of *liumin*, the decline of the family-based LAP. (See, for example, *Hanshu* [The history of Han] – *Shihou zhi*, *Songshu* [The history of Song] – *Fubi zhuan*, Lu 1947, 493–6, Fan 1965, 207, and Jian 1984, 29–30).

20. Some Chinese scholars believe, in the Marxist tradition, that *zigengnong* was only a "transitional" institution and a "supplement" to the landlord vs. *diannong* class structure. (Hu 1979, 131). This argument, however, clearly overlooks the fact that *zigengnong* were the majority of population for the largest part of most dynasties in China until the twentieth century. Furthermore, the "inherent" destruction of *zigengnong* took a long time to develop and was usually reversed by the political power of a new regime, including the CCP from 1946 to 1953. Some argue that *zigengnongs* always existed in large numbers throughout Chinese history. See Huang 1986, 34–5.

21. Some, a minority, rented land directly from the imperial state.

22. This is a variation of the *diannong* system started around the eighth century, in which the user's right of the land could be inherited and

transferred by the *diannongs* as long as the landlord got the generally fixed rent. (Huang 1986, 123–4).

23. For a discussion on *diannong* in the Song dynasty (tenth to thirteenth centuries), see He Zhongli et al.: *Songshi lunji* [On Song history], Zhenzhou, Zhongzhou Books, 1983, 267–70.

24. Common village names such as *Tiejanying* [blacksmith village] or *Jianhuchun* [craftsmen village] outside the city of Beijing, for example, are illustrations of such a specialized village-based labor allocation.

25. For example, see *Huangqing jingshi wenbian*, vol. 34. Cited in Hu 1979, 132.

26. Influential Chinese intellectuals like Hu Shi and others have used this fact to criticize Marxist-Leninist interpretation of Chinese history. See Guo Murou et al. 1956.

27. For a general overview of the slavery system in Chinese history, see Liu Weimin: *Zhongguo gudai lubi zhidu shi* [The history of the slavery system in ancient China], Hong Kong, Nonmen Books, 1975.

28. For a thorough examination of the history of science and technology in China, see Needham 1956–1984.

29. For example, some of these workers could get a "vacation" every year from some emperors while others were treated strictly like slaves (Zhu 1988, 41–3).

30. Si Maqian: *Shiji* [History]. vol. 129, *Shihouzhi*.

31. Fu Yiling: *Mingdai jiangnan shimin jingji shitan* [A preliminary study on the urban economy in the Jiangnan region during the Ming dynasty], Shanghai, Shanghai Renmin Press, 1957, 45.

32. A leading Chinese intellectual, Lu Xun, wrote in the early twentieth century that the 2,000-year-old Chinese culture was a "cannibalistic," inhuman culture. (*Kuanren riji* [The Dairy of a Crazy Man]). A similar argument was also made by Wu Yu, another leading scholar, as late as 1936 (*Wuyu wenxuan* [Selected works of Wu Yu]). For some rather harsh criticism against Confucianism at early twentieth century, see Fu Yunlong et al. 1995, 93–8.

33. For a historian's account of such institutional changes in an inland area in China at the time, see Pomeranz 1993.

34. CCP Shanghai Committee: *Qinggong zhenzhi lunxun jiaocai* [Textbook for political education of the young workers], Shanghai, Shanghai Renmin Press, 1985, 322–3.

35. Sun Yutang: *Zhongguo jindai gongye shi ziliao* [Historical data on Chinese modern industry], vol. 2, Shanghai, Science Press, 1957, 1201.

36. Chen Da: *Zhongguo laogong wenti* [The issue of Chinese labor], Shanghai, Shangwu Press, 1927, 7–20.

37. Chen Zhen ed.: *Zhongguo jindai gongye shi ziliao* [Historical data on Chinese modern industry], vol. 4, Beijing, Sanlian Books, 1961, 53.

38. Staff editors: *Jiuzhongguo jizi mianfeng gongyi tongji ziliao* [Statistical data on the mechanized flour mill industry in old China], Beijing, Zhonghua Books, 1966, 36–38.

39. Mao Zedong: "*Zhongguo shehui ge jieji de fengxi* [An analysis of the classes in China]," (1929) 1965.

40. Shanghai Social Science Academy ed.: *Shanghai jiefang qianhou wujia*

ziliao huibian [Data on prices before and after the Shanghai liberation], Shanghai, Shanghai Renmin Press, 1958, 50–1.

41. For a treatment of the origins of the Leap and its manifestation in one illustrative province, Henan, see Domenach 1995.
42. For a CCP account of the reform measures attempted by Liang Shuming and Yan Yanchu see Wang 1984, 312–15.
43. Mao (1973, 1075–76) argued in 1945 that a restoration of the *zigengnong* system was most appealing to the peasants and a major objective for the CCP.
44. Su Xin: *Woguo nongye de shehui zhuyi gaizhao* [The socialist reform of our country's agriculture], Shanghai, Shanghai Renmin Press, 1977, 13.
45. At Chen Yun's suggestion, the PRC adopted this policy in the fall of 1953, setting the stage for agriculture collectivization. See *Chenyun wenxuian 1949–1956* [Selected Works of Chen Yun], Beijing, Renmin Press, 1983, 209.
46. Deng Zihui: Report to the National People's Congress on Collectivization, 1956.
47. Chen Boda: "*Zai Maozedong de qizhi xia* [Under the banner of Mao Zedong]" in *Hongqi* [Red Flag] magazine, Beijing, July, 16, 1958.
48. Basil Ashton et al.: "Famine in China: 1958–61" in *Population and Development Review*, vol. 10(4), (Dec.) 1984, 613–45; John Aird: "The Preliminary Results of China's 1982 Census" in *China Quarterly*, No. 96, (Dec.), 1983, 613–40. A thorough study concluded that the "abnormal death toll" during the three years of the Leap was around thirty-five million. See Ding Shu: *Renhuo* [Man-made disaster], Hong Kong, The Nineties Press, 1995.
49. The Central Committee of the CCP: "*Guangyu gaibian nongchun renmin gongshe jiben heshuan danwei de zhishi* [Instructions on changing the basic accounting units in the rural people's communes], Feb. 13, 1962. In Huang et al. 1989, 169.
50. This is especially the case in those areas where a whole production team or even a whole brigade would be basically just an extended family.
51. For descriptions of these father-figure or "boss-like" rural cadres, see "Qingfa" in Chan et al. 1992, "Boss Geng" in Friedman et al. 1991, and the rural cadres in Oi 1989.
52. See *Sanlianglai xinzhongguo jingji de chengjou* [The economic achievement of the new China in the past three years], a collection of articles edited by the CCP. Beijing, Renmin Press, 1953; and Xia 1991, 84.
53. The State Council: "*Guanyu laodong jouye wenti de jueding*" [The decision on labor and employment issues], Beijing, July 25, 1952.
54. *Xinhua Yuebao*, Beijing, Xinhua News Agency, October 1954, 233.
55. *Renmin Ribao*, December 16, 1956. Later, the payment was extended to 1965, and finally stopped in September 1966 (Xia 1991, 85).
56. Thomas G. Rawski: *Economic Growth and Employment in China*, The World Bank and Oxford University Press, 1979, 131–2.
57. Zhou Enlai: "Guanyu laodong gongzi he laobao fuli wenti de baogao,"

Xinhua yuebao [Xinhua monthly], Beijing, Xinhua News Agency, September 1957.

58. For a long time, Mao and the CCP were treated literally in the PRC's propaganda as parents of the Chinese people. For example, a very popular political song has been "I take the party as my mother."

59. In the Chinese urban areas, the main problem was the extremely short supply of goods and widespread malnutrition, rather than massive death as in the rural areas. In fact, shortages in the Chinese economy began to emerge as early as in 1956, the time of the completion of socialist reform. That year, according to the State Planning Commission, the majority of the 235 products under state-centralized distribution and rationing were either in short supply or totally lacking. (Huang et al. 1989, 87, 110).

60. For an impressive discussion on the "positive" impact of this delayed institutionalization of the PRC regime, see Shirk 1993.

61. *Renmin Ribao* Oct. 31, 1990, 4.

62. Shue (1988, 105) argues that due to the heavy legacy of the past, China today is still basically an enduring, localistic, solitary, and resistant cellular society. This view contrasts Walder's argument (1986) that contemporary China is a new, party-dominated, divided, yet compliant network society – although both agree that the Chinese economy has been fundamentally a nonmarket economy which shaped patterns of social and political relationships in that country.

63. See the reflective thinking on this in the aftermath of the tragedy of June 4, 1989 (Kane et al. 1990, 3–5).

64. Jin 1987 and Zhang Minyuan 1990, 6–7.

65. Weber: "Konfuzianismu und Taoismus," cited in Moore 1967, 220.

66. For this subject, see J.J.M. Degrute: *Chinese Religion*, New York, Macmillan, 1910.

67. For instance, in the famous *Xuankongsi* [Mid-air temple] in Shanxi province in North China, all three religions are displayed together, enshrined, and worshipped in the same complex. (*Shanxi Ribao*, No. 15033, 1992.) In Taipei, the famous Lunshan Temple enshrines not only Buddhist gods and goddesses, Taoist figures, but also a local goddess, *Mazhu,* and many other legendary gods.

68. For a good survey of Chinese views on life and death and their impact on the overall Chinese culture, see Yuan Yang 1996.

69. Max Weber: The *Protestant Ethic and the Spirit of Capitalism*, New York, C. Scribners, [1905] 1930.

70. For how merchants were prosecuted, not encouraged, by Protestant political authorities – the General Court in Boston and the Protestant Church – for charging "too much" interest on loans in 1639, see Bailyn 1955, 41–4.

71. August Giebelhaus is acknowledged for this point.

72. Chen Bojun: "Who Opened the Bottle of the Devil?" *Wenxue Pinglun* [Literature Review], Beijing, No. 3, 1990, 30.

73. The five cardinal relationships are: ruler guides subjects, father guides son, husband guides wife, elder brother guides younger brother, and senior friend guides junior friend. The five constant virtues are: benevolence, righteousness, propriety, wisdom, and fidelity.

74. The conceptual difference between "being right" and "having right" (Kratochwil 1989, 156–70) is very meaningful. The former dictates people's behavior by emphasizing the importance of "doing the right thing" in a traditional society; the latter grants individual autonomy within a formally defined, institutionalized or legalized, structure in a human grouping (nation).
75. *Liji- Liyuan pian* (The Book of Rites – Liyun Section).
76. Kratochwil (1989, 165) made the distinction between "in authority" and "having authority." "In authority" means that the authority is gained through arrangements such as inheritance, designation or seniority. "Having authority," on the other hand, emphasizes much more the sources of authority beyond arrangement, that is, the authority generated by knowledge, achievement, and capability.
77. For a sincere and deliberate lifelong exploration of the "Chineseness" of the Chinese by a keen observer and an involved American, see Barnett 1990.
78. Luo Guoji, president of the Chinese Society on the Study of Ethics: "Quanju yishi, zhengti jingshen – tan Zhonghuo minzhu lunli sixiang hexin" [Overall viewpoints, entity senses – on the core of the Chinese ethics], in *Renmin Ribao-Overseas*, July 29, 1995, 3.
79. Cf., for example, Lucian Pye 1981 and 1985.
80. Kung Te-cheng: *Confucius: His Life, Thought, and Influence*, Taipei, Taiwan, Government Information Office, 1991, 29–39.
81. This has been one of the major debates in Chinese history after the middle of the nineteenth century. Almost all the important Chinese political leaders, intellectuals and scholars participated in this debate in one way or another. The most famous concepts developed in these debates can be summarized as follows: *quanpen xihua* [wholesale Westernization]; *biguang zishou* [close the door and take care ourselves]; and in a practical sense the most influential idea – *zhongxue weiti, xixue weiyong* [Chinese culture as the essence using Western culture as the means] – systematically summarized by Zhang Zhidong in 1898 in his famous *Quanxue Pian* [Encouraging learning]. For more on this intellectual debate, see Lu Xuehai ed.: *Quanpen xihui yanlunji* [Collections on wholesale Westernization], three vol, Guangzhou, Ningnan University Press, 1934. This debate is still very much alive in today's Chinese press and publications.
82. One author identified two major "factors that contributed to the stability in traditional Chinese social life": the family structure and "a relatively flexible class system." (Shu-min Huang 1989, 3)
83. Qiang Mu: *To Understand Chinese National Spirit and Chinese Culture from the Perspective of Chinese History*, Taipei, Taiwan, Jinglian Press, 1979, 17.
84. Sun repeatedly hand-wrote the *Liji-Liyun pian* as his political blueprint and ideological inspiration. It is still regarded as an official ideal by the Taiwanese government.
85. Chiang Kai-shek: *The Fate of China*, Nanjing, Government Information Office, [1943] 1948.
86. Liu Goying: *Lun Zhonghuo wenhua* [On Chinese culture], Kuala Lumpur, Malaysia, Chinese Association, 1986, 34–5.

87. *Mingshi* [The History of Ming] – *Taizhu benji*.

88. Fang Hao: *Zhongxi jiaotong shi* [History of China-West interactions], vol. 3, Taipei, Zhonghua Wenhua Shiye Committee, 1953, 175–8, 180–212.

89. Wang Zengcai: *Zhongwai jiaotong shihua* [History of Sino-foreign interactions], Taipei, Jingshi Books, 1988, 25–6.

90. *"Mingwei gui, shiji cizhi, junwei qing,"* (people is to be respected, the state follows, the monarchy is the least important) in *Monfucius – Lianghuiwang.*

91. The terms of "state" or "absolutist state" obviously have different meanings in the Chinese context. They do not necessarily carry the same specifics as in the case of Louis XIV's France.

92. *"Putian zhixia, mufei wangtu, shuatu zhibing, mufei wangcheng,"* in *Shijing* [The classic poems]. About the sixth century BC.

93. For an account of the Chinese political structure before the twentieth century, see Tsurumi Naohiro's "Rural Control in the Ming Dynasty" and Shigeta Atsushi's "The Origins and Structure of Gentry Rule" in Grove and Daniels 1984, 245–78 & 335–86 respectively. Fairbank (1983, 32) described this different "gentry class" in Chinese society as "connected both with land holding and with office holding." Pye (1981) also attributed a significant role to this gentry class in Chinese political structure. Shue (1980, 343) found that in contemporary China, "village cadres" have been playing a role similar to that of gentries in the past, to "glue and hold" the peasants and the CCP-ruled state together.

94. In comparison with other premodern nations, given its huge population, Chinese bureaucracy is relatively small (Fairbank 1983, 36–8). For an examination of the bureaucratic system in contemporary China, see Richard Kraus in Nee & Mozingo 1983, 132–47.

95. The famous Confucian teaching to the Chinese élites – "cultivating oneself, taking care of one's family, managing the state, and quieting the world" – reflects this kind of value standard.

96. For an examination of the unique features of factionality and informality in Chinese politics, see Pye 1981, 1983 and Woetzel 1989, 135.

4 Institutional Reconfiguration: Labor Allocation Patterns and Chinese Modernization

Against the institutional background of a premodern domestic organizational structure, the PRC Government started a cautious but quickly extensive institutional reform at the end of the 1970s. The political reasoning responsible for this daring departure from Maoist policies was simple: to head-off a seemingly inevitable "dynasty change" caused by an unprecedented political, economic and ideological crisis. Beyond many CCP leaders' expectations, however, the reform has increasingly transformed so much of the Chinese domestic organizational structure that the CCP regime, though surviving its comrades in most other socialist countries, has lost much of its grip of the nation; even the party itself has been profoundly affected by these institutional changes.

The course of Chinese modernization appeared to have gathered its own momentum. A marketization of the Chinese economy, social life and even politics has advanced rapidly. The Chinese economy is gaining increasing autonomy from the sociopolitical complex via an emergence of the market, facilitated by the combination of spontaneous commercial activities and external forces represented by foreign direct investment. Social life is differentiating from the state in many ways under the cover of a heavy commercialization. Combined with societal forces, however, the Chinese state is bending or distorting the emerging market, with an interesting implication of a very "Chinese" modernity. By the late 1990s, the Chinese domestic organizational structure appears to have become a great mixture of the elements of the past as well as the future. A total of four major LAPs now exist in the PRC, reflecting the transitional nature of the Chinese domestic organizational structure. The PRC is at an institutional crossroads and the unique coexistence of four LAPs testifies to that fact.

This chapter elaborates our inquiry into the domestic organizational structure and its changes in contemporary China by examining the current LAPs in the PRC. Section I attempts some assertions

125

and working hypotheses about the Chinese domestic organizational structure and its transformation – the course of Chinese modernization. Section II outlines the currently coexisting four LAPs in the PRC: a restored family-based traditional LAP, an authoritarian state allocation, the community-based labor markets and an emerging national labor market. The focus of this section is an examination of the institutional significance of those four LAPs and the implications of their changes. Section III summarizes the chapter.

I. TO OBSERVE CHINESE MODERNIZATION: ASSERTIONS AND HYPOTHESES

To observe a modernization course as large and as complex as that of China is a rewarding but potentially hazardous effort. A further clarification of the questions and parameters of our investigation may help to reduce the almost inherent perplexity. As a brief display of the starting conditions of the Chinese reform, a general overview of Chinese domestic organizational structure by the end of the 1970s appears to be necessary. Some working hypotheses are developed as the premises of our inquiry and they will be revisited in the conclusion of the book.

China: An "Old" Latecomer

Institutionally speaking, China is an "old" latecomer in the effort to modernize. Chapter 3 has described the premodern domestic organizational structure of China (Figure 4.1). This undifferentiated and well-preserved organizational structure has been widely viewed as responsible for the stagnation of the Chinese economy. The market institution was repeatedly suffocated and brilliant ideas of science and technology were sacrificed for the sake of this institutional arrangement that was highly legitimized by its deep internalization – the formation and perpetuation of the Chinese culture. There has never been a well-developed differentiation of economy-state-social life relationship, nor a market as the dominant economic institution, in Chinese history. The Chinese institutional arrangement features a giant, unified, stable, family-like complex; that is, it is a highly developed but premodern domestic organizational structure. The emergence of the market and the associated social and political changes could not meaningfully occur within such an

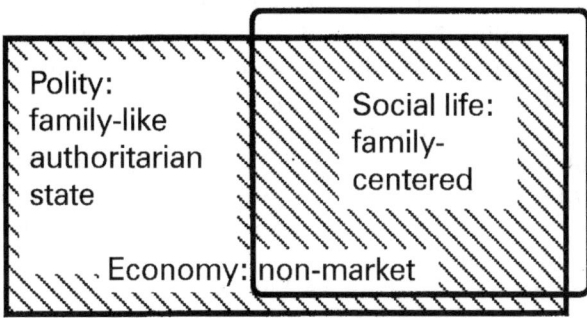

Figure 4.1   Chinese domestic organizational structure prior to the 1980s

institutional framework, despite cyclical dynasty changes and desperate rebellions. Social life and economy were under direct and authoritarian control of a unified and centralized imperial political authority. This largely continued in an extreme fashion under Mao. Prior to the 1980s, China was indeed a "communist neo-traditional" nation (Walder 1989, 242–64).

It was what W.W. Rostow called "sharp stimuli" from outside, beginning in the mid-nineteenth century, that posed a serious question to the Chinese: to change or to die as an independent nation. Although some believe it started much earlier (Spence 1990), Chinese modernization became a life-and-death priority to the Chinese by the late nineteenth century. The long absolute age of the Chinese premodernity and a long relative age (that is, started institutional differentiation long after many nations have largely completed it) forced the Chinese to search for a state-led modernization route. The decaying Qing Dynasty, the chaotic republican regimes, and especially the KMT's Republic of China all attempted a state-led modernization. They failed on the Chinese Mainland because of inability, ill luck, or insincerity. The Chinese domestic organizational structure remained to be an undifferentiated institutional complex under the rule of a family-like authoritarian state.

After bloody struggles with foreign enemies over the nationhood of China and with domestic enemies over what needed to be done, the CCP won the Chinese Revolution by establishing a powerful revolutionary state, the PRC. The PRC started to promote Chinese modernization with an unprecedented zeal and political power, also along a state-led route. Although on the appropriate track of state leadership, the CCP pushed in the wrong direction, with phenomenal political power and extraordinary human and material costs. Instead of introducing the market and institutionalizing and rationalizing the state, the CCP under Mao made an astonishing effort to eliminate the market and to deinstitutionalize the state – to re-integrate the economy, polity, and social life. An idealized premodern societal institution, *datong* [Great Harmony], from the philosophy advocated by Confucian scholars over 2,000 years ago, was adopted as a major tenet of the Maoist ideal domestic organizational structure.[1] A failure was inevitable, and Mao himself did not escape from the tragic dynasty cycles of Chinese history.[2] Essentially, the CCP searched in the past and wished for a miracle rejuvenation of the old Chinese organizational structure to develop China economically. This strategy failed miserably; the Chinese unfortunately missed the great worldwide technology revolutions after World War II, and thus lagged further behind many other nations. This gross error almost cost the political life of the CCP in the 1970s.

What Deng Xiaoping and his associates have accomplished since 1978, most importantly, is the reversal of direction on the track of state-led modernization.[3] The market is being introduced by the combined effort of the state, foreign influence exemplified by foreign direct investment, and indigenous entrepreneurs; it has grown steadily to be the major, if not dominant, economic institution for the 1.2 billion Chinese (Lardy 1991; Shirk 1993, 5–6). The indisputable efficiency and innovation of this emerging market has sealed the Chinese market-oriented economic reform into an irreversible course and stabilized the political regime of the CCP, at least for the time being. As Figure 4.2 shows, the current Chinese domestic organizational structure has been in transition, with a market emerging strongly. The authoritarian PRC state is challenged by the increasing force of market institutions, and by socialist or traditional Chinese social institutions, which are themselves under a powerful commercialization impact of the market. Given the short period of time and the long premodern history, what the Chinese have achieved in the two decades after 1978 is genuinely remarkable. The impressive economic gains and social changes are evidence of the power of the proper strategy on the appropriate track. The political institutions of the CCP-PRC state have now been recognized as a major reason for the impressive success of a gradual but steady reform of a socialist nation (Shirk 1993, 22, 329–50).

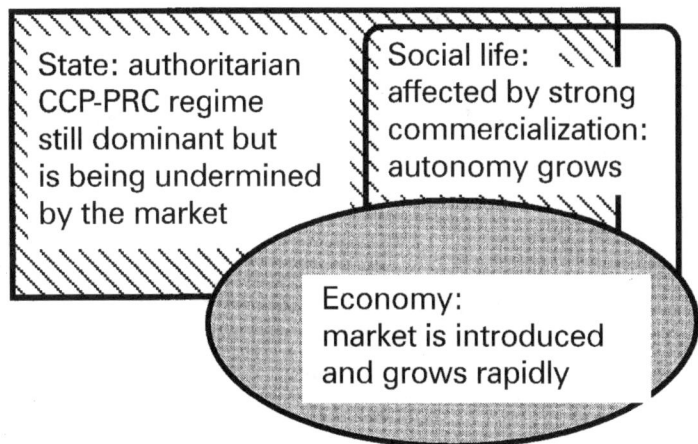

Figure 4.2 Changing organizational structure in the PRC – the first
step of a state-led modernization in the 1990s

Chinese Modernization: A Speculation

As an old latecomer, China has managed to start its modernization
with a tumultuous yet spectacular record. Assisted by the Chinese
in Hong Kong and Taiwan,[4] the Mainlanders have accomplished a
great deal in establishing and utilizing the market. The market
institution, ironically under the protection and facilitation of a
"socialist" state, has gained sufficient legitimacy in the PRC to function
as a major engine of further institutional changes in China. It is
likely to become the main institution of the Chinese economy, or
even social life and polity,[5] thus completing the first step of Chinese
modernization, in the not very distant future. It appears that the
CCP state wants economic development with decreased concern for
social institutions and social values. But as an authoritarian state,
Beijing strives to regulate the emerging market institution actively,
while the newly emerged market itself has yet to be institutionalized and matured in a way that leads to a differentiated yet interactive relationship among the market, the state and social institutions.
Truly exclusive private property rights and a national market, especially a national labor market, have yet to become the dominant
economic institutions in China. The PRC is still ruled mainly by ill-
prepared politicians rather than rationalized and institutionalized

experts/technocrats. Finally, the CCP may lack the organizational and ideological capacity to guide an emancipated market. To date, the CCP has merely given the market a chance to grow. Much of this "retreat" by the CCP has been forced by foreign influences, such as foreign direct investment. Among the three crucial conditions of successful state-led modernization mentioned in Chapter 1, the all-important third (continuous and effective guidance of the market by a transforming state) still appears to be in question. The sweeping commercialization force of the market, however, threatens the completion of the Chinese state-led modernization by undermining the social and political institutional bases necessary for this completion. The healthy development of a market economy, therefore, may be in jeopardy. The state-led modernization may derail since the rigid CCP-PRC state could lose its ability and/or willingness to lead and especially to guide the market.[6] The question then tends towards the profound issue of timing or sequence: What should be done next for the state-led Chinese modernization to succeed?

Based on the above thoughts, we can make some preliminary observations and tentative speculations concerning the future of Chinese modernization. It is rather clear that in nations like China, the three basic human institutions (economy, polity, and social life) can be built into a differentiated and interactive relationship only gradually and in sequence, with a visible time gap and order since no one can accomplish such an institutional change at once. The improvement of the internal structures of the three would take even more time and much more effort. For a state-led modernization to proceed, political democratization and social liberalization often need to be deferred or limited for a considerable time to let the new market advance and grow up nationwide under the guidance of an effective state and the less resisting social institutions. This is because a productive market is needed to meet basic human needs tangibly and quickly and thus legitimize the whole modernization approach.

A state-led modernization needs to have the market as the main economic institution to bring about the desirable effects: to separate the economy from polity and social life and to generate the resources, efficiency, and innovations that could enable the emergence of a participatory polity and a civil society. Yet the market can only be successfully established and institutionalized as the main economic institution through the reforming and protective role of the state. For latecomers, the state's help is especially crucial because many previously existing favorable conditions, such as low entry cost to the international market and "safety valves" such as colonies, are gone, while expectations of the populace are aroused by awareness of the advanced nations. A stable and effective state power, a "rational" and market-friendly authoritarian regime, is the key – even if the state may be still under the control of an undesirable ruling group for some time. Therefore, if there is a conflict between political stability and political reform, the prudent policy choice is rather obvious. We may want to recall the argument on the functional desirability and practical inevitability of institutional exclusions in Chapter 1 of this book.

Struggling to follow a promising state-led route to modernity, China is emulating Japan and other Asian NICs. Nonetheless, the current Chinese political system adds tremendous uncertainty to the prospect for success, mainly because what is required of the state is probably too much for the CCP regime to handle. Although a rapid political democratization may not be wholly constructive, substantial political reform, including meaningful political participation and more political transparency, may be very advisable.[7] But a thorough reform of the state to reduce that uncertainty might cost the effectiveness and stability of the state in guiding the market.

Two likely scenarios can now be contemplated from the institutional perspective about the prospect of Chinese modernization moving towards the twenty-first century. This book does not intend to and cannot provide comprehensive and convincing evidence to validate the speculation on either scenario. Nevertheless, the subsequent examination of the current institutional arrangement of the Chinese domestic organizational structure and its changes, reflected by the competing four LAPs, may provide some suggestive evidence and a stage for further inquiries.

An *optimistic scenario* assumes that the CCP-PRC state moves toward further institutional changes of its own, in the direction of institutionalizing an authoritarian administration with legal construction as its new power base. Rationalization and professional effectiveness are achieved and the traditional mechanisms of corruption are curbed.[8] The state may continue its strong influence over social institutions, while market distortions are devised by the state and/ or social institutions to guide the market. Then we will see a substantial and sustained growth of a national market economy in China with a global importance that could not be exaggerated. The institutional differentiation of the market, the state, and social life is

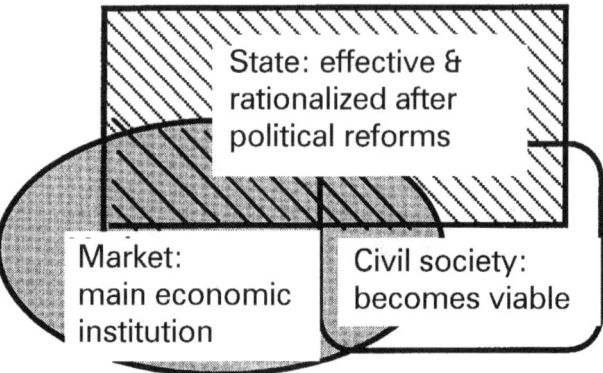

Figure 4.3   An optimistic scenario: The arrival of Chinese modernity

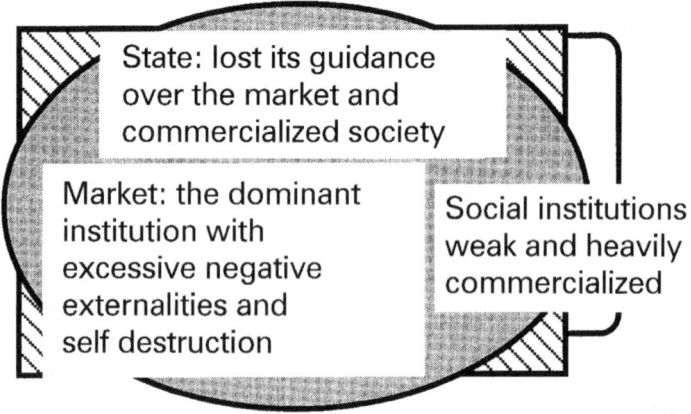

Figure 4.4   A pessimistic scenario: The delay of Chinese modernity

likely to occur to the point of forming a modernized organizational structure for the Chinese. The Chinese modernization is then successfully advanced as the overall foundation is cemented firmly (Figure 4.3).

The *pessimistic scenario* (Figure 4.4) however, is that the CCP sticks to or is forced to stick to its old-style administration, which produces incompetence, corruption, and illegitimacy. Then Beijing's ability to guide the market shrinks further and eventually an unguided and poorly institutionalized market takes over as *the* institution for Chinese economy, politics and social life. A weak state, perhaps "democratic" and "liberal" or perhaps simply warlordism, unleashes so many other destructive forces so early that they soon make the market dysfunctional. A Chinese modernity is then delayed, if not denied. A market-driven modernization may then become an alternative, but the timing is a major disadvantage and the prospect is highly improbable. In a country of 1.2 billion people who have just pulled their heads above the water in terms of meeting basic needs, political and economic disorganization – caused by either sociopolitical disintegration or an unrestrained market – would mean the perishing of millions and shock waves felt all over the world. It is too gruesome a picture to imagine, but a dark lesson of history is that humans have demonstrated the capability of visiting such tragedies upon themselves in the past, in China and other places.

II. MIXED LAPs IN THE 1990s: INSTITUTIONAL CONTINUITIES AND CHANGES

With the two scenarios identified above in mind, we are now to analyze the current Chinese domestic organizational structure through examining the Chinese LAPs in the 1990s after two decades of reform. During this period of PRC history, the relationship among economy, polity, and social life began to experience a major transformation – a real differentiation, perhaps for the first time in the Chinese history. China began "an exceedingly rapid retreat from the brink of . . . 'revolutionary-feudal totalitarianism'." Deng's reforms "mark the reversal of a fundamental trend in China in the twentieth century toward increased penetration of politics into other spheres of society" (Nee & Mozingo 1983, 54–5). An examination of Chinese LAPs since 1978 will reveal if such an institutional transformation has indeed taken place and, if so, how broad and how deep it has been. This examination hopes to capture the institutional alteration of the relationship among the Chinese economy, polity, and social life – the course of Chinese modernization.

The Reform and the Coexistence of Four LAPs

Chinese Reform started by the joint efforts of spontaneous activities of the people and major policy shifts in Beijing. A very important move was to reopen the college entrance exam to every Chinese from the ages of 16 to 36, or even older, at the end of 1977.[9] In October 1978, Beijing decided to halt "sending the youth to the countryside" and began to implement some pragmatic policies on labor allocation (Yuan 1987, 216). More importantly, desperate peasants and some sympathetic local cadres in Anhui and Sichuan provinces, with tacit support from the reformers in Beijing, started a decollectivization in the rural areas. Finally, in December 1978, the CCP launched a comprehensive reform under a more pragmatic leadership of Deng Xiaoping. The Third Plenum of the Eleventh CCP Central Committee decided on a series of reform measures, formally beginning the Chinese Reform that continued into the late 1990s.

After 1978, Deng Xiaoping's new pragmatism of "seeking truth from the practice/reality" was established as the new official ideology for the CCP.[10] In 1992, Deng openly applied that pragmatism to promote a "socialist market economy" with a rather classic Chinese statement of changing things through simply altering the names:

> More planning or more market is not the defining difference separating socialism from capitalism. Planning economy does not equal socialism, capitalism has planning too; market economy does not equal capitalism, socialism has market too. Planning and market are only economic means. (Deng 1992, 257)

The "working focus" of the CCP and the PRC was shifted from "class struggle" to "economic construction." Guided by the new "working focus," economic reforms featuring experiments based on a market orientation began. Most of the old political persecutions, including the "Anti-Rightist Movement" in 1957, were reversed and their verdicts dropped. Experimentation, as summed up by Deng himself as "crossing the river by groping of the stones," was encouraged. The centuries-old prejudice against commerce and material gains was tossed away and Deng declared that "there can be no socialism with pauperism. So to get rich is no sin."[11] The grand goals of the "Four Modernizations" were re-emphasized with a slightly different order.[12] Political power became favorable to altering old social contexts for the purpose of increased economic output and efficiency. Both "economic reforms" and "political reforms" were launched by the CCP. Social equality was traded for better economic efficiency, as illustrated by the drive for "breaking the iron rice-bowl and big rice-pot" to create a competitive working ethic in the "socialist" economy (Howard 1988). Politically, however, the fundamental organizational principle of the Chinese political structure was still the Leninist idea of "democratic centralism," at least within the ruling CCP. As one author puts it, "the principle of democratic centralism is clearly more centralist than democratic" (Nee & Mozingo 1983, 35). Furthermore, Deng laid down the limits of the Chinese political and economic reforms, the so-called "Four Cardinal Principles," as early as March 1979.[13] Finally, and perhaps most important, the "opening to the outside" policy greatly accelerated China's economic interactions with the rest of the world.

In a little over ten years, China rapidly moved from near autarky to a major participant in international trade. In 1990, the total Chinese import-export figure was over $115.4 billion, with a $13.1 billion surplus,[14] and trade began to increase at an annual rate of over 11 percent. By 1994, China had become the 11th largest world trader. Massive foreign direct investment contributed fundamentally to the alteration of the Chinese LAP. In 1986–90, over 230,000 Chinese workers were exported to work on projects abroad.[15]

In just over one decade, Chinese Reform has led to profound institutional changes. Perhaps the most important achievement was the initiation of a state-led modernization through introduction of the market. The CCP regime, forced by its failures in the past and longing for more economic power, altered substantially the Chinese domestic organizational structure to let the market grow through its "new pragmatism," its "new mercantilist" international economic policies, and its willingness to address the lack of efficiency and innovations in its state-owned economy. Great changes took place in the rural areas, and the family-based peasants regained substantial institutional autonomy from the state by the 1990s. The economy gained a great deal of autonomy from the CCP-dominated sociopolitical complex. The depth of the reform is particularly evident in the expansion of the private economy, and in the emergence of a commodity market, heavily commercialized culture, and newly emerged market-oriented LAPs. A huge nation with a history of thousands of years certainly cannot be transformed completely in only a decade or two. Although there was impressive advancement of the market and visible autonomy of the economy, the Chinese domestic organizational structure remained largely premodern or, more appropriately, in a transitional status. The sociopolitical complex was basically intact, with the CCP still monopolizing political power in the late 1990s.

New employment and labor policies

After the two unemployment peaks in the history of the PRC (1950 to 1952 and 1958 to 1962), a third peak was reached in 1978 and 1979, when the urban unemployment rate exceeded 5.9 percent. This seemingly small figure was actually very serious for two reasons. First, gross underemployment was already a widespread feature of labor allocation in the state-owned enterprises (Yuan 1987, 206–7). Second, a majority of the unemployed were younger than 35, mostly angry youth returning from the countryside and new graduates of middle and high schools. Its legitimacy and prestige already in serious trouble because of the "Cultural Revolution," the CCP Central Committee and the State Council summoned a "National Labor and Employment Conference" twice, in 1980 and 1981. Afterwards, Beijing proclaimed a new "Triple Combination" policy which stated that; "under state general planning and guidance, we will use a new employment guideline which combines the efforts of the state labor authority's arrangement, self-organized employment, and self-employment" (Yuan 1987, 217–19; Yuan 1990, 7.)

Under this three-combination policy, the newly-restored family-based traditional LAP was legalized in the rural and urban areas; the community-based societal LAP flourished in both urban and rural economies; private employment greatly increased; and employment by foreign investors expanded. State-owned enterprises also began continuous reforms of their labor practice. The CCP tried to "increase the incentives" for hard-working employees among the massive and very inefficient state labor force, and to promote economic development by granting more managerial and financial autonomy to state-owned enterprises (Walder 1989, 242–3 & Wang et al. 1986). Along the same lines, Beijing even began to try some quite "nonsocialist" measures in its economy, such as the new "labor contract system" in state-owned enterprises (Gordon White 1987, 365).

The official objective of the Chinese labor and employment policies shifted from pursuing a "socialist full employment" to the delicate goal of "considering both economic efficiency and social stability at the same time." The goal was "to expand employment at the expense of some economic efficiency when the waiting-for-job [unemployed] people are many and the national economy is not very good; to stress improving efficiency when the national economy is developing smoothly and the waiting-for-job people are few" (Yue 1989, 18). As the new "father," Deng Xiaoping himself posed this question as early as 1979: "Modernized production only needs fewer laborers, but we have so many people. How to consider both of these two issues at the same time?" (Deng 1985, 150). Apparently, the objective was a combined one of developing the economy through utilizing the market, while stabilizing CCP rule in the name of "socialism" and preserving the traditional social harmony, valued highly by the traditional Chinese society and Chinese culture. Distortion of the market in allocating labor, by the state and societal institutions, was therefore inevitable, but generally perceived to be desirable.

For these purposes, the Chinese state tried to consolidate its control over the most important urban industrial labor force and educated professionals, apart from the rural labor force, while promoting its market-oriented economic development strategies. The authoritarian state LAP remained the most important vehicle to achieve that goal in the eyes of the CCP leadership. Most of the PRC's "labor policies" or "employment policies" were therefore designed primarily for the urban population. Forced by the lack of resources and by social and economic needs, Beijing allowed a societal LAP to function at the local community level and within the CCP's political framework. Local authorities, the "neo-gentry class," were supposed to directly control the labor forces allocated by the community-based LAP in a way more or less modeled after the major labor and employment policies designed for the state LAP. The real control of the societal LAP, however, has declined rapidly. Besides policies dealing with labor management and employment *per se*, the state exercised control over Chinese labor allocation in the 1990s through a combination of party organizations and other devices such as the national *hukou* (household or residential registration) system; the *dangan* (dossier) system; the state monopoly on banking, insurance, and other financial institutions.[16] Allocation of the huge rural labor force, however, was largely left to the agrarian economy, rural nonstate institutions such as the villages, the underdeveloped Chinese market institutions, and especially the family structure.

The coexistence of four LAPs in the PRC
As a direct consequence and a major part of the reform, Chinese labor allocation evolved into a rare coexistence of four distinguishable patterns allocating as many as 825 million laborers – the largest labor force in the world:[17] a restored family-based traditional pattern, the authoritarian state allocation, the community-based labor

markets, and an emerging national labor market. The four LAPs can be divided into two groups: the old and the new. The basic information and institutional characteristics of them are summarized in Table 4.1. A comprehensive treatment of the four LAPs is in the sister volume of this book, Wang 1998, Chapters 1–4.

The rare coexistence of four different LAPs illustrates the institutional configuration and institutional continuities in the PRC. The family-based traditional LAP is currently numerically the largest one but is experiencing a steady decline. Restored by the rapid decollectivization at the end of the 1970s, this LAP has its roots in the century-old *zigengnongs* and *diannong*s. It gains its legitimacy primarily from its institutional foundation – the Chinese social institution of family. It currently covers the vast majority of the rural laborers, in the form of family responsibility system, and sizable urban workers in the form of *getihu* (private household economy) or *zhuanyehu* (specialized household). The inherent instability of the small family-based economy and the overall advance of the market institution, however, have inevitably made the family-based LAP a springbed for market-oriented labor practice. Increasing numbers of surplus laborers are leaving the families to seek better jobs thus provided the supply pool for the labor market. Many *getihus* have started to hire help and become part and parcel of the native private employers on the emerging national labor market.

The authoritarian state LAP is still politically and economically the most important LAP in China. It allocates the majority of the urban workers and professionals in a basically authoritarian and political way, despite the visible market-oriented reform measures. The now all "contracted" employees of the state still basically work and live in those socialist *"danweis"* and controlled by their party appointed supervisors, the more empowered *danwei* bosses, with the help of the *hukou* and *dangan* systems. Facing the increasingly strong competition from other LAPs especially the market-oriented LAPs, the authoritarian state LAP has been heavily reliant on the political and especially financial support from the CCP state. Overall, this socialist LAP is stagnant and has been widely viewed as the leading cause of the massive inefficiency in the state-owned enterprises. It is clearly under pressure to change, yet the political logic of the PRC has forced Beijing to be very cautious and slow in reforming this LAP. Increased bankruptcies of the state-owned enterprises and significant unemployment of the former state-employees have started by mid-1990s. But great caution and resistance

Table 4.1 Chinese patterns of labor allocation

LAP	Old LAPs		New LAPs	
	Authoritarian state LAP	*Family-based LAP*	*Community-based labor markets*	*National labor market*
Size	114* (1994)	480* (1993)	158* (1993)	85–9* (1995)
Ranking	third	largest	second	smallest
Growth	slow	declining	rapid	very rapid
Institutional foundation	the state (polity)	family (social life)	community and the market	the market (economy)
Historical origin	royal shops and *guanying qiye*	*zigengnong* and *diannong*	villages and CBEs	FDI & *getihu*
Birth date	mid-1950s	restored in late 1970s	mid-1950s, CLMs in 1980s	late 1980s
Age	four decades	centuries	two decades	one decade
Main location	urban	rural	urban and rural	urban and rural
Main industries	non-agriculture	agriculture, handicrafts	non-agriculture	non-agriculture
Economic significance**	largest	third	second	smallest
Political status	highest	lowest	third	second
Social status	second	lowest	third	highest
Main implication	authoritarian "socialism"	Chinese premodernity	distorted and localized markets	autonomy of national economy
Prospect	diminishing and transforming	reduced existence	new dominant LAP in China?	increased size and role

Source: Wang 1998, 308
* Numbers are in millions.
** Measured in their current shares of the Chinese GDP (gross domestic product).

are clearly seen.[18] Newly emerged labor mobility has yet to mean-ingfully alter what Andrew Walder (1986, 5, 7, 13) described as the "organized dependence" of the labor force and their families on the state.

The community-based labor markets (CLMs), which grew out of the societal LAP, are growing very rapidly, and have the likelihood of becoming the future dominant LAP in China by 2010. It is cur-rently the second largest LAP and covers labor allocation in the urban and rural areas. Workers generally have achieved a community-based labor mobility. Many CLMs have increasingly blended into the national labor market by hiring equally from outside the local communities, while most CLMs still demonstrate a clear social or communal distortion of the local labor markets. The urban collective enterprises and especially the TVEs generally practice a strong community-based discrimination against the outsider job-seekers. The state-owned enterprises that practice some CLMs also almost exclusively hire from local residents. The existing institutional devices such as the *hukou* system are still very important to the functioning of the CLMs.

Finally, a national labor market has emerged while its maturation or institutionalization have yet to be completed. Primarily started by the entry and operation of FDI and later practiced by the massive native private employers and some collective and even state-owned enterprises, the newly-emerged Chinese national labor market grew at an astonishing speed of at least 250 times (or as many as 500 times) during the past 15 years (Wang 1988, 254–257). It has now become a leading job creator and offers the most attractive jobs especially to the professionals and skilled laborers. Because of the politically sanctioned high desire for more FDI, the new national labor market has acquired very strong and persistent support from the CCP state, despite the fact that the labor market is undermining the whole Chinese premodernity. The national labor market has provided a realistic national labor mobility to the Chinese workers. The incompletion of the institutionalization of the Chinese national labor market has directly led to the lack of labor protection in the "socialist" PRC. A massive number of "floating laborers" primarily from the rural areas have become a profound by-product of this national labor market.

In short, labor allocation in the PRC by the late 1990s has entered an era of multi-LAP. Four institutionally different LAPs have appeared to carve up the largest labor force in the world. The old LAPs, the family-based LAP and the authoritarian state LAP, are still the dominant ones. But they are either shrinking or stagnant. The new LAPs, the national labor market and the CLMs have been growing at a very high speed. Together the new LAPs have already allocated over 240 million Chinese workers who are among the most productive. The future of the four Chinese LAPs, and the fate of the market economy may have indeed been written on the wall.

The coexisting four Chinese LAPs formed in the reform era are likely to advance and sustain the mixed Chinese domestic organizational structure into the twenty-first century, reflecting the process of Chinese modernization. Both the institutional continuities and changes of the Chinese domestic organizational structure are seen through the prism of the PRC LAPs. The two old LAPs, with their dominant position, still maintain a domestic organizational structure that is family-like and institutionally premodern. The new market-oriented LAPs have enabled a more efficient and more promising economic growth, with profound implications for an institutional transformation in China. The mixed Chinese LAPs crafted a complex transformation with a state-fostered advancement of the market as its clear direction, although the official CCP rhetoric may have created a deceivingly different impression. Scholars have suggested that China has a "neotraditional" society, a "socialist economy" in its "primary stage," and a "communist" authoritarian polity. China, in fact, came to have all these elements, as the four different LAPs illustrated. Chinese modernization, however, picked up its own momentum and steadily advanced institutionally, as the reformation of Chinese LAPs in the 1980s to 1990s exhibited. The unique coexistence of these four LAPs demonstrated well the fact that the Chinese domestic organizational structure was at an institutional crossroads. Modernity may eventually arrive in China, but an examination of the Chinese LAPs indicates that modernity is likely to be very "Chinese" indeed.

The Old LAPs: The Continuity of Institutional Premodernity

The family-like Chinese domestic organizational structure continued for centuries, as being reflected by the continuity of the family-based traditional LAP as the dominant LAP in the history of China. Under Mao's regime (1949–76), the Chinese premodernity was forcefully reinforced and "rejuvenated," as being reflected by the singular existence of an authoritarian state LAP in the PRC cities and its rural version – the communes – in the countryside. This authoritarian state LAP (and the "collective" LAP in the rural areas) may be viewed as an enlarged, distorted and centralized nation-based traditional LAP. This "revolutionary" but nonetheless traditional LAP, instead of developing along the lines of dispersed social institutions like the family, was organized around the centralized political institutions – the family-like PRC state. The family-like Chinese domestic organizational structure was therefore intensified and pushed to the extreme. This "new" Chinese premodernity was destined to be much less viable than the "old" premodernity, because of its extremism and radicalism and also the much changed external environment. An accelerated institutional explosion, another costly "dynasty cycle" soon began to loom on the horizon.

Deng Xiaoping's reform started to dismantle Mao's centralized nation-based traditional LAP and restored the traditional family-based LAP in the rural areas where the majority of Chinese lived and, to a lesser extent, in the urban areas as well. Consequently, much of the Chinese "old" premodernity and its "super-stability" was perpetuated, as much of the pre-1950s Chinese domestic organizational structure was restored. The authoritarian state LAP, however, continued to be the most important urban LAP in the PRC by the mid-1990s.

Both the authoritarian state LAP and the family-based LAP are now experiencing tremendous pressures for changes and reforms. The family-based traditional LAP declines as the market economy develops. The authoritarian state LAP stagnates as the inefficiency of the state-run economy has become increasingly apparent, despite the numerous reform measures. The new and competing LAPs (the community-based labor markets and the national labor market) are on the rise to undermine these two old LAPs that have constituted the basic characteristics of the premodern but stable Chinese domestic organizational structure. Where and how the declining family-based LAP and the stagnant urban authoritarian state LAP move, among the four LAPs existing in the 1990s and beyond, will naturally determine much of the future of China – the likelihood and the features of a Chinese modernity.

Family-based LAP: The issue of "Chineseness"

The institutional implication of the family-based traditional LAP in contemporary China is that it reflects the so-called "Chineseness," namely, the fact that the PRC still keeps the peculiar Chinese premodernity. While maybe hindering the advancement of the market institution, this LAP produces the traditional stabilizing effect for the CCP authoritarian regime. Under this LAP, especially among the majority of Chinese – the rural population, the traditional Chinese domestic organizational structure was largely restored. Powerful old norms and behavior patterns are rejuvenated, as are the central roles of the family institution and its internalization – the Confucian culture. While families have always been the cells of the Chinese nation and the ruling families/groups enjoyed stable and often unquestioned power, however, "the ruler or government, as the grand family/clan head (*dajiazhang*), has an obligation to work for the well-being of its subordinate members . . . [Thus the] legitimacy of the government does not come from votes but from promoting the welfare of the people."[19]

Mao forcefully attempted to abolish the layers of the gentry class and even the family/clans, in an attempt to organize a national family of Maoism. Collectivized communes and party cadres were used to control the citizens (especially the peasants) directly, under the giant family-like state power of the CCP.[20] The only hope left for "good" rule is how to refine and purify the top leader(s) of the CCP, the family head, since his authority tends to be unchecked and should be that way. To some, that explains Mao's constant, nearly paranoid, internal struggles aimed at producing new generations of revolutionaries to lead the nation (Wang Shan 1994, 178–80).

Agricultural decollectivization restored the family-based LAP and also restored many traditional Chinese social relations and much of the traditional political structure. Contrary to the optimistic belief of some that agriculture decollectivization made the Chinese peasants "free,"[21] the traditionally paternal families, instead of the CCP lineage, once again became the cells of the authority relationship in Chinese politics and social life.[22] A family-based "capitalist patriarchy" replaced Mao's "patriarchal socialism" to regulate basic social relations such as those between the sexes (Brugger & Reglar 1994, 304). It gave back a certain degree of economic freedom, bounded by the family institution, to the peasantry. It returned traditional sociopolitical autonomy to the villages, headed by the new gentry class that included clan heads, village and township officials (who are mostly still CCP members), rich peasants, and other "reputable" families.[23] Family/clan institutions rearranged social and political relations in the Chinese rural areas, and a clear and deep "familization" or "kinsfolkization" (*qinshouhua*) began taking place among the majority of the Chinese, the peasants (Xiaoyi Wang 1994, 52). Not only were the rural social control mechanisms, social stratification and authority structure again based on family institutions, but economic connections and property ownership were largely reorganized and redefined along family lines in the villages (Chen 1994, 57).

The peasants, according to survey studies, became more "democratic" in their economic, social, cultural, and political lives than their counterparts in the cities. The advancement of the Chinese rural "democratic" politics on the micro level is certainly interesting and provocative, since conventional democratization theory asserts that cities offer better social and cultural conditions for microdemocracy than the countryside.[24] The "democracy" in the Chinese villages was very much like the traditional village "self-governing" under the élite – the gentry families in the past, and later the families of cadres and clan heads, most of whom were indigenous CCP party members. Those village self-governing bodies were still basically undifferentiated economic-political-social structures with a social institution (the family and clan) as their basic organizational principle. Once the bonds of the labor force were loosened, the state retreated and was limited while a visible independence of the economy and social institutions developed in the rural areas, based on the restored traditional structures of the family.[25]

Culturally, the family-based LAP has associated with a restoration of ancestor worship, tomb building, nominal kinship building, and concubines.[26] Related to the restoration of the family-based LAP, a "renaissance" of Confucian culture took place in China. Chinese officials and intellectuals reassessed Confucianism with the intention of revitalizing it. The economic success of Korea, Taiwan and even Japan is believed to have direct links to Confucian culture or a "new Confucianism," which had been unfortunately almost "lost" in its homeland.[27] A nationwide "reeducation" of Confucian teachings got under way. Official publications were filled with the "fine and glorious traditions" stemming from Confucianism that every "modern civilized" Chinese needed to remember and act on.[28] The government-run Readings for the Rural Press even published a *Xing xiaojing* (New book on filial piety) in 1994 to educate the peasants more easily and more extensively about the classic virtues of respecting ancestors and obeying the elderly. A similar publication on "traditional morals and patriotism, socialist ethics, and modern civilized norms," *Xing sanzijing* (New three-word verses), edited by the Propaganda Department of the Guangdong CCP Committee, sold 10 million copies in Guangdong in 1994 alone and another 10 million copies in the first five months of 1995.[29]

Concerning the state-led Chinese modernization, perhaps paradoxically, a durable family-based LAP with its superior ability to absorb surplus labor, and turn them into bearable underemployed rather then unbearable unemployed, tended to stabilize the power of a "retreated" authoritarian state in Beijing. Restoration of traditional Chinese culture also effectively served this purpose. As a popular political writer put it, "the 800 million peasants are China's live volcano" that could very well destroy the relatively modernized Chinese urban sector and the whole hope of Chinese modernization (Wang 1994, Chapter 2). In the absence of massive emigration to other countries and before any new legitimate institutional framework can settle in, the stabilized, though underemployed, rural "surplus" laborers – estimated to be as many as 150 to 240 million – (Wang 1988, 71) is saving the overall Chinese domestic organizational structure from crashing.

Under the family-based LAP, it is unlikely that the hundreds of millions of Chinese peasants will invade the cities at once, despite the fact that many are living below the poverty line with little hope of change. Even in more developed areas such as Fujian province, the transfer of rural labor has demonstrated a slowing down trend since 1988, and there has been a sizable "reverse current" of peasants returning to the villages. One of the major reasons identified for this reverse current was the "confining" effect of the family-based LAP, which pulled many peasants back to the villages.[30] The traditionally paternal families, as the cells of Chinese social life, came to function as millions of minireservoirs for rural labor. They have a remarkable ability to absorb the surplus laborers, feed them, and then turn them into reasonably satisfied underemployed rather than unemployed workers.

The families provided perhaps the best cushion against the sufferings produced by political injustice and economic hardships, since sacrifice is among the glorious norms a family sanctions for its members. The millions of families adequately served the purpose of diverting social pressures and energies, thus mitigating many conflicts that had potential institutional implications. The golden rule of family-based behavior, "to stay together," has a strong restrictive impact on labor mobility. Thus a large portion of the "surplus labor" could be absorbed by the families and never flood the emerging Chinese market.[31]

Families are small groupings, and the abundant differences among them make it hard for them to form meaningful groups or become politically militant. The family/clan institution has historically played the important role of "reducing social shocks" through sharing, mutual assistance and other altruistic but "rational" activities of the members and member families. Thus, "family has been the most effective and most rational organizational structure of the traditional rural society" (Li 1994, 2). Therefore, the family/clan institutions have helped soothe the emergence of the market institution and to reduce significantly the social and political costs of a state-led modernization, at the expense of the stabilized but marginalized rural laborers. The rural economy was once again dispersed and the traditionally segmented Chinese socioeconomic structure has been perpetuated. The release of the alarming number of surplus rural laborers is, therefore, unlikely to be a sudden or total explosion. Thus the development of the Chinese market, paradoxically with the help of the family institution, may practically gain precious room and time to take its course.

*Authoritarian state LAP: Bureaucratic socialism and a
state-subsidized marketization*

The Chinese authoritarian state LAP has been a cornerstone of the peculiar premodern domestic organizational structure in the PRC: the so-called "bureaucratic socialism."[32] It affects fundamentally the possibility and the nature of a Chinese modernity. The Chinese authoritarian state LAP enabled the state, through the managers and foremen in the *danweis*, to "play a direct role in social stratification." Workers' life chances were determined by the political authority of the state under a CCP dictatorship, rather than "being determined by the conditions of labor and commodity markets" (Walder 1986, 29, 95–102). Under this LAP, both vertical and horizontal mobility of the urban labor force have been very low and largely involuntary.

Recent reforms changed some of that. But for the three-quarters to two-thirds of urban laborers allocated and managed under this authoritarian state LAP, their *danweis* remained essentially their lifetime employer and the universe of their political and social activities. Mobility was basically still a luxury for a few, and very high transaction costs were attached to it.[33] Apparently, now it is the authoritarian state LAP that makes China "socialist." Combined with the family-based traditional LAP in the rural areas, the dominant authoritarian state LAP in urban areas constitutes the institutional foundation for Deng Xiaoping's "socialism with Chinese characteristics." Essentially, the authoritarian state LAP and the family-based traditional LAP together forged an indeed unique Chinese premodernity – a "socialist" premodernity centered on the family-like state and based on a rigid administrative hierarchy.

As one of the "evolutionary universals," wrote Talcott Parsons, "a bureaucratic system is always characterized by an institutionalized hierarchy of authority, which is differentiated on two axes:

level of authority and 'sphere' of competence" (1967, 490–520). Through the authoritarian state LAP, the CCP leadership externalized such a bureaucratic "hierarchy of authority," at least in the urban areas. A centralized authoritarian political authority, based on personal power and will and revolutionary ethics has dominated the PRC. Economic and social desires and needs were often compromised, even replaced, by political needs and desires. Rewards and penalties were distributed through administrative channels and by administrative rank, decided by the centralized state authority. Everyone was equal, not in terms of money as in a market-dominated economy or law as in a democratic polity, but in terms of the superiors' authority. Things were greatly simplified and unified along the lines of the administrative bureaucrats. Everyone had a direct attachment to the state authority for meeting his basic needs and for the possibility of satisfying his desires. Everyone's behavior was contained, restricted, and even directed by the state authority, personified by the superiors. The state thus acquired its dominant position versus the economy and social life. Political logic became the most important logic in the Chinese urban universe. The urban Chinese domestic organizational structure was, therefore, an undifferentiated and state-centered complex under which people tended to be categorized and stratified into a rather rigid hierarchical order.

Bureaucratic ranks became basically the indicator of people's social status, power, ability, and material worth – the so-called *guanbenwei* [bureaucrat standard]. Despite the challenges from the emerging market institution, a rampant corruption of officials in the government and the state-owned *danweis*,[34] the new links ("quasi-equals-sign")[35] between administrative power and wealth only enhanced the bureaucratic standard. Many newly emerged "socialist millionaires," such as rich private businessmen, soon formally became part of the bureaucracy to acquire power and social status. In 1994, for example, the CCP "approved" twenty successful businessmen to become "leading" cadres or bureaucrats by making them "people's deputies" or members of the "people's consultation conference" (Qiao et al. 1994, 84–9, 171). By late 1990s, for the majority of the Chinese, the bureaucratic standard was still the standard by which everyone was to be evaluated. In many cities, public cemeteries have a specially designed, exclusive "senior cadres'" (*gaogan,* above the bureau or prefecture level) section, fenced or walled off from the rest of the graves. Thus, senior cadres kept their bureaucratic standard even after death, enjoying better-designed and exclusively maintained resting places at only a fraction (often about 10 percent) of the market price charged for a similar tomb.[36]

Contributing crucially to the CCP regime and the bureaucratic socialism, the authoritarian state LAP nonetheless has had some new developments that have produced an interesting and facilitating impact on the Chinese state-led modernization through a state-subsidized marketization of labor allocation.

Significant underemployment of the best educated Chinese workers is protected by this LAP. An official report revealed in 1995 that employees in state-owned enterprises only worked 81.7 percent of their "working time," and as little as 40 to 60 percent of their total time on the job hours was "effective working hours."[37] The gross inefficiency and chronic loss of so many state-owned enterprises that still over employed so many workers may be viewed as a state subsidy for development of a market economy. Practically, a massive number of workers allocated and managed by the authoritarian state LAP have joined the market in their "spare time" and generally at their own initiative. In all of China's major cities, as many as 26 to 70 percent of state-employed cadres and workers have become *de facto* workers allocated by the emerging market in the name of "second jobs." The common phenomenon of moonlighting has contributed to a boom in many TVEs and private business that are operated in basically a market-oriented way. In one TVE in Sichuan, 70 percent of its employees were also "full-time" employees of several state-owned enterprises.[38] The state and the authoritarian LAP effectively guaranteed the minimum income, benefits and job security for those workers; thus they were willing and able to "dive into the sea" (*xiahai*) of the turbulent and risky market economy.[39] "On leave without pay," open or secret moonlighting, part-time entrepreneurship or farming, and early retirement[40] are ways those guaranteed state employees contribute to the market economy.

Institutionally, there is clearly a strong incentive for the *danwei* bosses to "allow" their employees to be on leave or moonlighting, since the *danweis* can keep the wages of those people or use part of that money to hire the much cheaper labor of the peasants. This is just another form of "eating the state" by the *danweis*. Even foreign-invested enterprises have managed to hire many of their employees, usually some of the best, from state-owned *danweis* on a full-time or "part-time" basis. Many urban Chinese families have adopted an even more aggressive strategy called "one family, two systems" (paralleling Deng Xiaoping's "one country, two systems" policy regarding Hong Kong and Taiwan). With this strategy, one spouse would "suffer" low wages by staying with a secure state job to keep the cheap housing and many other benefits provided by the *danwei*, while the other would "dive into the sea" to make the risky but bigger money on the market.

The authoritarian state LAP, despite the CCP's politically motivated rescue efforts and economically driven reform measures, has become a state-subsidized national insurance for urban workers allocated and managed by the emerging market. This has meant tremendous savings for private and foreign employers, since the state provided extensive "socialist" benefits to their employees one way or the other. The large number of those "secure" laborers has greatly increased the supply of skilled but not very demanding workers. Labor in a "socialist" nation has thus paradoxically become very "weak" in its position versus the non-state employers on the market, as concluded by an official investigation in Guangdong province in 1993 (Qiao 1994, 286–7). A boom in the market-oriented economy in the PRC thus ironically happened with significant "help" from the authoritarian state LAP, but without replacing it. This is an interesting and indeed unique transformation towards a market economy by default.

Such development of a "Chinese" and "socialist" market economy may tend to have long-term and unique impacts on Chinese labor allocation and the overall domestic organizational structure. At this point, we may be able to only make two general speculations. First, the possibility of a Chinese modernity may be paradoxically enhanced by the authoritarian state LAP. Without a revolutionary destruction of this LAP, tremendous institutional changes have taken place in urban labor allocation. More and more workers, though remaining "secure" by staying with a *danwei*, have been earning most of their income through market-oriented economic activities. They have also experienced a welcome decline of state authority and a decrease in the ability of the *danwei* bosses to control their lives. All these significant institutional changes of labor allocation have occurred under the unintended "protection" of the secure authoritarian state LAP. The advancement of the Chinese market could therefore be expected to be fast, relatively less painful to the ordinary urban workers, and thus smooth.

Second, the rapidly advancing Chinese market-oriented labor allocation appears to have been profoundly distorted by the authoritarian state LAP. Those distortions are likely to have impacts on the future of the Chinese domestic organizational structure. Namely, if the Chinese can establish a modernity, it would have some distinctively different features. The relationships and distance among the state, market and social institutions may be less like those of the West but more like those of today's Taiwan and/or earlier Japan.[41] The authoritarian state LAP, given its status and its vital political utility, is unlikely to be abandoned by the Chinese in the near future. It may continue to be a main LAP in urban China, with decreasing economic significance but still powerful political and social presence.

The New LAPs: The Prospects for Chinese Modernization

The two-decade reform provided the opportunity for two new LAPs to emerge and grow in the PRC, reflecting the institutional changes that have taken place in the Chinese domestic organizational structure. The two new LAPs are both market-oriented but differ not only in scales. They demonstrate the complexity of the Chinese institutional transition and foretell substantially about the possibility and the nature of a Chinese modernity.

Directly growing out of the community-based societal LAP, numerous CLMs have flourished in China and especially in the vast rural areas. The CLMs are local labor markets constrained by the community-based political and social institutions. The CLMs, precisely because of their community-based nature and the associated distortions, have appeared to be fitting into the existing Chinese domestic organization structure well, while representing a gradual but profound institutional change of that structure. Currently already the second largest LAP in China, this market-oriented LAP is expected to become the dominant LAP in the near future (Wang 1998, Chapter 3), signaling a much increased labor mobility and economic autonomy at least on the local level. Nevertheless, the CLMs tend to obstruct the development of an economically more rational national labor market. The CLMs have also apparently contributed to the development of regionalism which may threaten the very course of Chinese modernization and the unity of the Chinese nation.

A national labor market has grown even faster in the PRC in the past two decades, leading the way of Chinese modernization. Initially as an institution "imported" by FDI, national labor market has its roots in the pre-PRC years. Now widely practiced by the FDI enterprises, open or hidden private enterprises, and even partially by many state-owned enterprises, the national labor market is in a rapid institutionalization. Tremendous legitimacy has been accumulated and substantial new institutions have been created. Political and social resistance to this LAP, however, is still plenty even by the late 1990s. Though unlikely to become the dominant LAP in the PRC soon, a further development and maturation of the national labor market seems to be crucially beneficial to Chinese modernization in terms of cementing the autonomy of the Chinese economy and the unity of the Chinese nation.

CLMs: A key to seeing the future of Chinese modernization
Contributing to political order and social stability in the history of the PRC, the CLMs created room outside the authoritarian state LAP for social institutions to survive and function, and thus mediate between the authoritarian state and the traditional families, or between the CCP dictatorship and the individual's rights and demands. Labor acquired economically important mobility within the communities, greatly enhancing the economic viability of those communities. But across the communities, the flow of labor was still institutionally restricted, even by the late 1990s. To belong to a "good" community or *danwei* was clearly as crucial as belonging to a good family. Group identity and the related, almost predetermined, position in the premodern Chinese organizational structure were still more important than an individual's quality, ability or effort. The rise of labor productivity in the CLMs thus had not yet institutionalized individualism significantly in China. Under the CLMs, therefore, the institutionally and functionally undifferentiated families, groups and communities continued to be the basis for the premodern Chinese domestic organizational structure, despite the visible increase of labor mobility and productivity within the communities.

How to solve the gradual and slow breakdown of the family-based traditional LAP has been a key to the preservation of the family-based Chinese culture, and thus the family-like Chinese premodernity. Cyclical dynasty changes were basically the results of the inherent difficulty of this task. Mao's collectivization and authoritarian state LAP may have helped to forestall that problem, but ruined the development of the Chinese economy. The community-based societal LAP, as spontaneous as it was initially, consolidated the social institutions on the community level in the

face of an intrusive and active PRC state. The stability and continuity of the Chinese premodernity (rather than its radical version
advocated by Mao) thus were maintained, at least in the local communities. The social harmony and equality maintained by the societal
LAP and the flexibility and diversity provided by the coexistence
of large numbers of communities are two of the leading institutional advantages the societal LAP/CLMs have generated for the
Chinese. The rural communities, equipped with the family-based
traditional LAP and the economically more advantageous CLMs,
seem to have the potential to provide a paradise for Chinese premodernity and the CCP regime.

By the late 1990s, despite the social distortions – which may actually
be necessary "modifications" – the CLMs have become an effective avenue for the Chinese market to grow, allocating and managing the most consequential economic resource – labor. As perhaps
one of the most important and most stable "socialist" practices in
China, CLMs may have represented an effective yet smooth way to
utilize the market institution without eradicating long-existing, thus
quite legitimate, social and political institutions. More interestingly,
the deep legitimacy of the pre-existing social and political institutions may have effectively legitimized the newly introduced market
institution, thus greatly facilitating the rather smooth progress of
marketization of labor allocation.

If all the Chinese communities had developed well towards institutionalized CLMs, then practically all the Chinese labor force
would be largely allocated and managed by the market institution.
A Chinese market would then be established in allocating the labor
force through the CLMs', suboptimal but nonetheless very feasible,
labor markets. It would be a great achievement if the Chinese could
have a market-oriented LAP, perhaps fragmented by community-
based social institutions, with help rather than obstruction or even
destruction from powerful social and political institutions. Institutional differentiation could develop among the economy, polity, and
social life in the communities. A balance could be struck on the
community level leading to a Chinese style of modernity. Following that logic, a young scholar asserted, since "the ownership of
modern corporations is in essence a collective one," an employee
ownership and management like the CLMs could be a viable alternative to the privatization reforms tried by Eastern Europeans.[42]

The growth of the CLMs has reduced the CCP state's role in
allocating labor resources and in managing the entire Chinese

economy. Yet this process has been slow, and the guise of "collective ownership" has been comforting to CCP leaders who thus far have few incentives to stop the costly process. But that reduction of control reached a critical mass by the late 1990s in both the cities and the rural areas. Foreign media have reported about the growing political autonomy of Chinese villages since the 1980s. The family/clan heads, the TVE managers – the financially "capables" – and the community-based CCP cadres have formed a new trinity replacing the CCP authority from above in the local communities. In some areas, the election of local CCP cadres was even subject to the approval of all the villagers, party members or not.[43] A "civil society" could even emerge strongly in the PRC as a result of the development of the CLMs.[44] The new development of "rich" villages/TVE corporations "annexing poor villages", first reported in 1995,[45] in addition to the "conversion" of many state-owned *danweis* to CLMs, may have indicated a unique but solid development of a market in a rather Chinese way.

Significant to not only the future of Chinese modernization, but even the unity of the Chinese nation, the CLMs may have already contributed to the increase of regionalism that emerged as a result of unevenly accelerating development of the Chinese economy in the past two decades. Despite the concentrated efforts of Beijing toward more balanced development between the booming east[46] and the slow central and western provinces, the gap of investment, growth, and technology levels between the two regions and among the provinces has continued to grow.[47]

All top ten provinces/metropolises in economic development and income were on the east coast, while the growth rates of the six to ten central and western provinces were declining in the early 1990s.[48] The share of the eastern region (36.7 percent of total population and 10.7 percent of territory) in the Chinese GNP rose from 52.3 percent in 1980 to 60.1 percent in 1993, while the share of the west (25.2 percent of the total population and 69.1 percent of the land) declined from 16.5 percent to 13.1 percent. Among the 100 "most prosperous counties" in 1993, the western provinces had none. Ninety percent of the 592 "poor counties" were in the west. Prosperous areas like Sunan (Jiangsu province) in the east had a per capita income nearly six times that of poor areas like Simao (Yunan province) and Biji (Guizhou province) in the west.[49] The average wage during the reform years in the more open coastal province of Guangdong was more than twice that in neighboring Jiangxi province.[50] The Government-mandated legal minimum wage also varies drastically across regions, separated by *hukou* and other community barriers. The highest legal minimum monthly wage (in Shenzhen) in 1995 was more than four times of the lowest (in Guizhou and Yunnan).[51] The CLMs, by definition, tend to encourage and promote divisive regionalism in a vast and diversified nation like China. Apparently, Chinese scholars have yet to include the impact of the CLMs in their discussion on the uneven development of the Chinese economy.[52]

The CLMs have been largely beneficial to the quiet but extensive growth of the market institution in China. The advantages and achievements of the CLMs are likely to make this LAP a dominant Chinese LAP in the near future. While promoting the market institution, the CLMs may have only limited effect on the differentiation of the Chinese domestic organizational structure beyond the community level. A resilient but nonetheless distorted and even controlled local market may survive and develop in the local communities, leading to visible and consequential differentiation of the economy, state, and social life in the communities. But beyond the communities, CLMs may actually help to consolidate the national premodernity by limiting the development of a national labor market. Perhaps a community-based modernity would be the future of Chinese modernization. If that is to be the case, the unity of China and the centralized political system and culture may all be seriously questioned.

The national labor market: to differentiate the Chinese premodernity

The disproportionately profound institutional impact the emerging national labor market has had on the premodern Chinese domestic organizational structure is difficult to exaggerate. Besides the direct facilitation of the development of new laws, values, and legal and behavioral norms, it has contributed fundamentally to the emerging differentiation of the Chinese premodernity. First, it led directly to the increasing autonomy of the Chinese economy from the institutional confines of the political and social institutions. If the national labor market is generally the last component of a national market institution, then the further institutionalization of the Chinese national labor market may also institutionalize the autonomy of the Chinese economy, hence completing a major step of Chinese modernization. Second, it created new social classes that are likely to reconfigure those social and political institutions. Finally, some of the basic fabric of the PRC organizational structure (such as the *hukou* and *dangan* systems) have been adjusted and even altered by the emerging national labor market.

The advance of the national labor market signals the emergence of the autonomy of the Chinese economy from the premodern sociopolitical complex. This labor market has enabled the PRC to become the second largest recipient of FDI in the world by the mid-1990s. The booming private economy of the PRC could not survive without the national labor market. The collective enterprises and even many state-owned enterprises, could not function well without the cheap and flexible "peasant workers" available on the national labor market. Both the state-planned "socialist" economy and the family-based moral economy are shrinking, replaced by the market economy in the allocation and utilization of consumer goods, capital goods, and now labor.

The Chinese market economy has yet to mature but the national labor market should be the last jigsaw piece to portray the overall framework and magnitude of a relatively autonomous new Chinese economy. Official statistics showed that the PRC state's control of industrial production declined from 70 percent in 1979 to 5 percent in 1995, and control of retail pricing fell from 95 percent in 1979 to less than 6 percent in 1994.[53] For perhaps the first time in Chinese history, millions of productive people are allocated and managed by neither the state authority nor the family institution nor the communities. Those millions, with the personal freedom they acquired from traditional social, political and even communal confines, have become the active agents of transformation of the Chinese domestic organizational structure and its internalized version, the Confucian culture. A great differentiation of the premodern Chinese domestic organizational structure is, therefore, underway.

The operation of the emerging national labor market has directly led to a social restratification that is likely to alter the configuration of Chinese social and political institutions and thus affect the overall domestic organizational structure. An increasingly powerful new bourgeois class is emerging. The private employers, who have few direct links to the capitalists of the pre-PRC era, have formed a special group which is gaining an increasingly important role in the Chinese economy, social life and even politics (Zhang 1994). Prior to the 1980s, the CCP, utilizing the authoritarian state LAP, effectively "bought off" the Chinese industrial working class and distorted it into a privileged group organized in a communist neotraditional or semifeudal fashion (Walder 1986). The CCP then avoided, for most of its nearly half century rule, any major confrontation with the Chinese industrial working class. Another achievement of this "buying off" strategy was to exclude the working class from really participating in the PRC's political process as an independent group. A significant result, therefore, is that although the PRC is supposed to be led by the proletarian class, the product of capitalist development, it is in fact ruled by a revolutionary political and military party that represents a precapitalist domestic organizational structure – the family-like Chinese premodernity. Ironically, and remarkably, the proletarian class "disappeared" in the PRC after 1949.

By the late 1990s, however, a "new" and real proletarian class, which reminds one of the British working class in the eighteenth and nineteenth centuries and the American working class before the New Deal, has been emerging as the result of the emerging national labor market. The market-oriented LAP, especially the crude version practiced by Chinese private employers, is giving rise to a steady formation of workers who are really in conflict, as a group, with the employers. This independent working class is emerging outside the direct control of the CCP and the CCP lost its ideological appeal to this new class, because the party is now a ruling party that resembles the employers rather than the employees. We may soon see the evolution of a real labor movement that may well lead to the growth of genuine trade unions in China. The consequences will be crucial to the whole process of Chinese modernization, since it will contribute not only to the advance of the market institution but also to the separation of the state from social institutions. Whether the CCP can capture the political strength of this new proletarian class, as it did before it came to power in 1949, may determine the historical fate of the CCP in the years ahead.[54] Most CCP propagandists and officials, however, have yet to act on this new development, either because they have not realized the institutional difference between this new working class and the "working class" under the authoritarian state LAP, or they are wishfully pretending that somehow the CCP will be able to control it. It is only a matter of time before they wake up to the altered reality.

III. SUMMARY

The modernization course in contemporary China has been largely a state-led modernization, one currently heading in the new direction of creating a market institution. The first step of that course, introducing the market, has made impressive gains but potential hazards loom. The premodern Chinese domestic organizational structure has demonstrated an institutional transformation so fundamental that the economy has evidently gained great autonomy from the sociopolitical complex, as reflected by the changes in the PRC's labor allocation patterns. The market-oriented LAPs (the CLMs and the national labor market) have had a phenomenal growth, yet elements of the peculiar Chinese premodernity powerfully exist at the end of the twentieth century. China now appears to be at a significant institutional crossroads. The family-based traditional LAP and the authoritarian state LAP still reflect the foundation of the CCP's political regime and the Chinese premodernity.

As an institutional retreat from Mao's failed experiment in institutional revolution, the traditional Chinese family-based LAP was restored after the end of the 1970s as the largest LAP. The traditionally social, mainly family-oriented, norms and considerations regained influence on the minds and behaviors of the Chiense people. The family institution and the clan institution continued to be the institutional foundation for an undifferentiated organizational structure governing the majority of Chinese in economy, politics, and social life. With its massive ability to absorb "surplus" or underemployed labor, this LAP has stabilized the power of the CCP state in controlling the national economy and social life on the macro level, although it may lessen state control over the peasants on the micro level. The traditional authority structure and social stratification have been restored as the relative economic autonomy of the peasant families and the limited self-governing of the villagers was revived.

The family-based LAP explains why there seems to be so much continuity of history in modern China, which many scholars have considered a great enigma.[55] Nevertheless, the small and stagnated family-based production should be a ready springboard for development of a market-oriented larger division of labor, utilizing the millions of cheap rural laborers. The stable family/clan institution, at the cost of confining and distorting the market, has provided a much-needed cushion against the shocks of the advancing market, thus smoothing the progression of an institutional differentiation of the Chinese domestic organizational structure. Labor mobility has increased under this restored family-based LAP but is unlikely to cause explosive labor floods that might destroy the newly emerged market institution or the whole domestic organizational structure. The authority structure of the Chinese nation, as reflected by that within and among families, has demonstrated significant changes in the direction of emphasizing "having the authority" based on resource and knowledge more than "being the authority" based on status and seniority.[56] The Chinese, as an inference from these observations, may construct a domestic organizational structure in which the basic units are groups with clear features of social institutions – the families or reformed clans (the villages/communities) – rather than individuals (Xiaoyi Wang 1994, 57). Those signals may actually foretell the fate and the unique nature of Chinese modernity and even the Chinese nation.

As an extremist version of the century-old family-based LAP, the authoritarian state LAP has been allocating the better educated Chinese urban labor force since the 1950s. Political authority and logic constituted the basis of this authoritarian state LAP. The authoritarian state LAP has been the social and political basis of the authoritarian political system and the bureaucratic socialism in China. It shaped the urban Chinese organizational structure as a "neotraditional communist" one, or as a "socialist society at its primary stage," as the CCP termed it. The *danwei* "ownership" of laborers and the state policy against labor mobility made market operation difficult. The ultra-economic means of control and the political and personal dependence created by this LAP ensured that the CCP-ruled authoritarian state had a solid domination over the premodern Chinese organizational structure.

During the two decades of reform and opening, the authoritarian state LAP has endured tremendous pressures and competition. For economic reasons, the CCP has attempted to reform the LAP with certain market mechanisms, but political concerns have limited the scope and the effectiveness of those reforms. By default, however, the authoritarian state LAP has been significantly eroded by advancing market forces. In fact, this LAP has contributed to the phenomenal development and success of the Chinese market by providing millions of willing, secure, and capable urban workers who could be allocated by the market at a low, state-subsidized, labor cost. A great differentiation of the Chinese urban organizational structure has been taking place as the *danweis* have begun losing their institutional importance while the whole authoritarian state LAP remained a powerful politically stabilizing force.

The community-based societal LAP and the CLMs historically have provided substantial breathing space for the Chinese economy. Having demonstrated the ability to absorb large numbers of laborers in fairly efficient urban collective enterprises and especially in the TVEs, the CLMs have become a pivotal part of the PRC's job-creation strategy.[57] In a nation that has more than 200 million "surplus labor" in the rural areas and more than thirty million underemployed urban laborers, the fast-growing, job-generating CLMs have naturally become the great hope.

As a community-based, market-oriented yet semisocialist LAP, the CLMs have grown to be an alternative to the authoritarian state LAP in the cities and to the family-based traditional LAP in the countryside, representing progress in both cases. They break away from both the confines of the family and the control of the state in a way quite acceptable to most Chinese, who are influenced by the harmony-valuing localistic culture. The CLMs permit the existence of variety, diversity, and competition, yet do not cause much breakdown in the premodern Chinese domestic organizational structure, which still appears to have deep legitimacy. This LAP calls for efficiency and optimal management while incorporating the local community-based socialist style of welfare, or "moral economy" characteristics in Chinese economy and social life. CLMs substantially promote a quasi-market economy with only limited political "damage" as viewed by the "neotraditional communist" state, since the "production means" are still owned by the "collectives" rather than by individual capitalists. Therefore, though not as spectacular and "clear" as a total and sudden privatization to many Western observers, the CLMs, as a distorted or "Chinese style" market-oriented LAP, have the realistic potential to function as the new fabric of the Chinese domestic organization in the near future. A further study of CLMs and their operations, therefore, perhaps should be a requisite for those who want to understand the future and the nature of a possible Chinese modernity and even the unity of the Chinese nation.

An emerging national labor market has led the trend in Chinese labor allocation for the past two decades and is likely to continue its rapid growth and comprehensive institutionalization. Primarily facilitated by FDI, the emergence of the Chinese national labor market demonstrated the strong institutional role of internal-external interactions between the international market and a nation's domestic organizational structure. The Chinese national labor market has contributed greatly to the institutional transformation of that premodern nation. The economy is gaining autonomy from the sociopolitical complex, while a separation between the CCP state and Chinese social life is occurring.

Many of the Chinese values and norms have been affected by the labor market. We are witnessing in China the rise of a new class of market-oriented, middle-income earners and a group of rich private property owners, a massive private economy, a genuine working class that is outside the "buying-off" scheme of the CCP regime and the related (still hidden) trade unions and labor movements. National labor mobility, social liberty and political participation are likely to continue to increase, facilitated by the national labor market. As a result, the political scene of China is likely to be more colorful and dynamic in the future.

Although the Chinese national labor market is perhaps unlikely to become the dominant LAP in the near future, it is institutionally desirable for it to be a larger and more important LAP than the family-based traditional LAP and the authoritarian state LAP. Furthermore, a nationally based market institution tends to unite a nation powerfully because of its ceaseless expansion and assimilation. The lingering and extensive political and social distortions of the labor market may be necessary and even inevitable in China, just as in other East Asian nations. But the difference is that the national-based unified distortions of the labor market may increase national unity and curb destructive regionalism and social polarization, while the community-based distortions tend to decrease national unity and fuel regional divisions. Therefore, not only the future of Chinese modernization and the nature of a possible Chinese modernity, but also the future of the Chinese nation, may rest heavily on the development of the Chinese national labor market.

NOTES

1. It is extremely interesting to notice that in today's Taiwan, the family-based *datong* ideals are still the official ideals. The *Liji-Liyun pian* (The book of rites – Liyun section) describing the "age of *datong*" by

Confucius, handwritten by Dr Sun Yat-sen, is displayed as official doctrine by the Taiwanese government in almost all government buildings, schools, monuments, and other public places.

2. Many scholars outside China have long pondered the view that the PRC is much more of a traditional Chinese regime than a socialist or a "communist" regime. See, for example, Tang Tsou in Womack 1991 and, in a narrower sense, Walder 1986. Many Chinese scholars have also, mostly indirectly, argued that the Chinese premodernity is clearly perpetuated in the era of the PRC. For a well-known and more direct Chinese assertion, see Wang Shan 1994, a now politically controversial best-seller in China originally published as a "translated" work by a nonexistent German scholar.

3. Chinese scholars, in internal publications, have rather clearly argued for a conscious state-led modernization route. Planning, authority, labor control, and support and guidance of the market have been listed as some of the roles a strong state needs to play in China. See, for example, Ren Xiao: "Lun houfazhan guojia jingji chengzhang de zhengzhi tiaojian" [On the political conditions for the economic growth in the latecomer developing nations], in *Shanghai lilun neikan* [Shanghai internal journal of theories], Shanghai, No. 4, 1994, 47–50.

4. For works on the great achievements of state-led modernization in Taiwan, see Gold (1986) and Hartland-Thunberg (1988).

5. Meaning the market is replacing social and even some political institutions. The widespread social crimes and political corruption are indicators of such a consequential replacement.

6. A representative view on this pessimistic prospect is Richard Hornik's "Bursting China's Bubble" in *Foreign Affairs*, May–June 1994, 28–42.

7. Besides effectiveness, stability and commitment, the state needs to open itself, however gradually, to the citizens to enhance the legitimacy of its leadership in the modernization process. Raymond W. Baker is acknowledged for this point.

8. There is hope that this may happen since some CCP leaders are aware of the need for institutional changes to strengthen the PRC state to guide the market. See, for example, Part Two of Li Tieying's long speech at the 1994 Beijing Advanced Economic Forum, "The Reform of Chinese Economic System and the Construction of Socialist Market Economic System," Beijing, May 11, 1994. As a major statement, Jiang Zemin emphasized the links among "reform, development, and stability" and the need for a "macro regulation of the market economy" in his speech to the Fifth Plenary Session of the Fourteenth CCP Central Committee, September 28, 1995. in *Renmin Ribao-Overseas*, Beijing, October 9, 1995, 1.

9. The *77 Ji* [Class of 1977] thus became the first "genuine" college students in more than ten years. A major breakthrough was therefore achieved by the reformers. CCP Central Committee and the State Council: *Guangyu gaige gaokao zhidu de tongzhi* [Notice on the reform of the college entrance exam], *Hongqi* [Red flag] magazine, Beijing, October 1977.

10. This Chinese pragmatism is illustrated by a well-known slogan of Deng's: "It doesn't matter whether the cat is black or white, it is a good cat

as long as it catches the mouse." One of the CCP's major "magic weapons," as Mao called it, is the "mass line" which simply calls for consciously reconceptualizing practical concerns in the terms of ideological theory and then generating solutions from this kind of reconceptualization. (Shue 1980, 334–5).

11. Deng's interview with Mike Wallace of CBS, September 26, 1986. In Ogden 1995, 80.

12. The outline of "Four Modernizations" was first proposed by the late Premier Zhou Enlai in 1964 and restated by him in 1975. However, no attention was really paid to it until 1978 when the order was modified. Previously, it had called for the modernization of industry, agriculture, national defense, and science and technology. After 1978, the value of "science and technology" was put ahead of national defense.

13. Deng Xiaoping: "Upholding the Four Cardinal Principles," in Deng 1985, 144–70.

14. *The 1990 Statistical Communiqué of the National Economy and Social Development*, The PRC National Statistical Bureau, Beijing, Feb. 22, 1991.

15. *Xinhua Daily Telegraph*, Jan. 6, 1991.

16. By the mid-1990s, foreign banks began to be allowed to operate in the PRC. The first "people owned" (private) national bank, Minsheng Bank of China, was formed in 1996 with the political support and apparent "leadership" of the CCP. See *Renmin Ribao-Overseas*, Beijing, January 13, 1996, 1.

17. By 1994, the Chinese labor force – all the men from 16 to 59 and women 16 to 54 (Yuan 1990, 6) – was 825 million, while the total number of "workers" was 614.69 million, including more than 487.68 million (69.2 percent) in the rural areas and 217.8 million in the urban areas. (Labor Ministry's 1994 Annual Report, cited in *Renmin Ribao*, Beijing, May 11, 1995, 1) The urban unemployment rate was about 3 percent and as many as 30 percent of the rural laborers were idling or "underemployed." (*Renmin Ribao* March 2, 1995).

18. By 1996, officially, there were at least more than 7.43 million state employees were either dismissed or *xiagang* (off duty). The author's field work (1996–7), however, found that this figure to be an underestimated one. For example, in Shanghai, the unemployed (or *xiagang*) workers were 300,000 in 1996. But the officials told the author in private that the real number was between 600,000 and one million. In Beijing, the gap between the real and published figures was roughly the same in 1997.

19. Ren Xiao: "Zhenzi wenhua de fangxeng" [A reflection on political culture], in *Zhongguo shuping* [China book reviews], Hong Kong, 1994 (1), 117.

20. For case studies illustrating such efforts, see Shue 1980, Oi 1989, Friedman et al. 1991 and Chan et al. 1992.

21. For a representative view on this point, see Ruan Min: *Deng Xiaoping diguo* [The Deng Xiaoping empire], Taipei, Times Newspaper Press, 1992, 76 (An English translation of the book was published by Westview Press in 1994).

22. A recent semi-official publication cried out for more "social stability" through stabilizing further the "cells of the society: the families" despite the fact that even in the more open urban China "only slightly more than 10 percent of marriages were based on love" (Qiao et al. 1994, 198–200).

23. Chinese scholars began to refer to these people as "populist ruling elites" that had become a new "middle layer" between the state and the masses. See Sun Liping: "Gaige qianghou Zhongguo guojia, minjiantongzhi jingying ji minzhong jian hudong guangxi de yangbian" [The evolution of the interactive relationship among the Chinese state, populist ruling élites and the masses before and after the reform], in *Zhongguo shehui kexue jikang* [Chinese social sciences quarterly], Beijing & Hong Kong, 1994 (1).

24. Anne Thurston: "Village Elections in Lishu County: An Eyewitness Account" in *China Focus*, Princeton, NJ, Vol. 3(5), May 1, 1995, 3, 5.

25. For an official report on the "self-governing" of the Chinese villagers in the 1990s, see Wang Zhongtian: "Yifa zizhi: Xinshiqi nongchun chunji zhuzhi jiangshi de xinsilu" [Self-governing by law: The new thinking of the construction of village organizations in the new era] in *Zhongguo shehui fazhan zhanlui* [Development strategy of Chinese society], Beijing, No. 3, 1994, 14–18.

26. For some of the most vivid descriptions of these "traditional" institutions and behaviors in the Chinese urban areas, see Yao & Murong 1993.

27. For a representative analysis on the important role played by Confucianism in the Japanese modernization, see Cui Xinjing: "Lun ruxue guanlian yu riben de xiandaihua" [On the Confucian ideas and the Japanese modernization], in *Riben Yanjou* [Japan studies], Shengyang, No. 4, 1993, 112–19.

28. For example, see articles in the series "Tigao quanmin shuzhi, yingji 21 shi ji" [Improve the national quality, to prepare for the twenty-first century], *Renmin Ribao*, Winter, 1994–Spring 1995. For a more systematic effort, see Fu et al. 1995, 234–52.

29. Guangdong People's Deputy Guang Shanyue spoke at the group sessions of the CNPC meeting, March 9, 1995. Also, Zhongxin News Agency news, Guangzhou, May 5, 1995.

30. Lin Zhenping & He Qing: "Fujian nongye laodongli zhuanyi xianzhuan yu zhanlui tangtao" [The current situation and strategic discussion on the transfer of Fujian agricultural labor], in *Fazhang yanjiu* [Development studies], Fuzhou, 1993 (1), 17–20.

31. In the 1980s and 1990s, studies revealed that, even in the more "open" major cities, as many as 80 percent to 95 percent of parents said they would be against their children working outside their hometowns. See Mu Guanzhong: "Bei chonghuai de xiaohuangdi" [The spoiled little emperors], in *Huaxia wenzhe* [China news digest], an Internet weekly, Nos. 124 & 125, May 5 & 12, 1995.

32. By using "bureaucratic," this book does not suggest that Chinese political authority is in the hands of specialized bureaucrats who take politics as a vocation, as in Weber's terminology. Rather, in the PRC,

guan (官, official or bureaucrat) means far more than government officials and politicians. It has been the best vehicle to power *and* wealth and glamour in almost every profession and discipline. It is also the most common standard for measuring success, rank and social status. For a discussion on the notion and the theories of bureaucracy, see Abrahamsson 1993, 3–59.

33. Yang Qinfang, in *Guangdong shehui kexuie* (Guangdong Social Sciences), Guangzhou, No. 2, 1990, 140.

34. The corruption of CCP-PRC bureaucrats has become a major theme of the writings on current affairs in China. For example, see Zeng 1993, Yao & Murong 1993, and the ten books of the series on "the hot issues in economic life" published by the Renmin University Press in 1992. For a foreigner's examination of this issue, see Yufan Hao & Michael Johnston: "Reform at the Crossroads: An Analysis of Chinese Corruption," in *Asian Perspective*, Seoul, Korea, Vol. 19(1), Spring-Summer 1995, 117–49.

35. Qiao et al. 1994, 235. The book was published by the Central Party School of the CCP. It was recommended by a number of Chinese élites to the author in 1995 as a "good reflection" of the élites' thinking.

36. Author's field notes in Anhui and Jiangsu provinces, 1995.

37. *Renmin Ribao-Overseas*, May 26, 1995, 2.

38. Xin 1992, 28–31 & Zeng 1993, 33–64. Both reports and the author's field studies revealed that, for most of those "moonlighting" state employees, their state job had become basically "rest time" while they really worked hard on their "second jobs" to make most of their total income.

39. For how active, how many and how significant those "divers" have been to the PRC economy in the 1990s, see, for example, Zeng 1993 and the whole series of books on the "underground economy" published by the same press in 1993–4.

40. The so-called *"bingtui"* (early retirement due to disease) became a convenient way for many to stay connected to the security net of the authoritarian state LAP while joining the market economy to earn more income. See, for example, Cheng Jingchan: "Bingtui xingtailu" [The mentality of the *bingtui* people], in *Anhui Ribao* [Anhui Daily], Hefei, August 8, 1995, 6.

41. Both have had a remarkable record of high economic growth and low unemployment in nations with large populations. Cf. Cole 1971, 1979, Garon 1987, Gordon 1985, 1991, and Friedman 1990. For a Chinese scholar's interpretation of the "treasures" of Japanese labor allocation and management, see Yu 1991, 300–7.

42. Zhiyuan Cui: "Marx, Theories of the Firm, and the Socialist Reform," in *China Report*, Washington, DC, July 1990, 1.

43. *Shijie Ribao* [World Journal], New York, July 18, 1995, A11.

44. Primarily in the cases of the TVEs in the rural communities. See Brugger & Reglar 1994, 173–4.

45. In Shangdong Province, there were more than 300 "poor villages" annexed by the rich villages and/or TVEs by 1995. See *Wanhue Pao* [Wenhui daily], Hong Kong, December 12, 1995, 2. This extremely

significant development of the expansion of the rural CLMs through the expansion of the local communities, though still limited, may signal a new avenue for a national labor market to form in the rural areas.

46. Officially, the PRC calls all the 12 provinces/metropolises along the Chinese coast "eastern China": Beijing, Fujian, Guangdong, Guangxi, Hainan, Hebei, Jiangsu, Liaoning, Shandong, Shanghai, Tianjin, and Zhejiang. See Anhui Provincial Government: *1995 Anhui Shengqing Shouce* [Official Handbook of Anhui, 1995], an internal publication by the CCP, Hefei, 1995, 93.
47. Guo Tong: "Keji touru: Dongzhongxibu bupingheng" [R&D investment: Uneven among the east. central and west], in *Zhongguo xinxibao* [China information], Beijing, SSB, August 3, 1995, 1.
48. SSB: "1993 shehui fazhan shuiping baogao" [Report on social development in 1993], in *Liaowang* [Outlook], Beijing, February 10, 1995, 10–11.
49. Observations revealed that technological levels were much lower in the western provinces and income inequality among them was also larger than that in the east. Figures and speculations in Xu Fongxian & Wang Zhengzhong: "Jingti: Quyu fazhan chaju zhubu kuoda" [Warning: The regional gap of development is gradually enlarging], in *Zhonghua gongshan shibao* [China business times], Beijing, January 16, 1995, 5, and January 23, 1995, 5.
50. State Statistical Bureau data, in *Zhongguo xinxibao* [Chinese journal of information], Beijing, SSB, August 1, 1995, 1.
51. *Beijing Ribao* [Beijing Daily], December 2, 1994, 1; *Xinmin wanbao* [Xinmin evening news], Shanghai, March 3, 1995, 3; and *Xinan wanbao* [Xinan evening news], Hefei, June 6, 1995, 1.
52. For example, see Yu Zhongxian: "Shilun Zhongguo daludiqu jingji zhi bu junheng fazhang" [On the uneven development of the economy on the Chinese mainland], in *Jingji xuejia* [Economist], Chengdu, May 1994, 16–23.
53. *Xinhua Daily Telegraph*, Beijing, September 25, 1995, 1.
54. Yang Fan: "Laozi maodun jianchengwei woguo shehui maodun de jiaodian" [The capital-labor confrontation will become the focus of our nation's social conflicts], in *Yanhai xinchao* [New tides], Shantou, No. 2, 1995, 10–12.
55. For example, see Friedman et al. 1991, Dittmer 1993, and Dittmer ed. 1993.
56. Wang Xiaoyi: *Xuyuang yu diyuang* [Consanguinity and geopolitics], Hangzhou, Zhejiang Renmin Press, 1993, 147.
57. The CLMs have been officially reported to be more than ten times as efficient in creating jobs than the authoritarian state LAP in the 1980s and 1990s. *Xinhua Daily Telegraph*, Beijing, February 18, 1991.

5 Conclusion: The Dragon Enters the Nets

I have proposed an alternative analytical framework to observe modernization in general and Chinese modernization in particular from a perspective emphasizing the institutions and institutional changes of a nation's domestic organizational structure. Labor allocation patterns (LAPs) have been proposed and used as the indicators for this analytical approach. After a brief review of LAPs in the two-thousand-year history of China and an examination of the LAPs in contemporary China, I have come to the point of conclusion. Section I attempts an assessment of the analytical framework proposed and used in this book. Its explanatory power and limits will be discussed based on its application in the Chinese case. Section II briefly summarizes the main findings of this book. The institutional features and the comprehensive institutional changes of the Chinese domestic organizational structure will be briefly revisited and explained. These findings may help us to narrow the currently tremendous uncertainties in China studies. Section III revisits some of the questions posted in Chapter 4 and speculates about the future of Chinese modernization, based on the findings of this study.

I. INSTITUTIONS AND INSTITUTIONAL CHANGES: TO UNDERSTAND MODERNIZATION

A summary and a short assessment of the analytical framework proposed and applied in this book are attempted in this section. The more extensive assessment that counts, however, will naturally be that made by the reader.

An Institutional Approach

The analytical framework used in this book can be very briefly outlined as the following:

166

1. Human behavior including economic development is constrained and even defined by the human institution. The human institution is man-made and can be altered through planned or spontaneous collective actions. Time-based institutional legitimacy is the key to an existing human institution and its changes. Culture, a factor often used to explain human behavior, is understood as nothing but the internalized human institution.

2. The human institution, originated from the understanding of human needs and desires, can be divided into three basic elements or spheres: polity, economy, and social life. Each has its own objectives, organizational characteristics, functions, values, scope, and behavioral patterns. Internally, each has historically had varied organizational structures. Externally, the three may or may not be differentiated from one another. One of the three may even become *the* human institution to largely replace the other two – the phenomenon called premodernity.

3. A certain type of relationship among polity, economy, and social life – a differentiated yet interactive relationship – denotes the institutional notion of human modernity. Human modernity tends, so far, to be group-based and varies across historical and geographic settings. Preexisting institutions, timing (absolute and relative) of institutional changes, and the ways of reaching modernity (state-led or market-driven) determine the fate and the variety of modernity in a particular human group. Human modernity itself is a dynamic situation and is subject to pressures of the growth of population, the expansion of its scope through reducing institutional exclusion, the accumulation of knowledge (the development of technology), the interaction with other human groups (nations), and the collective decisions of the group. Thus human modernity is not guaranteed nor is it immune to destruction. The so-called "post-modernity" and its associated "new" issues are to be understood as either expansion or adjustment of a modernity (for example, the reduction of institutional exclusion) or a process of the destruction of a modernity (the domination of one institution, such as the market, over the other two).

4. Nations, as the highest level of hierarchical human grouping, are the unit of analysis for an institutional inquiry of human behaviors such as economic development and modernization. A nation's political, economic, and social institutions *and* the relationship among the three constitute the nation's domestic

organizational structure or the overall institutional framework of that nation. Modernization of a nation, the effort and process of reaching modernity, means the institutional transformation of the nation's domestic organizational structure in the direction of having a differentiated yet interactive relationship among the three institutions.

5. Modernization differs from development. Development is a ceaseless process of expansion, improvement, or invention of human behavior and its outcome. Modernization is institutional changes towards the optimization of the human institution with a particular form of the human institution – modernity – as its identifiable goal. Modernity may be reached at any level of development. Development and economic development may take place in a premodern or a modernized institutional setting with, naturally, different performance or pace. Development is endless and can take different directions with progression and regression both possible.

6. A state-led modernization is believed to be more appropriate for "latecomer" nations in their efforts to reach modernity. Using a capable state to establish, guide, and legitimize a market as the dominant economic institution, and thus to have an autonomous economy, is the crucial first step of such a modernization process.

7. A nation's domestic organizational structure and its institutional changes can be reliably observed by examining the nation's labor allocation patterns. A thorough understanding of a nation's LAPs would reveal the relationship among the polity, economy and social life in that nation. It would also yield substantial information about the internal features and mechanisms of the three elements of the human institution or three institutions in that nation. A historical observation of a nation's LAPs could demonstrate the tracks, directions and consequences of the institutional changes in that nation.

8. There are basically four LAP shaping and reshaping forces: "spontaneous" economic activities based on the accumulation of knowledge (the development of technology); political decisions by the state; societal influences; and forces generated by external factors, mainly the international political economy.

9. Historically, three types or modes of LAPs can be identified across nations: a premodern LAP that is primarily family-based; a labor market; and an authoritarian state allocation in a nationwide

planning economy. The three typical LAPs correspond to the different domestic organizational structures centered on social institutions, the market economy, and the state respectively. Although few nations have only one type of LAP, in most nations one tends to be dominant. The variations or deformed/distorted versions of the three typical LAPs, however, contain rich information about complex and varied relationships among the political, economic, and social institutions – the variety of premodernity or modernity.

An Initial Assessment

Initially and briefly, the application of the analytical framework outlined above in our case study of China has appeared to be very rewarding. Being a difficult but almost ideal case, China served as a good test for the analytical framework. The framework offered a persuasive way to understand some of the most important and debated characteristics, such as the long-term stagnation and the cyclical political changes in Chinese history. It explained the Chinese super-stable premodernity well and enabled us to appreciate the institutional uniqueness of the Chinese domestic organizational structure and its causes. Institutional similarities and peculiarities between China and other nations could now be recorded and recognized with much more certainty. After all, in the light of our institutional analysis, we can see that the Chinese domestic organizational structure has been constructed with the same components and mechanisms as the other nations. The "uniqueness" of the Chinese culture or historical legacy – products of the Chinese premodernity, still important to our understanding of the Chinese behavior and the future of that nation – lost much of its mystery in the light of this analytical framework.[1]

This analytical model also worked satisfactorily in describing the turbulent history of the PRC since 1949. High clarity is achieved concerning the political and economic development of the PRC under Mao and Deng. We now have acquired more confidence in analyzing the sources and the uses of political power in the CCP and the PRC. A solid base is thus constructed for making speculations about the future of Chinese modernization. Perhaps testifying to the great potential of institutional analysis in the study of China, there has been a surge of study and application of an "institutionalist approach" in the social sciences recently in Chinese academia.[2]

Besides shedding penetrating light on Chinese institutions and their changes, our analytical framework appears to have great potential for cross-national and cross-time studies of people's behavior in different national settings. The barriers and gaps[3] that have prevented the development of truly cross-national studies and even an integrated study of nations may begin to disappear. Based on this analytical framework, we now see that the differences among nations are mainly the result of their varied domestic organizational structures. Those often exaggerated national differences are easily reducible to institutional changes leading to similar domestic organizational structures.

Nations are therefore *the same* underneath our microscope of institutional analysis, just as all matter is the same at the level of its basic elements. Our understanding of human behavior, that is, the disciplines of the social sciences, could gain from this analytical potential. Many human behaviors and their consequences in "modernized" nations like the United States could be understood and explained by this analytical framework as well. For example, the worrisome problems of psychological diseases and narcotics abuse, brutal and often "senseless" crimes, the decay of inner cities, the crisis of public finance and American domestic terrorism like Unabomer and the Oklahoma City bombing of 1995 may be all understood as results of a deep erosion of American social life and polity by the market institution. This erosion is taking place in the context of a fully justified diminution of institutional exclusion in the American modernity.[4]

Furthermore, this analytical framework appears to work well in the long historical context of China. It could describe the centuries-old institutions and institutional changes there and explain Chinese behavior under such institutions during those centuries. This "ahistorical" feature of our institutional approach may give us some analytical ability to conduct long-term observation of human behavior while reducing the time-specific uncertainties often associated with observation and recording. The edge in explaining human behavior over time and across the nations may be a major strength of this model, as demonstrated in our case study of China.

As just one approach in our study of domestic organizational structures and their changes (the modernization process), the analytical framework used in this book obviously does not claim to replace all other approaches and perspectives based on just one case study. The indicators used, the LAPs, may have great power and reliability in revealing and reflecting institutional arrangements and their changes in a nation. But one set of indicators naturally cannot portray all the details of the whole picture. Several important issues concerning examination of a nation's domestic organizational structure, such as how and exactly why the three institutions interact with each other at a given point, could not be sufficiently or precisely answered by looking at that nation's LAPs alone. Many other tools are needed to utilize the potential of our analytical framework fully. What has been done in this study is just the first step in explaining human behavior from an institutional perspective by offering an observational and analytical framework. Only time and more work can tell how much better and more accurately this framework explains human behavior than other approaches.

II. TO EMERGE FROM PREMODERNITY: CHINA AND THE CHINESE MODERNIZATION

A few general findings may now be summarized about the institutional features of the transforming Chinese domestic organizational structure, as reflected by our study of the Chinese LAPs.

A Super-Stable Premodern Nation

A "super-stable" premodernity has existed in China for many centuries, reinforced by Confucian culture and by natural and self-imposed international isolation, as shown by the observation that there was basically only one dominant LAP, the family-based traditional LAP, for most of Chinese history. From the *zigengnongs* in the Qin and Han dynasties to the peasants in today's PRC, the family-based traditional LAP has allocated and governed the majority of the Chinese. As a result, a family-like societal institutional framework became *the* institution for the Chinese, upon which the whole premodern Chinese domestic organizational structure has been built and maintained.

The undifferentiated Chinese domestic organizational structure, centered on a family-like imperial state, entangled the Chinese economy, polity, and social life and institutionally restricted the mobility and creativity of the Chinese in all the three basic domains of human behavior. The hierarchical, highly centralized, and often irrational political system controlled the fate of a very productive nation. The Chinese premodernity repeatedly suffocated the institutional changes generally termed modernization. The undifferentiated family-like institutional framework eliminated the institutional conditions for the market to develop internally. A market-driven modernization eventually became impossible under the premodern but highly legitimized and centralized Chinese "world" system that effectively shielded the Chinese from very important international comparisons, competition, and alternatives. A state-led modernization could not take place either, until the end of the nineteenth century, simply because there was no internal need for the ruling families to alter the familiar and comfortable domestic organizational structure; nor (unlike the case of Medieval Europe) pressure from foreign competition.

Culturally, technologically, and administratively, the Chinese definitely reached one of the most sophisticated levels among the premodern nations. The nation acquired a remarkable institutional stability and cultural cohesion. Reproduction-centered social values and family-centered social institutions dominated people's political and economic behaviors. Great social harmony was achieved among the people as long as the premodern domestic organizational structure could withstand the institutional strains, and there was an almost unbelievable certainty or predictability in Chinese history.

The accumulated institutional strains, demonstrated by the decay and collapse of the family-based traditional LAP over time, led to periodic institutional explosions or implosions, but not much in the way of generating new institutions. The repetition of dynastic cycles and the alternation of political unity versus division have made the long history of China, the longest continuous civilization, colorful and dramatic but also paradoxically stale and dull.

Most of the Chinese domestic organizational structure and its internalized version, the Confucian culture, were somehow established some two thousand years ago. The basic values, institutions, means of ruling[5] and modes of production experienced very limited changes for the two millennia. The brilliance and diligence of the Chinese people produced some of the best artifacts, scientific findings, workmanship, and literary achievements in the world. But they failed to alter the premodern Chinese domestic organizational structure beyond often trivial and temporary repairs. The numerous rebellions, revolutions and wars – some of them among the bloodiest in human history – were classic examples of human tragedy in the sense that they seldom changed much institutionally even though they were terribly destructive of property and lives. This destruction, as a historical anomaly, then produced the motives and conditions for reestablishment of the family-based LAP and the overall family-like premodern domestic organizational structure – which was only to be destroyed in a few more generations by new rebellions, wars, or famines. Over time, the super-stable Chinese premodernity was mythologized to become the fatalistic belief in the elusive "mandate of the heaven."

The unparalleled institutional stability and continuity of the Chinese premodern domestic organizational structure was perpetuated with a heavy price. After its peak of performance in the mid-Tang dynasty (eighth century), the Chinese premodernity started a continuous decline caused primarily by a simple but powerful factor – the growth of the population. New knowledge, especially innovation, was institutionally discouraged. At least since the early thirteenth century when the North Song dynasty collapsed, as the Chinese premodernity became increasingly rigid, centralized and internationally isolated, the people experienced centuries of technological and economic stagnation, brutal imperial despotism covered and legitimized with family institutions and values, declines in living standards, bloody wars and rebellions, as well as decay of arts and ethics in general.

People were organized to ensure the continuation of the family/nation. They could not have a participatory and rational politics nor an efficient and innovative economy. They survived as a nation supposedly like a giant family. But the cold rules of human politics produced some of the most brutal "fathers" or rulers, and equally brutal and rebellious "sons" or subjects, which really could result in making the "family-nation" a hell for its people. Chinese politics was generally painted with sweet "family values" but carried out with ruthless violence and vicious plots. A legitimized separation of words from deeds and of titles from contents[6] thus became an infamous but influential informal institution governing Chinese behavior. This deep philosophical and ethical tradition led to pragmatism, but often also led to the destruction of legal systems and the rise of personal rule and the infamously crucial role of "connections" (*guanxi*) in daily Chinese life. For many of today's Chinese merchants, who are breaking many traditional values through their market-oriented business activities, a "dilemma" like that experienced by Puritan merchants in seventeenth century New England is observable.[7]

Social life was negatively affected by the Chinese premodernity as well. Economically, premodern China after the thirteenth century degenerated into a poor, stagnated and even malnourished nation. Nutritional intake declined chronically as per capita grain production in China declined after the Tang dynasty and rarely returned to that high level. As a result, the highest value of the family-centered Chinese premodernity, to reproduce more people, was greatly compromised and twisted. Quite "logically," tens of millions of people lost their lives at an accelerated speed in wars and famines; many needs of the majority people were systematically suppressed and many more desires were denied.

Most tragic of all, the huge toll of millions of human lives and the denial of the needs and desires of many more changed very little, very slowly. Institutionally speaking, China was static for many centuries despite the horrifying sacrifices. That, as demonstrated by this study, has been the origin of the long-term Chinese backwardness.

The Mixed and Transitional Domestic Organizational Structure of Today's PRC

We discussed, based on the sister volume studying labor allocation in contemporary China (Wang 1998), four coexisting patterns of labor allocation in the PRC in the 1980s to 1990s.

The coexistence of four major LAPs in today's PRC demonstrated that the Chinese domestic organizational structure is a mixed and transitional one. The family-based traditional LAP is currently numerically the largest one but is experiencing a steady decline. The authoritarian state LAP is still the most important LAP politically and economically but is stagnant and under pressure to change. The community-based labor markets (CLMs) are growing very rapidly, with the likelihood of becoming the future dominant LAP in China, but represent a social or communal distortion of the labor market. Finally, a national labor market is emerging but its maturation has yet to take place.

This unique phenomenon of the coexistence of four LAPs determines much of the Chinese politics, economic development and social life. We see the powerful, still dominant, presence of the CCP state in Chinese politics, economy and social life as reflected by the still-dominant authoritarian state LAP. A revitalization of the local- or region-centered Chinese institutional setting is on the rise, as the rapid development of the CLMs shows. The restored family-based traditional LAP restored much of the Chinese premodernity to the majority of Chinese in the rural areas. The rapid emergence of the national labor market convincingly illustrates the increasing degree of autonomy of the Chinese economy from the sociopolitical complex. A drastic differentiation of the Chinese economy from the sociopolitical complex is under way, as revealed by the rapid growth of the market-oriented LAPs, a national labor market and the CLMs. Large numbers of laborers are now allocated and managed by the advancing market institution, signaling that the final stage of the marketization of the Chinese economy has arrived.[8] But the strong presence of the nonmarket LAPs, the largest family-based LAP and the dominant authoritarian state LAP, is powerfully resisting and distorting the emerging market institution and greatly complicating the process of Chinese modernization.

The state, premodern and resembling a giant paternal family, has been the center of the Chinese domestic organizational structure, leaving its imprint on the formation and development of the Chinese LAPs. But some LAPs, especially those market-oriented ones, may have already reached the critical mass to grow out of the control of the CCP state. The Chinese are in a state-led modernization; but whether the state can continue its leading role is increasingly unclear, as the transformation of the Chinese domestic organizational structure is differentiating the economic institutions and even the social institutions farther and farther away from the state.

The transition of the Chinese domestic organizational structure, demonstrated by the four LAPs and their relative growth or decline, paints an interesting and profound picture of an ongoing modernization of a quarter of humankind. The phenomenal economic growth of the PRC in the past decade is a major tangible result.[9] The grand Chinese institutional changes could have several outcomes with varied implications for other nations. The dominant Chinese LAP in the near future appears to be the CLMs. If that becomes reality, would we see some regionalized Chinese politics and economy? Would a polity of federalism be possible in China? Or will China split? If the authoritarian state LAP continues its domination, the powerful central government of the CCP state may continue its traditional role in the Chinese domestic organizational structure. The rapid changes of the Chinese LAPs thus offer a reliable yet convenient way to see the future of China. While it is still too early to pick one of the two scenarios about the future of Chinese modernization described in Chapter 4, it is indeed a very interesting and rewarding time to observe China.

Issues of a State-led Modernization

As our examination of the history of the Chinese LAPs demonstrated, the Chinese domestic organizational structure began to show signs of transformation in the second half of the nineteenth century. The changes were difficult, slow, very bloody and almost theatrical. By the mid-twentieth century, the CCP forcefully restored the premodern Chinese domestic organizational structure in the PRC. However, new circumstances (an external environment of international political anarchy and an international market) and a new regime (an imported but nationalized communist revolutionary ideology), did not restore the super-stability of the Chinese premodernity.

After the failed institutional experiments under Mao, Deng Xiaoping and his associates changed direction at the end of the 1970s, putting China on the track of a state-led and market-oriented modernization. Since then, China has been experiencing rapid institutional changes of its domestic organizational structure. In its own way, China appears determined to follow the "proven" state-led modernization route of its East Asian neighbors, as one scholar concluded, to have an economic development based on "the state and market" functioning as two "complementary and reinforcing" institutions.[10]

This study of the state-led Chinese modernization, based on the examination of the Chinese LAPs, has yielded some early findings concerning the state-led modernization approach in general terms.[11] Two such findings are especially worth mentioning. First, besides the importance of the pre-existing institutions, we see through our study the crucial role played by foreign influence in general and foreign direct investment (FDI) in particular. Since investors from Hong Kong, Taiwan and other overseas Chinese communities have made up the overwhelming majority of FDI in China, the development of Chinese modernization is likely to follow what happened in those Chinese "nations." The active role of an authoritarian but nonetheless effective state in encouraging, protecting and "utilizing" FDI has been a key to the development of the market in general and a national labor market in particular in the PRC. This is in strong contrast to economic reform in another heavily populated old premodern nation – India.[12] Unlike the Indian case, there were very few open attacks on FDI initially, and after nearly two decades the benefits of FDI have earned it a deep institutional legitimacy in China.

Second, a few uniquely Chinese institutions such as *hukou* (household or residential registration), *danwei* (units), and *dangan* (dossier) have affected the currents and the prospects of the Chinese modernization in many ways. The most important impact of those institutions has been their effective provision of special controlling mechanisms for the segmentation of the Chinese population by temporarily excluding or shielding many from the new but often painful institutional changes. The profound but perhaps ethically questionable issue of exclusion or discrimination in a nation's modernization process, may actually have been instrumental to the current success and the future development of Chinese modernization.

The importance of external influence

Primarily due to the push and pull of external influences, China started to change institutionally in the past century. The process was met with extraordinary domestic and international obstacles. Internally, the dysfunctional Chinese state could not pursue an effective state-led modernization, and strong resistance from societal forces made the advancement of the market slow and difficult. Internationally, the penetration of China by the international market was closely accompanied by foreign attempts at controlling China politically and even eliminating the Chinese nation-state. The great Chinese Revolution thus somewhat justifiably targeted the foreign influence that actually initiated the institutional changes in China.

When the CCP regime decided to open up China in 1978, foreign influence soon took a central role in the modernization process. This time, foreigners came as businessmen with capital, new technology, and alternative institutions, rather than with gunboats to threaten Chinese sovereignty. FDI was directly responsible for the emergence of market-oriented labor practice in the PRC. Foreign employers brought in market-oriented labor recruiting and management. Their socially accepted and glamorous operations soon added to the legitimacy of those practices. FDI's interactions with the CCP state led to the legalization of a national labor market, which was quickly and quietly used by native private employers (Wang 1998, Chapter 4). In the politically remote rural areas, the market-oriented labor practice was soon adopted by the township and village enterprises (TVEs) and the CLMs were thus born out of the formerly community-based societal LAP. Compared to the historical isolation, today's opening of China has sealed the Chinese institutional changes into a market-oriented course that is now far beyond the point of reversal. The decision by Beijing finally to knock down a major barrier of "containment" between the SEZs (special economic zones) and the rest of the nation illustrates the deep penetration of foreign influence and the rapid growth of a Chinese national market.[13]

FDI from Hong Kong, Taiwan and other overseas Chinese has constituted the majority of FDI in China. Those "Chinese foreigners" have brought much of their "modern" but Sinicized domestic organizational structures to China through their labor practice. Despite the fact that FDI employment is still treated by the CCP state as a temporary "concession," the impact of those "foreign" and "modern" but still essentially very "Chinese" institutions has been immense and lasting. The "digested" market-oriented LAP from those overseas Chinese seems to fit into the Chinese climate better than those that come directly from the West.

Hong Kong, which has over 60 percent of total FDI in China, legally became part of China in 1997. Will the Hong Kong "FDI" then still be treated with "temporary" or expedient measures as that of other foreign investors, or will the Hong Kong style of market institution become a permanent part of the changing Chinese domestic organizational structure? Either way, the market institution is likely to be much more important in the PRC. Conceivably, if the Chinese can successfully complete their state-led modernization, the PRC may just have a domestic organizational structure like that in today's Korea, Singapore[14] or Taiwan and perhaps yesterday's Japan. What would that imply for the rest of the world?

Hukou, danwei *and* dangan*: Tools of exclusion and market distortion*

As part of the pre-existing institutions, the *hukou* system, the *danwei* institution and the *dangan* mechanisms have all played important roles in the institutional changes concerning labor allocation currently unfolding in the PRC. Even by the late 1990s, when a national labor market has emerged and the CLMs are growing rapidly, those institutions still effectively separate the massive rural labor force from the urban economy and limit the internal migration of the people.[15] Furthermore, they are still important tools by which the state and all other types of employers in general can exercise ultra-economic controls over the workers. Those Chinese institutions have significantly smoothed the advancement of the market institution through their powerful functions of social control and exclusion, even though they created significant social injustice and regional differentiation among the Chinese. Indeed, social and political distortion of the emerging and imported market institutions has been a leading feature of the Chinese state-led modernization. The positive function of such distortion or deformation of the market may be a major lesson from our exploration of Chinese modernization.

The importance of social control in an era of reform is easy to understand. There must be a stable legal and political environment for the market economy to emerge and to operate. Political instability and uncertainty, rather than corruption or dictatorship, usually present the most hardship for the market economy. But institutional changes tend to cause strains and conflicts for existing social and political institutions[16] that could lead to massive social dislocation, drastic restratification, and political instability; this could eventually destroy the political and administrative effectiveness of the state that is crucial to a state-led modernization effort. The CCP, relying especially on the *hukou* system, managed to control the social mobility or dislocation caused by the advancing market economy and contain much of the "negatives" of the market into separate, thus easily manageable, areas. The political stability of the CCP regime, in comparison to many other communist regimes in reform, may be largely due to the function of the uniquely Chinese *hukou* system. Similar systems functioned similarly in other places like Taiwan and even Japan.

The three institutions, especially the *hukou* system, have had a strong effect of segmenting the general population, thus providing a basis for an institutional exclusion. An exclusive institutional arrangement appears to be a forgotten lesson from the modernization experiences of the advanced nations. Despite its current disrepute in the "modernized" nations, exclusion plays the valuable functional role of allowing for regionalized and sectioned institutional experiments – the so-called *"shidiang"* [testing points] in China.[17] This institutional feature of the Chinese domestic organizational structure provided the possibility for the gradualism of reform and Deng's "strategy of uneven development."[18] It also historically contributed to legitimizing new institutions with less cost by example-setting on smaller scales. Practically, it may have the even larger role of controlling the effects of the market, thus enabling a rapid and smooth institutional change. This is especially useful when the new market economy cannot quickly produce enough material benefits to convince everyone of its advantages, while inevitably causing dislocations and individual sufferings.

In an era when discrimination has become unacceptable and any institutional exclusion based on property ownership, race, education and gender can hardly be effectively implemented, the geographic and community-based exclusion or discrimination through *hukou* became a blessing from heaven for the Chinese. The exclusionary role of those three institutions in making the extensive institutional changes in China effective and smooth needs to be fully acknowledged. The gains have been, of course, built on the suffering and pain of those who were excluded or discriminated against. The rural labor force, especially in the less prosperous areas, are in a sense victims or the sacrificial lambs of Chinese modernization – at least for now.

The backwardness of the family-based traditional LAP is apparent, but it earns precious time for the emerging market economy by taking hundreds of millions of Chinese from unbearable unemployment to unfair but sustainable underemployment. The exclusion of the CLMs, an increasingly market-oriented LAP, clearly has its many downsides, including creating geographically based social injustice and inefficient utilization of human resources nationwide. But the CLMs and their exclusions enabled the smooth and orderly transformation of the nonmarket economy, as demonstrated by the gradual but steady decline of community-based labor discrimination in some advanced areas like Sunan. The discrimination of the authoritarian state LAP features more injustice and is even unethical. But the *hukou* and other tools maintained the stability of the overall Chinese domestic organizational structure, providing the legitimacy and time for the institutional changes to take place.

The Dragon Enters the Nets

My study of Chinese institutions and institutional changes through examining LAPs has confirmed the belief that China has gone through so much change that it is now departing from its long and glorious historical position as the stable but stagnant "center" of the world.

As the current Chinese LAPs and their changes demonstrated, despite all odds, China appears to have irreversibly entered a double net on its way to modernity. Domestically, the dragon of the Chinese state has entered the net of the market economy. Externally, the dragon of China has entered the net of the existing nation-state system based on international political anarchy and the international market economy.

Primarily in the past two decades, the family-like Chinese state, as the center of the premodern Chinese domestic organizational structure, has entered the net of a differentiating domestic organizational structure featuring a rapidly advancing market institution. The decline of the authoritarian state LAP illustrates that the autonomy of the Chinese economy and even social institutions has been on the rise. This is an unprecedented development in China's long history and the Chinese state, finding the net often uncomfortable and "degenerating," naturally kicks and screams all the way. Our analysis of the PRC LAPs, however, unmistakably points to the conclusion that the Chinese state is losing its traditional ability to be an almighty dragon versus other institutions such as the market, family, and social groups. The state itself, as already shown by changes in the authoritarian state LAP, has become more susceptible to economic and social forces. The widespread corruption and all sorts of "crimes"[19] and the continued and even increased importance of personal connections (*guanxi*)[20] vividly illustrate the much-reduced status of the Chinese state.

As the already disproportionate presence and effect of the foreign influence continue to grow rapidly, China has gingerly but irreversibly entered the net of the international market and international politics. The great institutional transformation of the domestic organizational structure, reflected by the emergence and development of market-oriented LAPs in the PRC, demonstrates the crucial and lasting role of foreign influence, especially FDI. The "unsocialist" and even un-Chinese labor market has now gained deep legitimacy, even among the CCP leaders. By making profound institutional changes to have market-oriented LAPs and thus a market-oriented economy, the Chinese appear to have wholeheartedly embraced the international market as the norm for their economic activities. After about 100 years, Chinese premodernity has finally and legitimately been accepted by the Chinese themselves as just one form of domestic organizational structure, not a way of life for everyone on Earth. Other than the traditionally leading but diminishing role of the state, international competition and the domestic market now appear to be the two new major driving forces for the continuation of the Chinese modernization.

III. THE DRAGON IN THE NETS: AN EPILOGUE

The massive scale and the heroic nature of the Chinese effort to emerge from premodernity have shaken the world for several decades. But it is after the 1980s that we see, probably for the first time, the rise of China as a potentially modernized nation. It has been termed the "largest emerging market economy," and the third largest of all national economies with the possibility of surpassing the size of the US economy by 2020.[21] If combined with Taiwan and Hong Kong, the Chinese economy could become the largest national economy in the world in the first decade of the twenty-first century.[22] The International Monetary Fund (IMF) concluded in 1995 that China has had the highest savings rate in the world since the 1970s.[23] The growth potential is thus still immense for the 1.2 billion Chinese. One must then ask: Where will China be in the twenty-first century?

From our understanding of the Chinese domestic organizational structure and its changes, we may make four general speculations here on the future of Chinese modernization. First, a differentiated and interactive economy-polity-social life structure is emerging and is likely to continue to develop into a modernity-type of domestic organizational structure. The leading indicator for that is the emergence and development of the market-oriented LAPs. Second, the potential Chinese modernity is far from certain. Several already existing obstructions could well delay or even derail the state-led Chinese modernization. The crucial transformation of the authoritarian state LAP is still a major bottleneck, and the massive family-based peasant labor force is accumulating explosive energy against the controlling mechanism, presenting a fundamental threat to the new and still poorly institutionalized Chinese market institution. Third, the modernity in China appears most likely to be a "Chinese" one with its own characteristics resembling those in some other East Asian nations. The CLMs, not a national labor market, appear to be the likely dominant LAP while other LAPs, especially the family-based traditional LAP, are likely to exist for quite some time to come. Finally, entering the nets of the market at home and the international political economy abroad, a modernizing China appears to be an increasingly powerful player internationally, with a fairly low likelihood of breaking the existing rules of the games.

An Emerging Modernity in China

By our analysis of Chinese LAPs up to the late 1990s, one can see that the arrival of a modernity-type of domestic organizational structure in China may have become just a matter of time. The market has become the leading, if not yet the dominant, economic institution in a nation where merely twenty years ago the market had only a marginal existence. Even the politically and socially most sensitive resource, labor, is now increasingly allocated and governed by market forces. As a result, the Chinese economy has definitely gained great autonomy versus the state and social institutions. Estimates by foreign observers have put the Chinese economic autonomy from the state in the neighborhood of the French and Italian economies. State planning used to allocate more than 700 kinds of commodities; by 1991, that list was already reduced to just 27,[24] and further reductions apparently continued in the 1990s.[25]

Beyond the economy, the emerging market has significantly affected Chinese politics and social life as a fully legitimized, powerful institution governing much of people's behavior outside the economic arena. The commercialization of social life in China is very striking, in contrast to the previous dominance of political norms and social values.[26] A vivid summary of Chinese behavior norms in the past five decades (Qiao 1994, 185) illustrates this well:

In the 1950s people helped each other; in the sixties people fixed up [struggled with] each other; in the seventies people lied to each other; in the eighties people took care of themselves only; in the nineties people overcharged each other.

The commercialized social life, in return, is gradually and steadily drifting away from the formerly centralized state control to assert its own autonomy in governing people's social activities. State officialdom, which traditionally monopolized the top position in the economic and social stratification, is now itself heavily eroded by the advancing market force; corruption of some sort, mainly financially motivated, has become an accepted behavioral norm for the majority of the CCP officials.[27] The widespread corruption of the CCP officials has at least partially explained why so many people now have a deep nostalgia for the Mao era.[28] We may not see a full blooming of social liberty in China before the end of the twentieth century. But recent empirical research leads us to believe firmly that Beijing has experienced a tremendous loss of control over much of Chinese social life.[29]

Now, a key to successful completion of modernization, as reflected by our analysis of the changes in the Chinese LAPs, is to cope effectively with the triumphing but inevitably self-destructive market. Sustained *appropriate* social and even political distortions of the market seem inevitable and highly desirable, though not necessarily "rational" from a pure economics viewpoint. A distorted but institutionalized market would eventually differentiate the Chinese economy from the state and social institutions without becoming *the* institution. An authoritarian but competent and autonomous administration by the state, accompanied by construction of a comprehensive and effective legal system, appears to be the political solution. To this end, extraordinary political wisdom, courage, initiatives, and skills are in great demand.

Major Obstructing Problems

Obviously, the arrival of modernity is not guaranteed. A number of obstructing problems may soon delay it. With bad luck, the whole state-led Chinese modernization course could derail. A worst case of degeneration of the process could cost, among other things, millions of lives. The logic of Chinese history has yet to be completely altered and the curse of bloody cycles has yet to be eliminated. Repeated calls from the CCP leadership for a "market socialism with Chinese characteristics"[30] indicates that Beijing has begun to realize more consciously the modernization track and direction they have taken and the possibility of a derailment of the political regime by the advancing market. The actions of the CCP, however, have been rather ineffective and inappropriate, largely because the state has yet to reform itself institutionally to cope with the market properly. The latest CCP efforts at fighting the rampant corruption,[31] for example, are still largely *ad hoc* and old-fashioned administrative measures that are probably doomed to be ineffective in a rapidly advancing but poorly institutionalized market economy. Serious danger exists that the existing institutions of the PRC may shrink or be incapacitated too quickly before any new institutions can be put effectively into place – an institutional implosion or explosion. It would be extremely unfortunate if China "changed" its course, by choice or default, to pursue an easy, "free" but ill-fated market-driven modernization at the end of the twentieth century. Such a pessimistic scenario would be a tragedy for the whole of humankind.

Internal problems[32]
The transaction costs of the historic institutional changes of a nation of 1.2 billion people naturally tend to be formidable. Devastation of the environment and increasing inequality of income, for example, are among the major negatives Chinese modernization has produced.[33] Directly related to our study, however, a major obstructing problem for the modernization has been the difficulty of transferring the hundreds of millions of surplus rural laborers quickly and efficiently.

Data suggest that, even under the strict family planning policy, the Chinese population will continue to grow by 25 million to 30 million every year until the middle of the twenty-first century. The booming TVEs relieved the pressure greatly by absorbing 74.68 million laborers during 1982–92, but the net increase of the Chinese rural labor force was 98.56 million during that period.[34] Creation of new jobs by the TVEs slowed down in the 1990s while the state-owned employers started to turn more and more underemployed workers into unemployed.[35] By mid-1997, there were already more than 14.5 million urban workers (7.5 percent) unemployed; and the rural "real" unemployment rate was 34.8 percent (Hu 1997, 12). The CCP's accelerated effort to reduce state employees (Jiang 1997) may further worsen the urban unemployment situation. The newly developed serious problem of the so-called floating people (*mangliu*), numbered to be 100 million by the late 1990s, began to cause extensive strains in the overall Chinese domestic organizational structure. This problem relates directly to the contradiction of having an efficient market allocation and management of labor in a nation that is filled with unskilled laborers who are unemployed or, more often, underemployed. Muddling through may be a solution but it is likely to be unsatisfactory to everyone. This single problem seems to have the potential explosive energy to destroy the premodern Chinese domestic organizational structure or even a Chinese modernity, were it to exclude large chunks of the population for too long.

Another problem, inferred from our study, appears to be the early and rapid decline of the PRC's central political authority. A major indicator has been the declining health of the central government's budget.[36] The inability of the state to control and manage the emerging market economy would soon deprive modernization of the leadership that is believed to be essential to its success. Many other problems could be alleviated or worsened, depending on the ability and the willingness of the state.[37] The outmoded communist ideology is apparently contributing to the decline of the PRC state as a capable manager of the market economy by limiting its representation and power base.[38] The internal structure of the state is urgently in need of major reforms to regain its legitimacy and capacity in the face of the rapidly advancing market institution. But such reforms appear to be difficult and imply huge risks of an institutional meltdown.

Third, the rise of regionalism poses a potential danger to the development of the Chinese market economy and the future of modernization. Institutional mechanisms useful for social control and market distortion, such as *hukou*, tend to contribute to the decentralization and regionalization of the state's public authority and the national economy.[39] The current development of the CLMs have just reflected that great potential. The increasingly striking gap in technology, growth rate, total income, and per capita income between the densely populated east coast areas and the vast central/western provinces which have most of China's natural resources, could have profound institutional impact on the domestic organizational structure. Even local agencies of the state, such as the courts, have engaged in the now common "local protectionism."[40] Some local law-enforcement agencies even used force to "protect" the wanted local VIPs against their colleagues from other regions.[41] If the CLMs, as this study found, are to be the dominant LAP in the future of China, then some effective reorganization of communities or other creative measures must be undertaken to counter the hazardous drifting apart of east and west.[42] If a Chinese modernity can succeed only in a decentralized or even a split nation, then the process could cause too much turmoil to justify the goal. Before the Chinese could culturally and psychologically change to the point of accepting a federalist political arrangement, modernization would be doomed by destructive forces released by regionalism.

Finally, the poorly institutionalized market institution in China has demonstrated its inevitably chaotic nature and especially an overemphasis on short-term gains. *Ad hoc* bargaining and personalization of economic and political transactions have become behavioral norms for many individuals and organizations in the PRC.[43] The prevalence of uninstitutionalized short-term behavior and rent-seeking not only greatly increases transaction costs, but also fundamentally damages the prospects for a legal system to institutionalize the market institution and, eventually, the differentiated yet interactive economy-polity-social life relationship. Premature consumerism and high expectation in a spectacularly commercialized society have made the Chinese élites, especially the underpaid and underrepresented intellectuals, a generally very impatient and unsatisfied group of able people. The bursting of their suppressed energy could powerfully disrupt the growth of the new institutions and cause an early total collapse of the state. If the institutional legitimization of the emerging market and the new domestic organizational structure could not progress for a prolonged period of time, the risk that *everyone* might spoil the future of a Chinese modernity for their short-term gains would be very high.

External problems

There are some conditions outside China that are unfavorable for Chinese modernization. A West increasingly hostile toward Chinese emmigration and many aspects of Chinese domestic politics[44] could conceivably hamper China's effort to use international resources to facilitate its market-oriented economic development. But, in the absence of a major international war or a Cold War type of international containment against China, the most important external issue that could severely affect China's opening policy and even its whole modernization is the matter of Taiwan.[45]

The Taiwan issue, a "domestic problem" in Beijing's official language, may force the Chinese once again to choose, painfully and at great cost, between opening up and their perceived national sovereignty, and between economic goals and political values. Worse, it could lead to a nationalistic and even bellicose China that might repeat the tragic history of Germany and Japan in their state-led modernization processes in the early twentieth century. Although what has happened in Taiwan's domestic organizational structure is widely and perhaps rightfully perceived to be the future of China, ironically, poor handling of the sensitive Taiwan issue could deprive the Chinese of that future and destroy the future of the Taiwanese.

A *Chinese* Modernity

We may now indulge in imagining what kind of modernity is likely to emerge in China in the not very distant future. Besides the institutional features of a modernity outlined in Chapter 1, a *Chinese* modernity may have the following particular characteristics. Any speculation about the future is inherently risky and subjective. Therefore, some readers may choose to skip this section and come to their own views about the nature of a Chinese modernity.

First, the Chinese market is likely to be strongly distorted or deformed by societal forces, in addition to the apparent political distortions (which may experience further abatement). Segmented community-based markets, especially for the allocation of labor, are likely to be the leading form of the new Chinese market. Social and even political institutions, through a variety of means, will continue to exercise lasting and deep penetrations into the market institution. The distance between the market economy and the social institutions and the state is expected to be close, and the interactions among them frequent and intense. Such a "Chinese" modernity and the route to it contain rich practical as well as theoretical lessons.[46]

Second, under a *Chinese* modernity, individual liberty is not likely to be as emphasized as in some other nations such as the United States. Groups like families, *danweis* (units), and local communities are likely to be more important and influential than individuals in a "modernized" China. A unified and almost singular social hierarchy and authority structure are likely to be maintained along the lines of the traditional patriarchy, reinforced by political power or wealth or both. The Western version of individualistic human rights is unlikely to be fully accepted, much less implemented.

Third, the Chinese polity, even after substantial institutionalization and rationalization, would retain much of its authoritarian tradition. In the near future, we may observe a clear lag of political changes. Political democratization may not fully occur long after an institutionalized differentiation and interaction have emerged among the state, market, and social life. Although the historical route of political development in another Chinese context – Taiwan – in the 1970s to 1990s may serve as a precedent for Chinese politicians, it is by no means guaranteed. Some have argued that political democratization in the East Asian context has produced significant negative implications for both economic growth and organized labor.[47] Willingly drawing from these kinds of "lessons," the Chinese, given their historical biases and distaste for the allegedly "congenital" chaos and disorder of political democracy, may hesitate to alter the internal structure of their polity for as long as possible.

Fourth, given the relatively small endowment of natural resources for the massive population, even if China manages to reach modernity peacefully, the living standard of the average Chinese would not be necessarily as high as those of other "modernized" nations. Modernity does not ensure a certain living standard or a certain level of economic and technological achievement; it only provides the institutional foundation for their maximization. This would perhaps be even more clear under a Chinese modernity. But a modernity will create the possibilities for a maximum achievement of these desirable outcomes in China, too. Therefore, the Chinese economic and technological development, and the Chinese living standard, should eventually approach the levels of any other similarly endowed modernized or "developed" nations. The Chinese plan to reach that goal by the 2030s to 2050s.[48]

Finally, if a federalist political system cannot take root in China,[49] the modernization process is likely to call for a new nationalism, a "patriotism," to strengthen national unity and the central political power of Beijing. A nationalistic, though "modernized," China may have some unforeseen but rather challenging foreign policy goals that deserve the full attention of the world, especially its neighbors.

China and the world

China has entered the nets of the market institutions internally and the international organizational structure externally. A *Chinese* modernity is emerging in this largest nation of the world. Undoubtedly, this grand yet peaceful institutional transformation will be among the greatest examples of development and achievement of human civilization. The economic power and technological innovations of 1.2 billion people likely to be unleashed under a modernized domestic organizational structure will surely shake, if not change, the world. What will a modernized China be? Will China, like some other modernizing nations before it, become an aggressive and even imperial challenger to the existing world organizational structure?

We can only very tentatively offer some speculative answers to these questions. First, based on our understanding of Chinese institutions and their changes, we probably can expect a rather conservative new China in the early twenty-first century. The dominant LAP in China, as described by this book, is likely to be community-based, thus socially and even politically distorted, labor markets. Such an institutional arrangement tends to sanction parochial orientations rather than global or cosmopolitan impulses. An imperialistic impetus may be possible but is likely to be rather limited under such a domestic organizational structure.

Second, in the foreseeable future, the obstructing problems discussed before and more new issues would keep the Chinese focused inward rather than outward. Even the thorny issue of Taiwan, from the Chinese point of view, is still a domestic, not international, issue. We naturally cannot ascertain now what else Beijing might want territorially if it were to establish full control of Taiwan and even the South China Sea islets. But it is rather difficult to see that the Chinese would have the ability and drive to expand territorially beyond their declared objective of "unifying the motherland." The family-like institutional tradition which is likely to continue to be powerful in China tends to stress social values like "just claims" and "propriety" over market values of constant expansion or political values of domination.

Third, there is a possibility, indicated by our analysis, for the Chinese to use their might to demand revisions of the world political and economic order. If a total revitalization of the family-like "Chinese World," which the Chinese used to find so comfortable, has become an impossibility, some institutional changes of the world organizational structure in that direction would be still desirable. Certain radical writings of nationalistic publications in China have hinted at that possible "Chinese" demand. Any efforts aimed at such changes would certainly cause significant conflicts in international relations. But under a modernity which results in the decline or even disappearance of the family-like institutions in China, at least in its economy, a Chinese drive to establish a family-like new world order is unlikely. Without a modernity, the Chinese may have a stronger interest in such a venture, but they would not likely have the ability to attempt it seriously. Modernized nations tend to have similar if not identical basic values. The Chinese absorption and implementation of "Western" values (Wang 1998(B)) have been good indicators.

Finally, the international environment and human knowledge (technology) in the twenty-first century would be more likely to discourage aggressive and disruptive behaviors like those practiced by Germany or Japan in the early twentieth century. Even with modernity, the Chinese are unlikely to become a number-one power in terms of its projectable military capabilities in the foreseeable future. Current military technology, mainly weapons of mass destruction, would force anybody to think twice before resorting to war for any international ambitions. The possibility of demands for reforming certain aspects of the existing world organizational structure from a "modernized" China do not warrant fear of a new superpower, or worse, any preemptive actions that might prove extremely counterproductive. Last but not least, humans can learn, and the international and domestic institutional settings tend to reward those who learn from the past.

In short, to end this book, we have found that the Chinese are proceeding along a state-led modernization track towards a national market economy. As a result of their collective actions, their modernization effort, the Chinese are approaching a modernity that would provide a brand-new institutional environment for 1.2 billion people. Though still not guaranteed to arrive, a *Chinese* modernity has appeared on the horizon. That is indeed profound news for humankind entering a new millennium.

NOTES

1. Others have made similar but somewhat narrower attempts to understand some of the peculiar Chinese behavior in varying historical settings from an institutional perspective. See, for example, Gates 1996.
2. The terminology of institutions and institutional changes used by most Chinese scholars is based primarily upon the early works of American scholars like Douglass North. See, for example, Fan 1990, Lin Yifu 1992, 1994, Wang 1992, and Li Chenggui: "Zhidu yangjiu zhongde rugang lilun wenti," [Some theoretical issues in the study of institutions] in *Jingji wenxian xinxi* [Information on works in economics], Beijing, August-September 1994, 49–56. For a counter-argument, see Cui 1995.
3. Those barriers and gaps are commonly caused by a specious belief that nations are so different that an integrated study of them is meaningless unless we consider first and foremost a variety of national characteristics such as their "culture" and "history." The underdevelopment of social sciences as a coherent science may be partially attributed to such a belief.
4. For an analysis along similar logic, see Robert Wright: "The Evolution of Despair" in *Time*, August 22, 1995, 50–7.

5. For a "conceptual reconstruction" of Chinese political thought that was basically formed in the Qin and Han dynasties (second century BC to second century AD), see Ames 1994.

6. The separation of *"ming"* (名, statement, name, title or words) from *"shi"* (实, reality, deeds, facts or contents) has been a foundation of Chinese pragmatism since the Warring States era (fifth to third centuries BC). The CCP, especially under Mao, utilized this tradition to its greatest advantage. Famous examples include the inventions of terms such as "people's democratic dictatorship" and "workers are the masters and the CCP officials are the servants."

7. For a historical discussion on such a moral dilemma in seventeenth century New England, see Bailyn 1955, 44.

8. By the mid-1990s, the commodity, real estate, information, and even the financial markets were being developed to be the dominant ways of allocating and utilizing those economic resources in the PRC. For a description of the development of those markets in China, see Hu et al. 1993, 475–637, 653–714.

9. According to the World Bank, the International Monetary Fund, and the Chinese government, China's GDP (gross domestic product) grew at an average annual rate of 9.3 percent from 1979 to 1993 (11.8 percent in 1994) while the average world annual rate of economic growth was only 2.6 percent (2.4 percent for the developed nations and 3.1 percent for the developing nations). Eliminating the inflation factor, the Chinese GDP increased 3.76–fold in 15 years. See *China in Brief: Factors Fueling China's Rapid Economic Development*, Beijing, New Star Publishers, 1995, 1–3.

10. Shalendra D. Shama: "Neo-Classic Political Economy and the Lessons from East Asia," in *International Studies Notes*, vol. 20(2), Spring 1995, 22–7.

11. For two semiofficial summaries of the "secrets of the success" of the Chinese reform, see Zhao Yao: "Zhongguo gaige shijian he chenggong aumi" [The secrets of Chinese reform and its success] in *Shehui kexue* [Social sciences], Shanghai, No. 10, 1994, 4–8, and Yang Xianqi: "Zhongguo jing jigaigede jibeng jingyan qianxi" [A preliminary analysis of the basic lessons of the Chinese economic reform], in *Jingji shehui tizhi bijiao* [Comparison of the economic and social systems], Beijing, March 1994, 3–7.

12. For a report on the difficulties caused by the various "nationalist" groups who used Indian "democratic processes" to oppose FDI in that nation, see "India's Economic Nationalists," in *Economist*, London, August 12, 1995, 27–8. The Chinese press also noticed such an "Indian resistance to opening." See the three articles in the full-page *"Haiwai liaowang"* [Overseas observation] column of the *Wenhui Bao* [Wenhui Daily], Shanghai, August 16, 1995, 9.

13. China started in 1995–6 to eliminate all the tax breaks it had granted to the SEZs for almost two decades. Those "abnormal" breaks were used to attract FDI and maintain a controlled regional market economy and "have become unnecessary." In *Renmin Ribao-Overseas*, September 22, 1995, 1. For some empirical reports on the slow-down of the lopsided

or artificial economic development and even recessions in the SEZs by mid-1990s, see *Xinshiji* [New century], Haikou, Hainan, No. 11, 1995, 7–11.

14. As an "industrialized" nation, as so termed by OECD (Organization for Economic Cooperation and Development), Singapore, retained much of the tight social and information control measures Beijing has been working hard to enforce in China. For example, the Singaporean control of cable and satellite TV and "pornographic materials" was very similar to that seen in China. But unlike the much more traditional regime in Beijing, the pragmatic Singaporean government did recognize the "need" for maintaining a government-inspected legal "red-light zone." Author's interviews in Singapore, 1995.

15. A "reportage" published in 1995 vividly demonstrated the effectiveness of the *hukou* institution in social and especially migration control. It described how a rural *hukou* policy branch in Hunan province "worried" about and investigated a newly arrived Buddhist monk who joined a local temple but had a problematic *hukou* identification. See Cao Jiangping ed. *Zhongda anjian zhenpou jishi (B)* [Reports on the resolution of major cases, vol. B.], Xining, Qinghai Renmin Press, 1995, 43–51.

16. Any structural or functional changes of an institution tend to impose strains that could crack it before the new structure or function could be legitimized. For a sociologist's view on this point, see Parsons 1951a, 507–9. For the general political "danger" of institutional changes, see Huntington 1968.

17. Most of the Chinese market-oriented institutional reforms have been put to such experiments first before being implemented nationally. The SEZs are famous cases of "testing points." In 1995–6, for example, Beijing conducted its experiment of state-owned enterprise reform in 159 *danweis*, its social security program in twenty cities, and its medical insurance program in two cities (*Renmin Ribao-Overseas*, September 25, 1995, 1).

18. Deng Xiaoping argued in 1978 that the CCP need to let some people, some enterprises and some regions "get rich first" (Deng Xiaoping 1992, 125). For an elaborated discussion on Deng's "uneven development strategy," see Yuan Enzheng: "Deng Xiaoping de feijunheng fazhan sixian" [The uneven development thought of Deng Xiaoping], in *Mao Zedong Deng Xiaoping lilun yangjou* [Theoretical studies of Mao Zedong and Deng Xiaoping], Shanghai, No. 5, 1994, 60–3.

19. On the one hand, the rise of crime in China has been clear and steady. The government indirectly admitted that there was a 19.75 percent increase of criminal cases in 1994 over 1993 (*Renmin Ribao-Overseas*, March 17, 1995, 1). On the other hand, a widespread sharp sense of insecurity and a justified "overreaction" by people who were used to security under the tight political control eroded people's faith in the authority of the state.

20. The statistical bureau in Shandong province in 1994 surveyed two thousand urban households in twenty-five cities/counties and concluded that the *renqingfei* [fees for human feelings, that is, for connections]

mainly gifts cost on average rose fourteenfold in thirteen years to be 5.6 percent (2.4 percent in 1981) of total household expenditures. *Xinan wanbao* [Xinan evening news], Hefei, June 15, 1995, 6.

21. Based on PPP (purchasing power parity), the World Bank has concluded that China had the third largest economy in the world in 1993. The economic development of China over the past two decades was described as among the "largest and fastest" economic successes in human history (*New York Times*, May 20, 1993, A-1, A-8). Also see World Bank 1994.

22. For a speculation by a group of leading economists from Taiwan and the Mainland on the future of a "greater Chinese economy," see Gang Yuanzhi: "Nianan xuezhe yuce Zhongguo jingji" [Speculation on the Chinese economy by scholars from the two sides of the strait], in *Xinshiji* [New century], Haikou, Hainan, No. 11, 1995, 3–6.

23. IMF reports concluded that the Chinese savings rate from 1989 to 1993 was as high as 35 percent of its GNP. *Xinhua Daily Telegraph*, Geneva, Switzerland, July 8, 1995.

24. *Economist*, London, November 28, 1992. For a feel for the advancing market in the PRC, see the ten-page "special report" of *Business Week*, "China, the Emerging Economic Powerhouse of the Twenty-first Century." New York, May 16, 1993.

25. For example, the state monopoly of steel was lifted in 1994–5.

26. For a vivid description of the seemingly overheated commercialization of social life and premature high consumerism in China, see Lu Xingsheng: "Xiaofei jingbao" [Alarms of consuming], in *Wenhua yu shenghuo* [Culture and life], Shanghai, No. 1, 1994, 12–13.

27. A mayor of a major Chinese city told the author in 1995 that, according to his estimation, so-called "gray income" would count for a substantial amount of total income for "all" PRC officials. Among the more than two hundred cadres the author interviewed or talked to in 1995–96 in seven Chinese cities, very few could credibly show that he or she was clean of all sorts of corrupt activities.

28. The resurgent popularity of the songs of Mao's era has existed in the PRC for most of the 1990s. It is reported that, in an abandoned coal mine in Henan province, two thousand volunteer workers with an approximately 20 million yuan donation built up a majestic temple called "*Sanyuanshi*" (the Temple of Triple Unity) to allow thousands of visitors daily to worship Mao Zedong and his close associates Zhou Enlai and Zhu De as three gods. See Liu Caiwen: "Mao Zedong zaishang shengtan?" [Mao Zedong returned to the divine altar?] in *Liangyu Weekly*, Taiyuan, Shanxi, No. 126, July 8, 1995, 1.

29. A major indicator is that there are now so many open social activities including "illegal publications," independent religious activities, gambling, smuggling, counterfeit products, prostitution, child labor, and of course official corruption that are not sanctioned and even openly criticized by the CCP central government. Author's field notes in China, 1992–7.

30. Jiang Zemin: "Speed Up Reform and Open and Modernize for Greater Victories of Constructing a Socialist Course with Chinese Characteristics," political report to the Fourteenth Congress of the CCP, Beijing,

October 12, 1992. He repeated the same thinking on the issues of "development" and "stability" in his long speech to the CCP's Fifth Plenary Meeting of the Fourteenth Central Committee on September 28, 1995.

31. "The Joint Decision of the CCP Central Committee and the State Council on Anti-Corruption Struggles," October 5, 1993. *Renmin Ribao*, October 23, 1993, 1. For a report on the measures and "successes" of the anti-corruption campaigns, see *Xinhua Daily Telegraph*, Beijing, January 24, 1996.

32. Some Chinese scholars have argued that there were eight "leading problems facing the Chinese economy" including the draining of state assets, stagnation and decline of the state-owned enterprises, and inflation. See Hu Zhaopei: "Woguo jingji miannin de bage wenti" [Eight problems facing our country's economy], in *Zhongguo jingji wenti* [Economic issues of China], Xiamen, No. 3, 1994, 3–13.

33. Some Chinese scholars believe that there were at least "four crises" facing the Chinese modernization effort in the late 1990s: the huge but "low-quality" population, the shortage of resources, the environmental crisis, and the fluctuation of the economic cycles. See Zheng Shiji & Zhang Rui: "Zhongguo shehui chixu fazhan zhanlui" [A sustainable development strategy of Chinese social development], in *Xuehai* [Sea of learning], Nanjing, No. 6, 1994, 34–40. For a discussion on the complexity of the "social problems" in China in the 1990s, see Tong Xin: "Lun dangqian Zhongguo shehui wenti de tediang he duice" [On the character and treatment of the current social problems in China], in *Jianghai xuekan* [Jianghai journal], Nanjing, No. 3, 1994, 36–41. For a report on the frightening environmental pollution in urban China, see A Ji: "Zhongguo chengshi wurang yangzhong" [The severe environmental pollution in urban China], in *Xinshiji* [New century], Haikou, Hainan, No. 11, 1995, 25–31.

34. See Zhang Luxong: "Nongchun gaige he fazhan suominnin de sida nanti" [Four major problems facing rural reform and development], in *Shehui kexue yangjou cankao ziliao* [Materials for social science studies], Chengdu, No. 21, 1994, 1–5. For a Chinese report and analysis of the growing disparity between the haves and the have-nots in the PRC in the 1990s, see Lin Qiping: "Shixi woguode pingfu caiyi" [On the gap between the rich and the poor in our nation] in *Jingji wenti* [Economic issues], Taiyuan, No. 5, 1994, 54–8.

35. Chen Dongqi: "Zhongguo jinhou 15 nian jouye xinshi yuchebaogao" [A forecast of Chinese employment in the next 15 years], in *Caijing kexue* [Financial and economic sciences], *Chengdu*, No. 1, 1995, 1–5.

36. For a discussion on the alarming decline of Beijing's financial power and authority, see Wang & Hu 1994. Recent evidence from the author's field studies, however, has suggested that the CCP leadership has a fairly good understanding of the problem. But judging from the speech by Zhu Rongji, the top CCP leader for economic policies, there seemed to be still serious problems for Beijing to get its "share" of the tax revenues. See *Wenhui Bao* [Wenhui Daily], Shanghai, December 15, 1995, 1. This issue was listed by a group of scholars close to the CCP

leadership as the most serious of all major problems China faced by the late 1990s (Xu 1997).

37. Some young Chinese scholars, becoming aware of this danger, have already started to argue for a restrengthening of the PRC central state's authority and capacity. Hu Angang: "Zhongyang zhengfu zai shichang jingji zhuangxing zhongde zhuyong" [The role of the central government in the transition of the market economy], in *Xuexi* [Study], Beijing, No. 2, 1994, 23–4.

38. The CCP Central Committee recently was reported to have issued a directive to exclude all private business owners and employers from party ranks because the "nature of the party" should not allow capitalists as members. See *Huaxia wenzhe* [China news digest], an Internet Weekly, No. 233, September 15, 1995, 2.

39. The provinces had long ago started their fight for resources. One example is that Beijing was forced by competing provinces to carry out its first ever strict drawing and clarification of provincial and county boundaries, a job Beijing promised to finish by 2001. (*Renmin Ribao*, Beijing, November 16, 1995, 4.)

40. As reflected by the official media. See, for example, *Renmin Ribao-Overseas*, September 19, 1995, 4.

41. Very often, one region's criminal could be a "hero" benefiting the economy of another region thus protected by the local government there. Author's field notes of 1993 and 1995. For a publicized case of how a group of convicted perpetrators of credit card fraud were fiercely protected for more than two years by the local government and police in Henan Province against the warrants issued by the court and the enforcing marshals of the neighboring Hubei Province, see Xiao Yong: "Aozhang Anyang" [Fierce battle in Anyang], in *Shenzhen Fazhibao* [Shenzhen legal daily], Shenzhen, December, 17, 1995, 3.

42. The so-called "river valley-based development" strategy (most Chinese major rivers flow from the west to the east) would be an effective way to reorganize the communities to incorporate the poor river-head areas in the West. Xu Fongxian & Wang Zhengzhong: "Jingti: Quyu fazhan chaju zhubu kuoda" [Warning: The regional gap of development is gradually enlarging], in *Zhonghua gongshan shibao* [China Business Times], Beijing, January 23, 1995, 5. For some other suggestions on closing the regional gaps, including "coupling" of communities between different regions, see Fang Ning: "1996–2010 woguo quyu jingjifazhan de jibeng silu" [Basic ideas on the regional economic development in our nation in 1996–2010], in *Shichang yu fazhan* [Market and development], Chengdu, No. 11, 1994, 16–18.

43. For a conceptual discussion on the widespread "irrational" short-term behavior in today's PRC, see Liu Yunlong: "Shilun rende xinwei jiading yu woguo jingji tizhi gaige" [On the assumptions of human behavior and the reform of our nation's economic system], in *Jingjixue qingbao* [Information on economics], Wuhan, No. 5, 1994, 13.

44. Among others, the Chinese "national policy" of family planning, which has its clear rationality in the Chinese context, has been drawing substantial criticism in the West.

45. For a discussion of the unlikelihood of an international containment against China, see Wang, 1998B.

46. For one example of the "rethinking" on the theoretical implications of Chinese modernization, see Cui Zhiyuan: "The Challenge of the Chinese Practice to the Neo-Classic Political Economy" in *Xianggang shehui Kexue xuebao* [Hong Kong Journal of Social Sciences], special issue, Hong Kong, July 1995, 1–33.

47. For an interesting argument on the negative impact on economic growth by political democratization in Taiwan and Korea, see Tun-jun Cheng: "Economic Consequences of Democratic Transition: The Case of South Korea and Taiwan," a paper presented to the annual meeting of APSA (American Political Science Association), Chicago, September 3, 1995. For two works on the unfavorable conditions for organized labor created by political democratization, see Hyunseog Yu: "Democratization and Labor," a paper presented to the annual meeting of APSA, Chicago, September 1, 1995. Chang-Ling Huang: "Who is Afraid of Corporatism – Labor Control in South Korea and Taiwan," a paper presented to the annual meeting of APSA, Chicago, September 3, 1995.

48. In 1992, Beijing drew up modest criteria for a "*xiaokan*" (comfortable) living standard to be reached by the year 2000: per capita GNP of 2,400 yuan (about $300), daily intake of 2,600 kilocalories and 75 grams of protein, per capita housing space of 15.5 square meters, Engel index of 40 to 49 percent, fewer than five criminal cases per ten thousand people, and life expectancy of 70. See *Xinhua Daily Telegraph*, December 21, 1992, and CCP Anhui Committee: *95 nian Anhui shengqing shouce* [Handbook on Anhui province 1995], an internal publication for cadres, Hefei, 1995, 106–10. By the end of 1995, among the more than two thousand counties/cities, eighty "basically achieved the *xiaokan* level." (*Renmin Ribao-Overseas*, Beijing, January 11, 1996, 8) Chinese scholars speculated that by 2030–50, China could reach the level of important indicators such as per capita GNP that "developed nations" like the United States enjoyed at the end of the twentieth century. See the National Conditions Study Team of the Chinese Science Academy: *Jiyu yu tiaozhan – Zhongguo zhouxian 21 shiji de jingji fazhang mubiao he jibeng fazhang zhanlue yanjou* [Opportunities and challenges: The economic development objectives and basic development strategies of China toward the twenty-first century], Beijing, May 18, 1995.

49. For a Chinese perspective on the relationship between the central and local governments and its reform, see Wu Guoguang & Zheng Yonglian: *Lun zhongyan-difang guanxi* [On the relationship between the central and the local], Hong Kong, Oxford University Press (China), 1996.

Appendix
A Methodological
Discussion on Chinese
Statistical Data

The accuracy of scientific observation is not guaranteed. The famous uncertainty principle of the physicist Werner Heisenberg asserts that some physical events can never be accurately observed because the scientist's intrusive eye changes the event itself. In social sciences, due to the difficulty of replicable experiments, the issue of accuracy and certainty is an even bigger problem. To study a nation as large and complex and with such a long history as China, good statistical analysis may serve as a sharp tool to reveal patterns, trends and basic indicators.

Since it is often difficult and or even practically infeasible for outsiders to conduct large-scale data collection in China, we must rely on the available statistics published by the Chinese themselves. This study has used such data extensively. Yet, as anyone who has studied China in some depth would testify, we must exercise great caution and make significant additional effort in reading the Chinese statistics to reduce the possibility of being misled. An accurate "feel" of China from interviews, and especially prolonged and unobtrusive field studies, is very crucial to a correct reading and use of the Chinese statistical data. Some knowledge of the patterns of distortion in the official statistics is important. A comparison between published (and used by scholars) and the unpublished (or internally published) versions of the same set of statistical data is also very helpful. With those cautions and methodological weighing, even propaganda publications can serve as a valuable source for statistical information on China. Some scholars have proven that we can use Chinese statistical data effectively and see through the apparent confusion and puzzles created by complicated, inaccurate, misleading and even contradictory figures.[1]

Before the PRC years, statistical data collection in China was at best very incomplete. The PRC government, primarily driven by the needs of national economic planning, started to collect and publish statistical data from the early 1950s. On the surface, there appear to be plenty of published statistics about almost every aspect of Chinese politics, economy and social life. Compared to other nations, even the former Soviet Union, however, the PRC's data-collecting agencies were poorly institutionalized and generally had very underdeveloped skills and techniques.[2] More problematically, PRC statistical data, especially the openly published versions, were historically subject to heavy use by politicians for their specific political needs. During the years of the "Great Leap Forward" (1958–61) and the "Cultural Revolution" (1966–76), published Chinese statistical data were so distorted that many figures now appear to be just purely imaginary. The major official newspapers and journals were filled with such fraudulent "statistics" to please Mao and his "left" radicals and to deceive the people.[3]

Although it is difficult to assess, the problematic reliability of certain PRC official statistics, especially those about the rural economy, has been widely recognized. The total number of the Chinese rural labor force, for example, has shown up differently in different official statistics. In 1982, such an "error" was caught by Chinese economists, as there were about 74 million people "missing" from the official data (Zhang et al. 1988, 99–100). Another example has been the important figures of the size of the Chinese cultivated land. Officially, the cultivated land shrank by as much as 5 percent in the 1980s: from 1,710 million *mu* in 1979 to the lowest point of 1,300 million *mu* in 1986. Per capita cultivated land was 2.7 *mu* in 1949 but only 1.2 *mu* by 1994.[4] But these worrisome figures may have been the result of a widespread artificial abridgment by the local officials who desire some "flexibility" in appropriating the land and in reporting an "increased" grain production in the future.[5] Different agencies of the government have officially reported wildly different figures on the size of the arable land in China.[6]

A great deal of information collected by the PRC through its official channels is generally not available to outsiders. The central government, the provincial governments and the official Xinhua News Agency all publish voluminous "internal" periodicals, books, almanacs and handbooks with varied degrees of classification. Careful reading and research may point to the existence of this rich "internal" information, but it is often difficult to use it in an open and academic study. For example, in 1994, there was a six-month national *"laodong yonggong da jiangcha"* [grand inspection on labor and employment].[7] It would be a very rich source of information for understanding current labor and employment issues in the PRC. But so far, only very limited findings of this inspection have been published in a very fragmented and periodical way. We acquired some useful findings of that inspection only through fieldwork and "internal" channels.

Worse, one often finds a huge artificial gap between the published figures and the "internal" numbers – the so-called "water" added in the published statistical data. This added "water" seems to be an identifiable pattern. Some published official statistics tend to have more water than others at a given time. The most diluted statistics appear to be the economic growth rate, the "gross product" and even the profit situation of state-owned enterprises. A classified internal document revealed in early 1995 that there was at least four percentage points of "water" in the 1994 growth rate of the Chinese industrial product. Moreover, because of the low efficiency of the growth (high cost and high amount of unsold goods in stock), absolute gains of 10 percent in the Chinese economy would roughly equal about 1 percent growth of the economies of the United States or Japan. By 2000, the PRC "internally" calculated, even at the current high rate of 9 percent a year, the Chinese GNP – currently $370.5 billion or 7.1 percent of the United States ($5,208.1 billion) and 10.33 percent of Japan ($ 2,976.4 billion) – would be only $877 billion, or 12.53 percent of the United States ($6,999.1 billion at a 3 percent annual growth rate) and 19.53 percent of Japan ($4,491.2 billion at a 4.2 percent growth rate).[8]

Those less sensitive, hard to alter and more verifiable figures, such as population, employment, and the numbers and dollar amounts of FDI, tend to be more accurate and consistent, with less added water. As revealed by a few other internal statistical reports the author acquired, the "good" news in the public press generally tends to be more truthful while the "bad" news often is underreported.[9] An acute understanding of the contemporary political environment and the CCP's policies is very important for assessing the amount of water in a particular set of statistical data.

The political abuse and distortion of statistics subsided somewhat in the past two decades. The basic statistics published by the official media has become generally reliable by the 1990s. With a cautious and critical perspective, the official publications such as *Renmin Ribao*, that were often filled with political lies and fictional statistics in the past, could be used as important sources of information.

Most of the officially collected statistics are no longer treated as national secrets, and both the ethics and methods of data collecting and reporting improved. The State Statistical Bureau (SSB) acquired its ministry level status in 1978 and has been publishing volumes of data with visibly improved accuracy and comprehensiveness. Zhang Sai, the director of the SSB, reported to the National People's Congress on June 28, 1995, that the SSB had improved its work based on international standards since the adaptation of the PRC Statistical Law of 1983. Population figures, grain production, rural per capita income, price index, and so on, are fairly accurate and more objective methods like sampling rather than reports of local cadres have been used by the two (urban and rural) independent "Economic Investigation Teams" of the SSB. But a strong political force exists in "some regions and *danweis*" to inflate or underreport certain information. In 1995, the production of the TVEs was found to be inflated and the birth rate of the rural population was found to be underreported in many areas. The figures of capital construction investment and grain storage were also "inaccurate." Certain "falsification trend in statistical data collection" still existed.[10]

One additional problem for proper use of Chinese statistical data has been that of terminology. For example, in the data used in the Chinese press and official and academic publications, the word "market" is often used loosely. The currently implemented "contract employment" system in the state-owned *danweis* has been called a "labor market" even by some of the best Chinese economists (Hu 1993, 649). But such a contract employment system, at best, is still just a modified authoritarian state LAP (Wang 1998, Chapter 2). Careless reading without a good understanding of terms and categories would, therefore, very easily mislead outside observers. Related to the issue of terminology, there has been a strong methodological bias in data collecting and reporting. Recently, survey-type polling and statistical investigation have developed in the PRC. But those surveys have been heavily biased against the rural population, the majority of the Chinese people. The samples are basically all urban residents. A pollster, the "*Lingdian* Corporation" in Beijing, concluded in 1995 that published survey results in today's PRC only represent about 120 million people who live in the major cities and the SEZs, out of a nation of 1.2 billion.[11]

Besides political interference, the inadequacy of objective standards and reliable techniques, and the problem of terminology, some uniquely "Chinese" factors may have contributed to the difficulty of data collection and record-keeping. One is the historical habit of approximation in Chinese archives. There are many examples of this tendency. Often the size of military forces, the number of famine deaths, or the size of mass gatherings was conveniently "rounded up." This inaccuracy and exaggeration, fortunately, now seems to be on the decline. But the subtle yet persistent impact of this tradition must be taken into consideration. One could easily encounter, in field studies, such approximation habit and the additional difficulty it often causes.

In the light of the above discussion, this study, like many other studies on China, has attempted to exercise special caution in using Chinese official statistical data. Combined with a good "feel" for China based on extensive and in-depth fieldwork and certain access to internal versions of the data in question, we are confident that official data can be used effectively as a major source of information in our academic exploration of China.

NOTES

1. See Nicholas Lardy's persuasive analysis on the real size of the Chinese GNP and the "openness" of the Chinese economy (1991, 150–5). For a discussion on the problem of underestimation (the real size may be four times larger than the official figures) of the Chinese GNP and per capita GNP, see Brugger & Reglar 1994, 83–4.
2. Yesheng Huang: "Information, Bureaucracy, and Economic Reforms in China and the Soviet Union," in *World Politics*, Princeton, NJ, vol. 47(1), October 1994, 102–34.
3. The official newspaper of the CCP, *Renmin Ribao*, published some "statistics" during the years of the Leap Forward that soon became common laughingstock. For example, it reported on September 18, 1958, that in Guangxi Province, the rice production "leaped" to the level of 130 thousand *jin* (about 143.3 thousand pounds or 65 metric tons) per *mu* (about 0.165 acre).
4. "Year-end Report" in *Xinhua Daily Telegraph*, Beijing, December 19, 1994.
5. One reporter concluded that in some areas, the "hidden" cultivated land can be as much as 50 to 75 percent of the reported acreage. See Ma Yuejun: "Huang tudi, he tudi" [Yellow land, black land], in Liu Ying ed.: *Dangdai Zhongguo yeshenghuo – Dangdai Zhongguo redian xiezhen chongshu* [Night life in contemporary China – The series on the hot issues in contemporary China], Beijing, Huayi Press, 1993, 8–9.

6. The gap between the SSB and the State Land management Bureau was reported to be 30 percent. Li Xiguan & Ni Xiaoyang eds: *Ji e hui chongxin kouxiang zhongguo de damen man?* [Will famine knock on the door of China again?], Beijing, Gaige Press, 1996, 80.

7. Some information about this event can be found in *Jingji Ribao* [Economic Daily], Beijing, Nov. 6, 1994, 7.

8. The published figure for Chinese industrial growth in 1994, 18 percent, was in the SSB's Statistical Communique on the 1994 Chinese Economy, in *Renmin Ribao*, March 2, 1995, 2. The actual growth rate of Chinese industry, according to this internal document, was less than 14 percent (the classified report by the chief of the State Economic and Trade Commission, January 1995.)

9. The classified reports of the State Council on economic and trade situations in the PRC by the State Planning Commission, the State Economic and Trade Commission, and the Ministry of Internal Trade respectively, Beijing, July 1995.

10. *Renmin Ribao-Overseas*, June 29, 1995, 4.

11. *Shijie Ribao* [World Journal], New York, July 18, 1995, A11.

Bibliography

Abrahamsson, Bengt: *The Logic of Organizations*, Newbury Park, CA, Sage, 1993.

Agrawal, Pradeep et al.: *Economic Restructuring in East Asia and India : Perspectives on Policy Reform*, London, Macmillan Press, 1995.

Almond, Gabriel A. & James S. Coleman: *The Politics of Developing Areas*, Princeton, Princeton University Press, 1960.

Alesina, Alberto & Enrico Spolaore: *On the Number and Size of Nations*, Working Paper No. 5050 of the National Council on Economic Research, Cambridge, MA, 1995.

Alt, James E. & Kenneth Shepsle: *Perspectives on Positive Political Economy*, New York, Cambridge University Press, 1990.

Ames, Roger T.: *The Art of Rulership: A Study of Ancient Chinese Political Thought*, Albany, NY, SUNY Press, 1994.

Amin, Samir: *Accumulation on a World Scale*, New York, Monthly Review Press, 1974.

Arrow, Kenneth J.: "The Division of Labor in the Economy, the Polity, and Society" in O'Driscoll Jr, Gerald ed.: *Adam Smith and Modern Political Economy*, Ames, IA, The Iowa State University Press, 1979.

Bachman, David: *Bureaucracy, Economy, and Leadership in China*, New York, Cambridge University Press, 1991.

Bailyn, Bernard: *The New England Merchants in the Seventeenth Century*, Cambridge, MA, Harvard University Press, 1955.

Barnett, Robert W.: *Wandering Knights: China Legacies, Lived and Recalled*, New York, M.E. Sharpe, 1990.

Becker, Gary Stanley: *The Economic Approach To Human Behavior*, Chicago, University of Chicago Press, 1976.

—— *A Treatise on the Family*, Cambridge, MA, Harvard University Press, 1981.

Bendix, Reinhard: *Nation-building and Citizenship*, Berkeley, CA, University of California Press, [1964] 1977.

—— "Tradition and Modernity Reconsidered" in *Comparative Studies in Society and History*, April, 1967.

Berliner, Joseph: *Factory and Manager in the USSR*, Cambridge, MA, Harvard University Press, 1957.

Bian, Yanjie: *Work and Inequality in Urban China*, Albany, NY, SUNY Press, 1994.

Bianco, Lucien: *The Origins of the Chinese Revolution*, Stanford, CA, Stanford University Press, [1967] 1971.

Black, Cyril E.: *The Dynamics of Modernization*, New York, Harper & Row, 1960.

Black, Antony, *Guilds and Civil Society in European Political Thought from the Twelfth Century to the Present*, London & New York, Methuen, 1984.

Breiger, Ronald L.: *Social Mobility and Social Structure*, New York, Cambridge University Press, 1990.

Brugger, Bill & Stephen Reglar: *Politics, Economy, and Society in Contemporary China*, Stanford CA, Stanford University Press, 1994

Brunner, Karl & Allan H. Meltzer eds: *Stabilization Policies and Labor Markets*, Amsterdam, North-Holland, 1988

Buzan, Barry et al.: *The Logic of Anarchy*, New York, NY, Columbia University, 1993.

Byrd, William A. & Lin Quinsong: *China's Rural Industry: Structure, Development, and Reform*, New York, Oxford University Press, 1990.

Cardoso, F.H. & Enzo Faletto: *Dependency and Development in Latin America*, Berkeley, CA, University of California Press, 1979.

Chan, Anita et al.: *Chen Village, under Mao and Deng*, Berkeley, CA, University of California Press, 1992.

Chandler, A.: *The Visible Hand*, Cambridge, MA, Harvard University Press, 1974.

Chase-Dunn, Christopher: "Interstate System and Capitalist World Economy: One Logic or Two?" in *International Studies Quarterly*, 25(1), 1981.

—— *Global Formation: The Structure of the World Economy*, New York, Basil Blackwell, 1989.

—— "The Limits of Hegemony: Capitalism and Global State Formation," in David Rapkin ed.: *World Leadership and Hegemony*, Boulder, CO, Rienner, 1990.

Chen, Junjie: "Jiazu chuantong yu nongcun qiye de jiazuhua" [Family tradition and the familization of the rural enterprises] in *Shehuixue yu shehui diaocha* [Sociology and social investigation], Beijing, 1994 (2): 57–9.

Clark, Hugh: *Community, Trade, and Networks: Southern Fujian Province from the Third to the Thirteenth Century*, New York, Cambridge University Press, 1991.

Cole, Robert E.: *Japanese Blue Collar: The Changing Tradition*, Berkeley, CA, University of California Press, 1971

—— *Work, Mobility, and Participation – A Comparative Study of American and Japanese Industry*, Berkeley, CA, University of California Press, 1979.

Connolly, William E: *Political Theory and Modernity*, Ithaca, NY, Cornell University Press, 1993.

Cook, Linda: *The Soviet Social Contract and Why It Failed: Welfare Policy and Workers' Politics from Brezhnev to Yeltsin*, Cambridge, MA, Harvard University Press, 1993.

Coughlin, Richard M.: *Morality, Rationality, and Efficiency: New Perspective on Socio-Economics*, Armonk, NY, M.E. Sharpe, 1991.

Cowen, Tyler ed.: *The Theory of Market Failure: A Critical Examination*, Fairfax, VA, George Mason University Press, 1988.

Cox, Robert W.: *Production, Power, and World Order*, New York, Columbia University Press, 1987.

Cui, Zhiyuan: "Market Incompleteness, Innovation, and Reform," in *Politics and Society,* March 1991.

—— *Dierci sixiang jiefang yu zhidu chuanxin* [Second liberation of thinking and institutional innovation], Hong Kong, Oxford University Press (China), 1995.

Dahl, Robert, *After the Revolution?* Yale University Press, 1970.

—— *Polyarchy: Participation and Opposition*, Yale University Press, 1971.

—— *Democracy and Its Critics*, New Haven, CT, Yale, 1989.

Davis, Deborah & Steven Harrell: *Chinese Families in the Post-Mao Era*, Berkeley, CA, University of California Press, 1993.

De Bary, Wm. Theodore et al. eds: *Sources of Chinese Tradition*, Two vols, Columbia University Press, 1960.

Delaney, C.E. ed.: *The Liberalism-Communitarianism Debate*, Lanham, MD, University Press of America, 1994.

De Neubourg, Chris: *Unemployment, Labour Slack and Labour Market Accounting: Theory, Evidence and Policy*, Amsterdam, North-Holland, 1988.

Deng, Yunte: *Zhongguo jouhuang shi* [Chinese history of famine relief], Shanghai, Shanghai Books, [1937] 1984.

Deng, Xiaoping: *Speeches and Writings*, Oxford, Pergamon Press, 1984.

—— *Deng Xiaoping wenxun* [Selected works of Deng Xiaoping], vol. 1, Beijing, Renmin Press, 1985; vol. 2, Beijing, Renmin Press, 1992.

Denham, Mark E. & Mark Owen Lombardi: *Perspectives on Third-World Sovereignty*, New York, St. Martin's Press, 1996.

Dittmer, Lowell: *China Under Reform: A Preliminary Reassessment*, Boulder, CO, Westview Press, 1993.

—— ed.: *China's Quest for a National Identity*, Ithaca, NY, Cornell University Press, 1993.

Domenach, Jean-Luc: *The Origins of the Great Leap Forward: The Case of One Chinese Province*, Boulder, CO, Westview, 1995.

Duara, Prasenjit: *Culture, Power and the State: Rural Society in North China, 1900–1942*, Stanford, Stanford University Press, 1988.

Dunning, John et al.: *Economic Analysis and the Multinational Enterprise*, London, Allen & Unwin, 1974.

—— ed.: *Multinational Enterprises, Economic Structure*, Wiley, New York, 1985.

Ebrey, Patricia Buckley & James L. Watson eds: *Kinship Organization in Late Imperial China, 1000–1940*, Berkeley, University of California Press, 1986.

Eckstein, Alexander: *Communist China's Economic Growth and Foreign Trade*, New York, McGraw-Hill, 1966.

Eisenstadt, Shmuel Noah: *Social Differentiation and Stratification*, Glenview, IL, Scott Foresman, 1971.

—— *Tradition, Change, and Modernity*, New York, Wiley, 1973.

Elster, Jon: "The Necessity and Impossibility of Simultaneous Economic and Political Reform" in Douglas Greenberg et al. eds: *Constitutionalism and Democracy*, Oxford, Oxford University Press, 1993.

—— & Karl Moene eds: *Alternatives to Capitalism*, New York, Cambridge University Press, 1989.

Ensminger, Jean: *Making a Market: The Institutional Transformation of an African Society*, New York, Cambridge University Press, 1992.

Epstein, Edward C. ed.: *Labor Autonomy and the State in Latin America*, Boston, MA, Unwin Hyman, 1989.

Esherick, Joseph W. & Mary B. Rankin eds: *Chinese Local Elites and Patterns of Dominance*, Berkeley, CA, University of California Press, 1990.

Esping-Andersen, Costa ed.: *Changing Classes: Stratification and Mobility in Post-Industrial Societies*, New York, Sage, 1993.

Etzioni, Amitai: *The Moral Dimension: Toward a New Economics*, New York, The Free Press, 1988.
—— & Eva Etzioni eds: *Social Change*, New York, Basic Books, 1964.
Evans, Peter: *Dependent Development, the Alliance of Multinational, State and Local Capital in Brazil*, Princeton University Press, 1979.
—— et al. eds: *States Versus Markets in the World-System*, Beverly Hills, Sage, 1985.
Fairbank, John King et al.: "Economic Changes in Early Modern China: An Analytic Framework," in *Economic Development and Cultural Change*. October 1960.
Fairbank, John K. & Kwang-Ching Liu eds: *The Cambridge History of China, vol. 10, Late Ch'ing 1800–1911, Part I*, New York, Cambridge University Press, 1978.
—— *The Cambridge History of China, vol. 11, Late Ch'ing 1800–1911, Part II*, New York, Cambridge University Press, 1980.
Fan, Gang: *Gongyouzhi hongguan jingji lilun dagang* [A theoretical outline for the macroeconomics of the public-owned economy], Shanghai Press, 1990.
Fan, Wenlan: *Zhongguo tongshi jianbian* [Brief history of China], Renmin Press. Beijing, vol. 1. (1957), vol. 2 (1957), vol. 3 (1965) the rest, 1978.
Fei, Xiaotong: *Xiao chengzhen siji* [Four records of small towns], Beijing, Xinhua Press, 1985.
Forbath, William: *Law and the Shaping of the American Labor Movement*, Cambridge, MA, Harvard University Press, 1991
Frank, Andre Gunder, *Capitalism and Underdevelopment in Latin America*, New York, NY: Monthly Review Press, 1967.
Freeman, John. R.: *Democracy and Markets: The Politics of Mixed Economies*, Ithaca, NY, Cornell University Press, 1990.
Freeman, Richard B.: *Labor Markets in Action*, Cambridge, MA, Harvard University Press, 1989.
Friedman, David: *The Misunderstood Miracle: Industrial Development and Political Change in Japan*, Ithaca, NY, Cornell University Press, 1990.
Friedman, Edward et al.: *Chinese Village, Socialist State*, New Haven, CT, Yale University Press, 1991.
Fu, Yunlong et al.: *Shehui zhuyi shichang jingji yu chuantong wenhua* [Socialist market economy and traditional culture], Beijing, Central CCP School Press, 1995.
Furtak, Robert: *The Political Systems of the Socialist States*, New York. St Martin's Press, 1988.
Gai, Jun: *Zhongguo gongren yundong shi jiaocai, 1919–1949* [Textbook on the Chinese labor movement, 1919–1949], Shanghai, Huadong Shida Press, 1988.
Gao, Shangquan et al. eds: *1993 zhongguo jingji tizhi gaige nianjian* [Yearbook of economic reform in China, 1993], Beijing, Gaige Press, 1993.
Garon, Sheldon: *The State and Labor in Modern Japan*, Berkeley, CA, University of California Press, 1987.
Gates, Hill: *China's Motor: A Thousand Years of Petty Capitalism*, Ithaca, NY, Cornell University Press, 1996.
Gerschenkron, Alexander: *Economic Backwardness in Historical Perspectives*, Cambridge, MA, Harvard University Press, 1964.

Giddens, Anthony: *Durkheim on Politics and the State*, Stanford, CA, Stanford University Press, 1986.

—— *The Consequences of Modernity*, Stanford, CA, Stanford University Press, 1990.

Gleick, James: *Chaos: Making a New Science*, New York, Viking, 1987.

Gold, Thomas B.: "After Comradeship: Personal Relations in China Since the Cultural Revolution" in *China Quarterly*, December 1985.

—— *State and Society in Taiwan Miracle*, Armonk, NY, M.E. Sharpe, Inc. 1986.

Goldstein, Avery: "The Domain of Inquiry in Political Science: General Lessons from the Study of China," *Polity*, Spring, 1989.

—— *From Band-Wagon to Balance of Power*, Stanford, Stanford University Press, 1990.

Gordon, Andrew: *The Evolution of Labor Relations in Japan, 1853–1955*, Cambridge, MA, Harvard University Press, 1985.

—— *Labor and Imperial Democracy in Prewar Japan*. Berkeley, CA, University of California Press, 1991.

Gould, Carol: *Marx's Social Ontology: Individual and Community in Marx's Theory of Social Reality*, Cambridge, MA, MIT, 1978.

Gourevitch, Peter A.: *Politics in Hard Times – Comparative Responses to International Economic Crises,* Ithaca, Cornell University Press, 1988

Grafstein, Robert: *Institutional Realism: Social and Political Constraints on Rational Actors*, New Haven, CT, Yale University Press, 1992.

Granick, David: "Multiple Labour Markets in the Industrial State Enterprise Sector," in *China Quarterly*, January 1991, 269–89.

Greenfield, Liah: *Nationalism: Five Roads to Modernity*, Cambridge, MA, Harvard University Press, 1992.

Griffin, Keith: *Institutional Reform and Economic Development in the Chinese Countryside*, Armonk, NY, M.E. Sharpe, 1984.

Grove, Linda & Christian Daniels eds: *State and Society in China – Japanese Perspective on Ming-Qing Social and Economic History*, Tokyo, University of Tokyo Press, 1984.

Guo, Moruo et al.: *Zhongguo nuli zhi yu fengjianzhi fenqi wenti lunwen xuanji* [Collections of the timing of slavery and feudal systems in China], Beijing, Sanlian Press, 1956.

Gupta, Kanhaya L.: *Industrialization and Employment in Developing Countries: A Comparative Study*, London, Routledge, 1989.

Hass, Ernst B.: *Beyond the Nation-State: Functionalism and International Organization*, Stanford, CA, Stanford University Press, 1964.

——"Regime Decay: Conflict Management and International Organizations, 1945–1981," *International Organization*, Spring 1983.

Habermas, Jürgen: *Knowledge and Human Interest*, Boston, MA, Beacon Press, 1971.

—— *Theory and Practice*, Boston, MA, Beacon Press, 1973.

—— "Toward a Reconstruction of Historical Materialism" in *Theory and Society*, vol. 2, 1975.

—— *Communication and the Evolution of Society,* Boston, MA, Beacon Press, 1979.

—— *The Philosophical Discourse of Modernity*, Boston, MA, MIT Press, 1987.

—— *On Society and Politics*, Boston, MA, Beacon Press, 1989.

Hadenius, Axel: *Democracy and Development*, New York, Cambridge University Press, 1992.

Haferkamp, Hans ed.: *Social Change and Modernity*, Berkeley, CA, University of California Press, 1992.

Haggard, Stephan: *Pathways from the Periphery – The Politics of Growth in the Newly Industrialized Countries*, Ithaca, NY, Cornell University Press, 1990.

—— & Robert R. Kaufman: *The Political Economy of Democratic Transition*, Princeton, Princeton University Press, 1995.

Hall, Peter: *Governing the Economy: The Politics of State Intervention in Britain and France*, New York, Oxford University Press, 1986.

Harding, Harry: "Book Review: On Chinese Studies and Scholars," *World Politics*, January 1984.

—— *China's Second Revolution*, Washington, DC, Brookings Institution, 1987.

Harrison, David: *The Sociology of Modernization and Development*, Boston, Unwin Hyman, 1988.

Harrison, Lawrence: *Who Prospers? How Cultural Values Determine Economic and Political Success*, New York, Basic Books, 1993.

Harrod, Jeffrey: *Power, Production, and the Unprotected Worker*, New York, Columbia University Press, 1987.

Hartland-Thunberg, Penelope: *China, Hong Kong, Taiwan, and the World Trading System*, New York, St. Martin's Press, 1988.

Hayek, F.A.: *The Fatal Conceit: The Errors of Socialism*, Chicago, The University of Chicago Press, 1990.

He Xin: "Dui xiandaihua yu chuantong wenhua de zaisikao" [A rethinking on the issues of modernization and tradition], in *Shehui kexue jikan* [Collections of social sciences], Beijing, No. 2, 1987.

—— *Zhongguo wenhuashi xinlun* [New thought on Chinese cultural history], Beijing, 1990.

Held, David: *Political Theory and the Modern State*, Stanford, Stanford University Press, 1990.

Heller, Agnes: *The Theory of Need in Marx*, translated by Allison & Rusby, New York, St. Martin's, [1974] 1976.

—— "On Formal Democracy," in John Keane ed. *Civil Society and the State*, London & New York, Verso, 1988, 129–46.

—— *Can Modernity Survive?* Berkeley, University of California Press, 1990.

Herzberg, Frederick et al.: *The Motivation to Work*, 2nd Ed, New York, John Wiley & Sons, 1959.

Hirschman, Albert O. *Essays in Trespassing*, Cambridge, Cambridge University Press, 1981.

—— *A Bias for Hope: Essays on Development and Latin America*. Boulder, CO, Westview, 1985.

—— *Rival Views of Market Society*, Cambridge, MA, Harvard University Press, 1992.

Hoffmann, Charles: *The Chinese Worker*, Albany, NY, SUNY Press, 1974.

Howard, Pat: *Breaking the Iron Rice Bowl*, Armonk, NY, M.E. Sharpe, 1988.

Howe, Christopher & Kenneth Walker: *The Foundations of the Chinese Planned Economy*, Basingstoke, Macmillan, 1989.

Howell, Jude: *China Opens its Doors: The Politics of Economic Transition*, Boulder, CO, Lynne Rienner, 1993.

Hsü, Immanuel C.Y.: *The Rise of Modern China*, 5th ed, New York, Oxford University Press, 1995.

Hu, Angang: *Tiaozhan Zhongguo: Denghou zhongnanhai mianlin de jiyu yu xuanze* [Challenge China: Opportunities and options for the post-Deng CCP leadership], Taipei, Xinxinwen Press, 1995.

—— "Xunquo xinde ruanzhuolu: jiangdi gaoshiyeleu shi jinhou hongguan tiaokong de shouyao renwu" (Seek a new soft landing: to reduce the high unemployment rate is the chief task of macro-regulations in the future), *Liaowang* (Outlook), Beijing, No. 31, 1997.

Hu, Ping et al. eds.: *Zhongguo shichang jingji quanshu* [The comprehensive book on the Chinese market economy], Beijing, Huaxia Press, 1993.

Hu, Rulei: *Zhongguo fengjian shehui xingtai yanjou* [A study on the structure of the Chinese feudal society], Beijing, Sanlian Press, 1979.

Hua, Shan: *Songshi lunji* [On the history of Song], Jinan, Qilu Books, 1982.

Huang, Daoxia et al. eds: *Zhonghua renmin gongheguo dashiji 1949–1989* [The chronicle of the PRC], Beijing, Guangming Daily Press, 1989.

Huang, Philip C.C.: *The Peasant Family and Rural Development in the Yangzi Delta, 1350–1988*, Stanford, CA, Stanford University Press, 1990.

Huang, Shu-min: *The Spiral Road: Changes in a Chinese Village*. Boulder, Colo. Westview Press. 1989.

Huang, Xiyuan, *Zhongguo jinxiandai nongyi jingji shi* (Modern history of agriculture in China), Zhengzhou, Henan Renmin Press, 1986.

Huntington, Samuel: *Political Order in Changing Societies*, New Haven, CT, Yale University Press, [1968] 1970.

—— et al.: *No Easy Choice*, Cambridge, MA, Harvard University Press, 1971.

Inglehart, Ronald, *Modernization and Pastmodernization: Cultural, Economic, and Political Change in 43 Societies*, Princeton, NJ, Princeton University Press, 1997.

Inkeles, Alex & David H. Smith: *Becoming Modern: Individual Change in Six Countries*, Cambridge, MA, Harvard University Press, 1974.

International Labour Office (ILO): *World Labour Report, 1–2*, Oxford University Press, 1987.

Jacobson, Harold & Michal Oksenberg: *Toward a Global Economic Order: China's Participation in the IMF, the World Bank, and GATT*, Boulder, CO, Westview Press, 1989.

Janoski, Thomas: *The Political Economy of Unemployment*, Berkeley, CA, University of California Press, 1990.

Jian, Bezan: *Qinghang shi* [The history of Qing and Hang], Hong Kong, China Books Press, 1984.

Jiang, Zemin: *Zhonggong shisida zhengzhi baogao* [The political report to the Fourteenth National Congress of the CCP], Beijing, Renmin Press, 1992.

—— *Zhonggong shiwuda zhengzhi baogao* (The political report to the Fifteenth National Congress of the CCP). Beijing, Renmin Press, 1997.

Jin, Guangtao: *Zhongguo de chao wendingxing jiegou* [The Chinese super-stability structure], Beijing, Dabeiku Press, 1987.

Johnson, Chalmers: *Peasant Nationalism and Communist Power*, Stanford, CA, Stanford University Press, 1962.

—— *MITI and the Japanese Miracle: The Growth of Industrial Policy, 1925–1975*, Stanford, Stanford University Press, 1982.

Jowitt, Kenneth: "An Organizational Approach to the Study of Political Culture in Marxist-Leninist Systems," in *American Political Science Review*, September 1974.

—— "Soviet Neo-Traditionalism: The Political Corruption of a Leninist Regime," in *Soviet Studies*, July 1983.

Kane, Anthony J. et al.: *China Briefing, 1990*, Boulder, CO, Westview Press, 1990.

Katzenstein, Peter J.: *Small States in World Markets: Industrial Policy in Europe*, Ithaca, NY, Cornell University Press, 1985.

Kautsky, John H.: *The Political Consequences of Modernization*, New York, John Wiley & Sons, [1972] 1980.

Keane, John ed.: *Civil Society and the State: New European Perspective*, London & New York, Verso. 1988a.

—— *Democracy and Civil Society*, London & New York, Verso. 1988b.

Keleinberg, Robert: *China's "Opening" to the Outside World: The Experiment with Capitalism*, Boulder, CO, Westview Press, 1990.

Kelliher, Daniel: *Peasant Power in China: The Era of Reform, 1979–1989*, New Haven, CT, Yale University Press, 1992.

King, Gary, Robert O. Keohane, and Sidney Verba: *Designing Social Inquiry: Scientific Inference in Qualitative Research*, Princeton, NJ, Princeton University Press, 1994.

Knight, Jack: *On Institutions and Social Conflict*, New York, Cambridge University Press, 1992.

Knox, F.: *Labour Supply in Economic Development*, Westmead, UK, Saxon House, 1979.

Kornai, Janos: *The Economics of Shortage*, Amsterdam. North-Holland, 1980.

—— *The Road to a Free Economy*, New York, Norton, 1990.

—— *The Political Economy of Socialist Systems*, Princeton, NJ, Princeton University Press, 1992.

Korzec, Michael: *Labour and the Failure of Reform in China*, London, Macmillan, 1992.

Kowalewski, David: *Global Establishment*, New York, St. Martin's Press, 1996.

Krasner, Stephen ed.: *Structural Conflict*. University of California Press, Berkeley, Calif. 1985.

Kratochwil, F.V.: "On the Notion of 'Interest' in International Relations," *International Organization*, Winter, 1982.

—— "Regimes, Interpretation and the 'Science' of Politics," *Millennium*, No. 2, 1988.

—— *Rules, Norms and Decisions*, Cambridge, Cambridge University Press, 1989.

Kratochwil, Friedrich & Edward Mansfield: *International Organization, A Reader*, New York, Harper-Collins College Publishers, 1994.

Kraus, Willy: *Economic Development and Social Change in the People's Republic of China*, New York, Springer-Verlag, 1982.

Krueger, Anne O. et al. eds.: *Trade and Employment in Developing Countries*, vol. 1, *Individual Studies* and vol. 2 *Factor Supply and Substitution*, Chicago, The University of Chicago Press, 1981 & 1982.

Lardy, Nicholas: *Foreign Trade and Economic Reform in China*, New York, Cambridge University Press, 1991.

Lavigne, Marie: *International Political Economy and Socialism*, New York, Cambridge University Press, 1990.

Lawson, Key: *The Human Polity: A Comparative Introduction to Political Science*, 3rd edn., Boston, Houghton Mifflin Co, 1993.

Lee, Hong Yung: *From Revolutionary Cadres to Party Technocrats in Socialist China*, New Haven, CT, Yale Press, 1990

Le Grand, Julian & Saul Estrin eds: *Market Socialism*, New York, Oxford University Press, 1989.

Lehmbruch, Gerhard: "Liberal Corporatism and Party Government," in *Comparative Politics Studies*, April, 1977.

—— "Corporation and the Structure of Corporatist Networks," in Goldthorpe, J. ed., *Order and Conflict in Contemporary Capitalism*, London: Clarendon Press, 1984.

Lerner, Daniel: *The Passing of Traditional Society*, New York, Free Press, 1958.

Levitan, A. et al.: *Human Resources and Labor Market. Labor and Manpower in the American Economy*, New York, Harper & Row, 1972.

Lewis, John Wilson ed.: *Party, Leadership and Revolutionary Power in China*, Cambridge, Cambridge University Press, 1970.

—— *Political Networks and the Chinese Policy Process*, Stanford, CA, Stanford University Press, 1987.

Li, Chenggui: "Chuantong nongcun shehui zongfa zhidu de lixing senshi" [A rational examination of the patriarchy system in traditional rural society], in *Minsu yanjiu* [Folklore studies], Jinan, 1994: 1–4, 38.

Li, Lanqing ed.: *Zhongguo liyong waizi jichu zhishi* [Basic knowledge on using foreign investment], with the preface by Jiang Zemin, Beijing, CCP Central School Press, 1995.

Liang, Chuanyun ed.: *The Guidebook for Managing Private Enterprises in China*, Beijing, Beijing University Press, 1990.

Lieberthal, Kenneth & David M. Lampton eds: *Bureaucracy, Politics, and Decision Making in Post-Mao China*, Berkeley, CA, University of California Press, 1991.

Lieberthal, Kenneth & Michael Oksenberg: *Policy Making in China – Leaders, Structures, and Process*, New Haven, CT, Yale Press, 1990.

Lin, Ganquan: "On the Economic Basis of Feudal Absolutism in Qin and Han," in *Qinhan shi lunchong* [On the history of Qin and Han], Xian, Shangxi Renmin Press, 1983.

Lin, Yifu: "Guanyu zhidu bianqian de lilun" [On the theory of institutional changes] in *Caichan quanli yu zhidu bianqian* [Property rights and institutional changes], Shanghai, Sanlian Press, 1992.

—— *Zhidu, jishu yu Zhongguo nongye fazhan* [Institution, technology, and the agricultural development in China], Shanghai, Sanlian Press, 1994.

Lindblom, Charles E.: *Politics and Markets: The World's Political-Economic Systems*, New York, Basic Books, 1977
—— ed.: *Democracy and Market System*, New York, Oxford University Press, 1991.

Lishisuo (The Institute of History, Chinese Social Science Academy) ed.: *Zhongguo ziben zhuyi mengya wenti lunwen ji* [On the sprouts of Chinese capitalism], three vols, Beijing, Renmin Press, 1963–5.

Little, Daniel: *Understanding Peasant China*, New Haven, CT, Yale Press, 1989.

Liu, Binyan: *China's Crisis, China's Hope*, Cambridge, MA, Harvard University Press, 1990.

Liu, Shaoqi: *Collected Works of Liu Shao-Chi 1958–1967*, Hong Kong, Union Research Institute, 1968.

Lomasky, Loren: *Persons, Rights, and the Moral Community*, New York, Oxford University, 1987.

Loveridge, R. & A.L. Mok: *Theories of Labour Market Segmentation: A Critique*, The Hague, Martin Nijhof, 1979.

Lu, Simian: *Qinahan shi* [The history of Qin and Han], Shanghai, Kaiming Books, 1947.

Lyons, T.: *Economic Integration and Planning in Maoist China*, Columbia University Press, 1987.

Mansbridge, Jane J. ed.: *Beyond Self-Interest*, Chicago, The University of Chicago Press, 1990.

Mao, Zedong: *Mao Zedong xuanji* [Selected works of Mao Zedong, 1949–1966], vols. 1–5, Beijing, Renmin Press, 1973–8.

Marglin, Stephen & Juliet Schor ed.: *The Golden Age of Capitalism: Reinterpreting the Postwar Experience*, New York, Oxford University Press, 1993.

Marx, Karl & F. Engels: *Selected Works*, London, Lawrence & Wishart, 1968.

Maslow, A.H.: "'Higher' and 'Lower' Needs," *Journal of Psychology*, vol. XV, 1948, 433–6,

McCarthy, Thomas: *The Critical Theory of Jürgen Habermas*, Cambridge, MA, MIT Press, 1978.

McCormick, Barrett L.: *Political Reform in Post-Mao China – Democracy and Bureaucracy in a Leninist Sate*, Berkeley, CA, University of California Press, 1990.

McNally, David: *Political Economy and the Rise of Capitalism*, Berkeley, CA, University of California Press, 1989.

Meier, Gerald M.: *Emerging from Poverty*, New York, Oxford University Press, 1984.

Migdal, Joel S.: *Strong Societies and Weak States: State-Society Relations and State Capabilities in the Third World*, Princeton, Princeton University Press, 1988.

Milor, Vedat: *Changing Political Economies: Privatization in Post-Communist and Reforming Communist States*, Boulder, Lynne Rienner, 1993.

Moon, Bruce E.: *The Political Economy of Basic Human Needs*, Ithaca, NY, Cornell University Press, 1991.

Moore, Barrington: *Social Origins of Dictatorship and Democracy*, Boston, MA, Beacon, [1967] 1993.

Moore, David & Gerald J. Schmitz: *Debating Development Discourse*, New York, St. Martin's Press, 1996.

Moors, Hein & Rossella Palomba eds: *Population, Family, and Welfare – A Comparative Survey of European Attitudes*, New York, Oxford University Press, 1995.

Morales, Juan Antonio & Gary McMahon: *Economic Policy and the Transition to Democracy*, New York, St. Martin's Press, 1996.

Murphy, James: *The Moral Economy of Labor: Aristotelian Themes in Economic Theory*, New Haven, CT, Yale University Press, 1993.

Myrdal, Gunnar: *Asian Drama*, two vols, New York, Oxford University Press, 1968.

Nam, Charles B. et al.: *International Handbook on Internal Migration*, Greenwood Press, 1990.

Nathan, Andrew J.: *Chinese Democracy*, Berkeley. University of California Press, 1985.

Nee, Victor & David Mozingo eds: *State and Society in Contemporary China*, Ithaca, NY, Cornell University Press, 1983.

Needham, Joseph: *Science and Civilization in China*, vols. I–V, Cambridge, University of Cambridge Press, 1954–95.

Nisbet, Robert A.: *The Sociological Tradition*, New York, Basic Books, 1966.

—— *Social Change and History*, New York, Oxford University Press, 1969.

Nolan, Peter et al.: "Towards an Appraisal of the Impact of Rural Reform in China." In *Cambridge Journal of Economics*, March, 1986.

—— & Dong Fureng ed.: *Market Forces in China: Competition and Small Business*, London and New Jersey, Zed Books Ltd, 1989.

North, Douglass: *Structure and Change in Economic History*, New York, Norton, 1981.

—— *Institutions, Institutional Change and Economic Performance*, New York, Cambridge University Press, 1990.

Nove, Alec: *The Soviet Economic System*, London, George Allen & Unwin, 1977.

—— *Socialism, Economics and Development*, London, George Allen & Unwin, 1986.

O'Brien, Kevin J.: *Reform Without Liberalization: China's NPC and the Politics of Institutional Change*, New York, Cambridge University Press, 1990.

O'Donnell, Guillermo: *Modernization and Bureaucratic Authoritarianism*, Berkeley, University of California, 1979.

Ogden, Suzanne: *China's Unresolved Issues: Politics, Development, and Culture*, Englewood Cliffs, NJ, Prentice Hall, 1995.

Oi, Jean C.: "Communism and Clientelism: Rural Politics in China," in *World Politics*, January, 1985.

—— *State and Peasant in Contemporary China – The Political Economy of Village Government*, New Haven, CT, Yale Press, 1989.

Packenham, Robert: *The Dependency Movement: Scholarship and Politics in Development Studies*, Cambridge, MA, Harvard University Press, 1992.

Palmer, Monte: *Dilemmas of Political Development*, 2nd edn, Itasca, IL, Peacock, 1980 and 4th edn, 1989.

Parish, William L. ed.: *Chinese Rural Development: The Great Transformation*, Armonk, NY, M.E. Sharpe, 1985.

Parnell, Martin: *The German Tradition of Organized Capitalism: Self-Government in the Coal Industry*, Oxford, Routledge, 1994.

Parsons, Talcott: *The Social System*, New York, Free Press, 1951a.

—— *Toward a General Theory of Action*, Cambridge, MA, Harvard University Press, 1951b.

—— *Social Structure and Personality*, New York, Free Press, 1964.

—— *Sociological Theory and Modern Society*, New York, Free Press, 1967.

Patterson, Perry ed.: *Capitalist Goals, Socialist Past: The Rise of the Private Sector in Command Economies*, Boulder, CO, Westview Press, 1993.

Peng, Huei En: *Taiwan fazhande zhengzhi jingji fenxi* [The political economy of Taiwan's development], Taipei, Taiwan, Fengyun Luntang Press, 1995.

Perkins, Dwight H.: *Agricultural Development in China, 1368–1968*, Chicago, Aldine Pub. Co., 1969.

—— ed.: *China's Modern Economy in Historical Perspective*, Stanford, CA, Stanford University Press, 1975.

—— *China, Asia's Next Economic Giant?* Seattle, University of Washington Press, 1986

—— & S. Yusuf: *Rural Development in China*, Baltimore The Johns Hopkins University Press, 1984.

Perry, Elizabeth: "State and Society in Contemporary China," in *World Politics*, July, 1989.

Perry, E. & Wong, C.: *The Political Economy of Reform in Post-Mao China*, Harvard University Press, 1985.

Perry, Elizabeth & Li Xun, *Proletarian Power: Shanghai in the Cultural Revolution*, Boulder, CO, Westview, 1997.

Picchio, Antonella: *Social Reproduction: The Political Economy of the Labour Market*, New York, Cambridge University Press, 1992.

Poggi, Gianfranco: *The State: Its Nature, Development, and Prospect*, Stanford, CA, Stanford University Press, 1991.

Polanyi, Karl: *The Great Transformation. The Political and Economic Origins of Our Time*, Boston, Beacon Press, 1957.

Pomeranz, Kenneth: *The Making of a Hinterland: State, Society, and Economy in Inland North China, 1853–1937*, Berkeley, CA, University of California Press, 1993.

Popkin, Samuel: *The Rational Peasant: The Political Economy of Rural Society in Vietnam*, Berkeley, CA, University of California Press, 1979.

Postone, Moishe: *Time, Labor, and Social Domination: A Reinterpretation of Marx's Critical Theory*, New York, Cambridge University Press, 1993.

Powell, Simon G.: *Agricultural Reform in China*, New York, St. Martin's Press, 1991.

Przeworski, Adam: "Could We Feed Everyone? The Irrationality of Capitalism and the Infeasibility of Socialism," in *Politics and Society*, March, 1991, 1–38.

—— *Democracy and the Market: Political and Economic Reforms in East Europe and Latin America*, New York, Cambridge University Press, 1991.

—— & Fernando Limongi: "Modernization: theories and facts" in *World Politics*, 49, January, 1997, 155–83.

Putnam, Robert D.: *Making Democracy Work: Civic Traditions in Modern Italy*, Princeton, Princeton University Press, 1993.

Putterman, Louis ed.: *State and Market in Development: Synergy or Rival?* Boulder, CO, Lynne Rienner, 1992.

—— *Continuity and Change in China's Rural Development*, New York, Oxford University Press, 1993.

Pye, Lucian, *The Dynamics of Chinese Politics*, MA, GH Inc, 1981.

—— *Asian Power and Politics*, Harvard University Press, 1985.

—— "On Chinese Pragmatism in the 1980s" in *The China Quarterly*, vol. 106, June, 1986, 207–34.

—— *China: An Introduction*, New York, Harper Collins, 1991.

Qiao, Lijun et al.: *Zhongguo buneng luan* [China cannot afford chaos], Beijing, Central CCP School Press, 1994.

Rawski, Thomas G.: *Economic Growth and Employment in China*, The World Bank and the Oxford University Press, 1979.

Reich, Robert ed.: *The Power of Public Ideas*, Cambridge, MA, Harvard University Press, 1990.

Reiman, Jeffrey: *Justice and Modern Moral Philosophy*, New Haven, CT, Yale University Press, 1994.

Rima, Ingrid H.: *Labor Market in a Global Economy*, Philadelphia, Temple University Press, 1996.

Ri, Shan ed.: *Zhuming xuezhe lun shichang jingji* [Famous scholars on the market economy], Beijing, Renmin Press, 1993.

Rogowski, Ronald: *Commerce and Coalition: How Trade Affects Domestic Political Alignments*, Princeton, NJ, Princeton University Press, 1989.

Rosen, George: *Contrasting Styles of Industrial Reform: China and India in the 1980s*, University of Chicago Press, 1992.

Rosen, Stanley: "Youth Socialization and Political Recruitment in Post-Mao China," in *Chinese Law and Government*, Summer, 1987.

—— & David Chu: *Survey Research in the PRC*, Washington, DC, USIA, 1987.

Rosenau, Pauline M.: *Post-Modernism and the Social Sciences*, Princeton, NJ, Princeton University Press, 1992.

Rostow, W.W.: *The Stages of Economic Growth: A Non-Communist Manifesto*, Cambridge, Cambridge University Press, 1960.

—— *The Stages of Economic Growth: A Non-Communist Manifesto*, 3rd edn, New York, Cambridge University Press, 1990.

Saith, Ashwani ed.: *The Re-emergence of the Chinese Peasantry – Aspects of Rural Decollectivisation*, London & New York, Croom Helm, 1987.

Sassen, Saskin: *The Mobility of Labor and Capital: A Study in International Investment and Labor Flow*, New York, Cambridge University Press, 1990.

Schmitter, Philippe et al. eds: *Trends toward Corporatist Intermediation*, Beverly Hills, CA, Sage, 1979.

—— "Neo-corporatism and the State," in Grant, W. ed., *The Political Economy of Corporatism*, New York, St. Martin's Press, 1985.

Scott, James: *The Moral Economy of the Peasants*, New Haven, CT, Yale University Press, 1976.

Seidman, Ann & Robert S. Seidman: *State and Law in the Development Process*, New York, St. Martin's Press, 1995.

Sen, Amartya: *Employment, Technology and Development: A Study for the International Labor Office*, Oxford, Clarendon Press, 1975.
—— *On Economic Inequality*, New York, Oxford University Press, 1993.
Shih Chih-yu: *State and Society in China's Political Economy: The Cultural Dynamics of Socialist Reform*, Boulder, CO, Lynn R ienner, 1995.
Shirk, Susan: *Competitive Comrades: Career Incentives and Student Strategies in China*, Berkeley, CA, University of California Press, 1982.
—— *The Political Logic of Economic Reform in China*, Berkeley, CA, University of California Press, 1993.
Shoji, Shiba: *A Cross-National Comparison of Labor Management with Reference to Technology Transfer*, Tokyo, Institute of Developing Economies, 1973.
Shue, Vivienne: *Peasant China in Transition: The Dynamics of Development Toward Socialism, 1949–1956*, Berkeley, University of California Press, 1980.
—— *The Reach of the State: Sketches of the Chinese Body Politic*, Stanford, CA, Stanford University Press, 1988.
Simai, Mihály ed.: *Global Employment: An International Investigation into the Future of Work*, Tokyo, United Nations University Press, 1995.
Sklair, Leslie: ed.: *Capitalism and Development*, Oxford, Routledge, 1994.
—— *Sociology of the Global System*, 2nd edn, Baltimore, Johns Hopkins University Press, 1995.
Skocpol, Theda: *State and Social Revolutions*, Cambridge University Press, 1978.
Smith, Adam, *The Wealth of Nations, Books 1–3*, New York, NY, Penguin Books, [1776] 1983.
Smith, James P.: *Female Labor Supply: Theory and Estimation,* Princeton, NJ, Princeton University Press, 1980.
Smith, Joan & Immanuel Wallerstein: *Creating and Transforming Households: The Constraints of the World Economy*, New York, Cambridge University Press, 1993.
Southall, Roger ed.: *Labor and Unions in Asia and Africa*, New York, St. Martin's Press, 1988.
Spence, Jonathan: *The Search for Modern China*, New York, Norton, 1990.
Squire, Lyn: *Employment Policy in Developing Countries: A Survey of Issues and Evidence*, New York, The World Bank & Oxford University Press, 1981.
SSB (State Statistics Bureau) ed.: *Zhongguo tongji zaiyao 1993* [A statistical survey of China 1993]. Beijing, Zhongguo Tongji Press, 1993.
Standing, Guy (ed): *Labour Circulation and the Labour Process*, London, Croom Helm, 1985.
Staudt, Kathleen: *Managing Development: State, Society, and International Context*, Newbury Park, Sage, 1991.
Steinmo, Sven et al. eds: *Structuring Politics: Historical Institutionalism in Comparative Analysis*, New York, Cambridge University Press, 1992.
Strange, Susan ed., *Paths to International Political Economy*, London, George Allen & Unwin, 1984.
—— *States and Markets*, New York, Basil Blackwell, 1988.
Sun, Zhumin: *Zhongguo nongmin zhanzheng wenti tangsou* [A study on the issues of Chinese peasant wars], Shanghai, Xing Zhishi Press, 1956.

Swann, Dennis: *The Retreat of the State: Deregulation and Privatization in the U.K. and U.S.*, Ann Arbor, MI, The University of Michigan Press, 1990.

Tang, Yijie ed.: *Zhongguo zhongjiao: Guoqu yu xianzai* [Chinese religion: Past and current], Beijing, Beijing University Press, 1992.

Tarling, Roger ed.: *Flexibility in Labour Markets*, London, Academic Press, 1987.

Tausch, Arno: *Towards a Socio-Liberal Theory of World Development*, New York, St. Martin's Press, 1992.

Taylor, Jeffrey: *Employment and Unemployment in China: Results from 10-Percent Sample Tabulation of 1982 Population Census*, Foreign Economic Report No. 23 by the US Department of Commerce, Washington, DC, 1985.

—— "Rural Employment Trends and the Legacy of Surplus Labor, 1978–86," in *China Quarterly*, December, 1988.

Thomas, S. Bernard: *Labor and the Chinese Revolution*, Ann Arbor, MI, Center for Chinese Studies, The University of Michigan, 1983.

Timmer, C. Peter: *Agriculture and the State: Growth, Employment, and Poverty in Developing Countries*, Ithaca, NY, Cornell University Press, 1991.

Tipps, Dean C.: "Modernization Theory and the Comparative Study of Societies: A Critical Perspective," in *Comparative Study in Society and History*, 1973.

Tomlins, Christopher: *The State and the Unions: Labor Relations, Law, and the Organized Labor Movement in America, 1890–1960*, New York, Cambridge University Press, 1985.

Tsou, Tang, *American's Failure in China*, Chicago: University of Chicago Press, 1967.

Turner, Lowell: *Democracy at Work: Changing World Markets and the Future of Labor Unions*, Ithaca, NY, Cornell University Press, 1991.

Twitchett, Denis ed.: *The Cambridge History of China, Vol. 3, Sui and T'ang China, 589–906*, New York, Cambridge University Press, 1979.

—— & Michael Loewe eds: *The Cambridge History of China, Vol. 1, The Ch'in and Han Empires, 221 BC–AD 220*, New York, Cambridge University Press, 1986.

Ullerich, Curtis: *Rural Employment & Manpower Problems in China*, Armonk, New York, M.E. Sharpe, 1979.

Ulman, Lloyd et al. eds: *Labor and an Integrated Europe*, Washington, DC, The Brookings Institution, 1993.

UN Development Program: *Human Development Report 1993*, New York, Oxford University, 1993.

Unger, Jonathan: *Education under Mao: Class and Competition in Canton Schools, 1960–1980*, Cambridge University Press, 1982.

Van den Doel, Hans et al.: *Democracy and Welfare Economics*, 2nd edn, New York, Cambridge University Press, 1993.

Van Ness, Peter ed.: *Market Reforms in Socialist Societies: Comparing China and Hungary*, Boulder & London, Lynne Rienner, 1989.

—— & David Stark eds: *Remaking the Economic Institutions of Socialism: China and East Europe*, Stanford, CA, Stanford University Press, 1990.

Vogel, Ezra, *Canton under Communism: Programs and Politics in a Provincial Capital, 1949–1968*, Cambridge, MA, Harvard University Press, 1969.
—— *One Step Ahead in China: Guangdong under Reform*, Cambridge, MA, Harvard University Press, 1989.
Wade, Robert: *Governing the Market – Economic Theory and the Role of Government in East Asian Industrialization*, New Haven, CT, Yale University Press, 1990.
Walder, Andrew G.: *Communist Neo-Traditionalism – Work and Authority in Chinese Industry*, New Haven, CT, Yale Press, 1986.
—— "Factory and Managers in an Era of Reform," in *China Quarterly*, June, 1989.
Wallerstein, Immanuel: *The Modern World-System: Capitalist Agriculture and the Origins of the European World-Economy in the Sixteenth Century*, New York, Academic Press, 1974.
—— *The Capitalist World Economy*, New York, Cambridge University Press, 1980.
Waltz, Kenneth: *Theory of International Politics*, New York, Random House, 1979.
Wang, Dingding: "Zhidu bianqian de yiban lilun" [General theory of institutional changes], in *Jingji yanjou* [Economic studies], Beijing, No. 5, 1992.
Wang, Fei-Ling: *From Family to Market: Labor Allocation in Contemporary China*, Lanham, MD, New York, NY, & London, UK, Rowman & Littlefield, 1998.
—— "To Incorporate China – A New Policy for a New Era," in *The Washington Quarterly*, CSIS (Center for Strategic and International Studies), Washington, Vol. 21–1 (Winter), 1998(B), 67–81.
—— "Four Cheers for International Political Anarchy," in *Journal of Chinese Political Science*, Vol. 1(2), ACPS, Fall, 1995.
—— "International Market and Domestic Changes: the Case of China", *In Depth*, Washington, DC, Vol. 4 (1) Winter, 1994.
Wang, Guichen et al.: *Zhongguo nongcun jingji xue* [Rural economics of China], Beijing, Renmin University Press, 1988.
Wang, Haibo et al.: *Xinzhongguo gongye jianshi* [A short history of industry in the new China], Beijing, Jingji Guangli Press, 1986.
Wang, Jianchu et al.: *Zhongguo gongren yundong shi* [The history of the Chinese labor movement], Shengyan, Liaoning Renmin Press, 1987.
Wang, N.T.: *China's Modernization and Transnational Corporations*, Lexington, MA, Lexington Books, 1984.
—— *Transnational Corporations and China's Open Door Policy.* Lexington, MA, Lexington Books, 1988.
Wang, Shan: *Disanzhi yanjing kan Zhongguo* [Look at China through the third eye], Taiwan edn, Taipei, Zhouzji Wenhua Co., 1994.
Wang, Shaoguang & Hu, Angang: *Zhongguo guojia nengli baogao* [An analytical report on the capacity of the Chinese state], Shenyang, Liaonong Renmin Press, 1993 & Hong Kong, Oxford University Press (China), 1994.
Wang, Weili: *Zhongguo xiandai shi* [Contemporary History of China]. Shengyan, Liaoning Renmin Press, 1984.

Wang, Xiaoyi: "Nongcun shehuixue zai Zhongguo de fazan" [The Development of Rural Sociology in China], in *Nongcun jingji yu shehui* [Rural economy and society], (4) Beijing, 1994.

Watson, James L. ed.: *Class and Social Stratification in Post-Revolution China*, Berkeley, CA, University of California Press, 1984.

Weber, Max: "Economic Policy and the National Interest in Imperial Germany," in Runciman, W., *Weber, Selections in Translation*. New York, NY, Cambridge University Press, 1977.

—— *Economy and Society*, Berkeley, CA, University of California Press, 1978.

Wellman, Barry et al. ed.: *Social Structures: A Network Approach*, New York, Cambridge University Press, 1988.

White, Gordon: "The Politics of Economic Reform in Chinese Industry: The Introduction of the Labor Contract System," in *The China Quarterly*, September, 1987, 365–89.

—— ed.: *Developmental States in East Asia*, New York, St. Martin's Press, 1988.

White, Stephen: *Political Theory and Postmodernism*, New York, Cambridge University Press, 1991.

White III, Lynn T.: *Careers in Shanghai: The Social Guidance of Personal Energies in a Developing Chinese City, 1949–1966*, Berkeley, CA, University of California Press, 1978.

Wilkinson, Endymion: *The History of Imperial China*, Cambridge, MA, Harvard University Press, 1991.

Williamson, Oliver E.: *Markets and Hierarchies: Analysis and Anti-Trust Implications*, New York, Free Press, 1975.

—— "The Vertical Integration of Production: Market Failure Considerations," in *American Economics Review*, vol. LXI(2), May, 1977: 112–22.

—— *The Economic Institutions of Capitalism: Firms, Market, and Relational Contracting*, New York, Free Press, 1985.

Winfield, Richard D.: *Freedom and Modernity*, Albany, NY, SUNY Press, 1991.

Wittfogel, Karl A.: *Oriental Despotism: A Comparative Study of Total Power*, New York, Vintage, [1957] 1981.

Woetzel, Jonathan: *China's Economic Opening to the Outside World – The Politics of Empowerment*, New York, Praeger Publishers, 1989.

Wolfer, Bertram: *Communist Totalitarianism*, Boston, Beacon, 1956.

Womack, Brantly: *Contemporary Chinese Politics in Historical Perspective*, New York, Cambridge University Press, 1991.

World Bank: *China Socialist Economic Development*, Three vols, Washington, DC, World Bank, 1983.

—— *The East Asian Miracle: Economic Growth and Public Policy*, New York, Oxford University Press, 1993.

—— *World Development Report 1994*, New York, Oxford University Press, 1994.

Xia, Jizhi & Dang, Ziaojie eds: *Zhongguo de jiuye yu shiye* [Employment and unemployment in China], Beijing, Laodong Press, 1991.

Xin, Changxing: *Jiuye shiye* [Employment and unemployment], Beijing, Renmin University Press, 1992.

Xu, Ming ed., *Guanjian shike: dandai zhongguo jidai jiejue de 27 ge wenti* (Crucial moment: the 27 issues that need to be urgently solved), Beijing Jingri Zhongguo Press, 1997.

Xue, Muqiao: *China's Socialist Economy*, Beijing, Foreign Language Publisher, 1981.

Yang, Mayfair M.: *Gifts, Favors, and Banquets: The Art of Social Relationship in China*, Ithaca, NY, Cornell University Press, 1994.

Yao, Wei & Murong Qiu: *Chaoji fuhao* [Super rich], Beijing, Tuanji Press, 1993.

Ye, Yaojun: *Zhongguo dushi fazhan shi* [The history of Chinese capitals], Xian, Shangxi Renmin Press, 1988.

Yi, Gang: *Money, Banking and Financial Institutions in China*, Boulder, CO, Westview Press, 1994.

Young, Oran: *Compliance and Public Authority*, Baltimore, Johns Hopkins University Press, 1979.

Yu, Ziming ed.: *Xiandai laogong renshi guanli* [Modern labor and personnel management], Tianjin, Tianjin Social Science Academy Press, 1991.

Yuan, Lunqu ed.: *Xinzhongguo laodong jingji shi* [The labor history of new China], Beijing, Laodong Renshi Press, 1987.

Yuan, Fang: "The Current Labor and Employment Issues In China," in *Beijing University Journal*, No. 4, 1990.

Yuan, Shouqi et al. ed.: *Laodongfa quanshu* [The complete book on labor laws], Beijing, Yuhang Press, 1994.

Yuan, Yang: *Shengsi shi da: shengsi zhihui yu zhongguo wenhua* [Life and death are major matters: the wisdom on life and death and Chinese culture], Beijing, Dongfeng Press, 1996.

Yue, Guangzhao ed.: *Labor Policy and System in China*, Beijing, Economic Management Press, 1989.

Zagoria, D. & Li Cha: *The Nature of Mainland Chinese Economic Structure*, New York, Columbia University Press, 1972.

—— "China's Quiet Revolution," *Foreign Affairs*, Spring, 1984.

Zaretsky, Eli: *Capitalism, the Family, and Personal Life*, New York, Harper & Row, 1986.

Zeng, Fanhua: *Tiefanwan, heifanwan, jinfanwan* [Iron rice bowl, black rice bowl, gold rice bowl], Zhenzhou, Henan Renmin Press, 1993.

Zhang Houyi: "Siying yezhu jiecheng zaiwouguo shehui jiegou zhongde diwei" [The social status of the private employers in our country], in *Zhongguo shehui kexue*, Chinese Social Science Beijing, No. 6, 1994.

Zhang, Jin et al. eds.: *Laodong renshi guanli zidian* [The dictionary of labor and personnel management], Chendu, Sichuan Keji Press, 1987.

Zhang, Mingyuan: *Huangse wenming – Zhongguo wenhua de gongneng yu moshi* [Yellow civilization – The function and models of Chinese culture], Shanghai, Shanghai Wenyi Press, 1990.

Zhang, Sai et al. eds: *1992 Zhongguo fazhan baogao* [China development report 1992], Beijing, Statistics Press, 1992.

Zhang, Siqian et al.: *Zhongguo nongye fazhang zhannue wenti yanjou* (A study on the strategic issues in the Chinese agricultural development), Beijing, Zhongguo Shehui Press, 1988.

Zhong, Nian: "Zhongguo xiangcun shehui kongzhi de bianqian" [The evolution of social control in Chinese villages], in *Shehuixue yanjou* [Sociology studies], Beijing, (3) 1994, 90–9.

Zhou, Enlai: *Selected Works*, Beijing, People's Publisher, 1981.

Zhu, Cishou: *Zhongguo gudai gongye shi* [Industrial history of ancient China], Shanghai, Xueling Press, 1988.

Zweig, David: *Agrarian Radicalism in China*, Cambridge, MA, Harvard University Press, 1989.

Index